T0367299

Deep Down in
BROOKLYN

Ed German

authorHOUSE®

AuthorHouse™
1663 Liberty Drive
Bloomington, IN 47403
www.authorhouse.com
Phone: 1-800-839-8640

© *2013 Ed German. All rights reserved.*

No part of this book may be reproduced, stored in a retrieval system, or transmitted by any means without the written permission of the author.

Published by AuthorHouse 3/7/2013

ISBN: 978-1-4567-5439-6 (sc)
ISBN: 978-1-4567-5438-9 (hc)
ISBN: 978-1-4567-5443-3 (e)

Library of Congress Control Number: 2011905380

Any people depicted in stock imagery provided by Thinkstock are models, and such images are being used for illustrative purposes only.
Certain stock imagery © Thinkstock.

This book is printed on acid-free paper.

Because of the dynamic nature of the Internet, any web addresses or links contained in this book may have changed since publication and may no longer be valid. The views expressed in this work are solely those of the author and do not necessarily reflect the views of the publisher, and the publisher hereby disclaims any responsibility for them.

Deep Down in Brooklyn

A memoir of mid-twentieth century Brooklyn and a revelation of urban transition during the black migration from the south. A look at life in the cellar for the first black family to live among the Jews and Catholics on a block of Willoughby Ave. Brooklyn, arriving from the Pine Barrens of South Jersey.

A resurrection of characters and institutions and an account of calamity and violence, of laughter and music, gangs and gamblers, and a testament from a generation mostly lost from the ravages of drugs, disease, homicide and war. A glimpse into the interaction of Blacks and Jews, Puerto Ricans and West Indians, Northerners and Southerners.

A documentation of events in a chapter of deep urban culture and street life. A story with a musical backdrop about war, survival, language and dress.

edwinsgerman@gmail.com

Acknowledgements

To my Son Vaughn for his loyalty, technical expertise, patience and encouragement for helping me in times of panic.

To my Sisters Sissy and Linda, my Brother Don and my Son Darren for finding long-lost photos of family and friends.

To my Brother Ronnie and my Cousins Cedric and Tony for reminding me of events and names and for clarification.

To Julie May of The Brooklyn Historical Society for helping me in photo research.

To Barbara Hibbert of the New York City Municipal Archives for her patience and help in photo research.

To Urban Archeologist and Historian Brian Merlis of Brooklynpix.com for photos and inspiration.

To Sister Constance Brennan of the Sisters of Charity Archives for photos of St. Joseph Hall.

To Jason Lorick of Brooklyn for giving me access to his backyard for photos of St. John's R.C. Church and for sending me even nicer ones.

To my friend Marty D'Giff of Bravo Company 1/4 for looking out for me.

To Dominick Mondelli of Brooklyn, and Our Lady of Loreto, for Brooklyn photographs.

The command chronologies of 1st Battalion, 4th Marines, Vietnam

Dedicated to Ma and Dad,

my sister Cathy, my girl Cathy,

Mickey and Reggie,

Chucky and Dice

And to all the young people of the boomer generation

whose lives were so surprisingly brief.

Deep Down

in

Brooklyn

Copyright, 2013 by Ed German

Prologue

All I wanted to do is be friends and be fair and have fun because I was healthy and free. This story is about people and times and places that meant a lot, to a lot of people, who aren't here to tell it today.

I don't consider myself an African American. I am an American Negro. We've been slaves and nigras and niggers and colored and spades and spooks and coons and splibs and Afro Americans and blacks, but Negro conclusively describes for me who I am and the journey that my continental ancestors took. Negro means black, anyway.

My parents, grandparents, great- grand parents and great-great grandparents were born in America. My flag is the Stars and Stripes, the only one I can claim. My father and all my uncles served in World War II and I served with the marines in Vietnam. When I was born in the spring of 1950 we lived in Bedford Stuyvesant, Brooklyn, at 522 Halsey Street.

522 Halsey Street bet. Lewis & Stuyvesant

Ma was pregnant with me for 10 and 1/2 months and said she didn't think I wanted to come into this world. She said when I was a baby I wouldn't let Daddy touch me. I had rickets, and wouldn't eat anything but pancakes and cornflakes.

My best friend Mickey was killed in Betsy Head swimming pool in Brownsville in 1974, five years after being wounded in the head in Vietnam while serving with the 9th Marines.

My brother Don and his best friend Chucky planned to join the Army together, but Chucky was shot to death by a Puerto Rican kid in 1975 as Don witnessed helplessly from our upstairs window. Chucky died under Daddy's car, running from the bullets. My sister Sissy had to hold Don back from jumping out the window.

Mike, my sister Cathy's boyfriend, was gunned down in his Cadillac in 1987 by some Colombians while they sat there talking. Cathy was able to jump out of the car and run down Howard Avenue. They weren't after Cathy.

My older brother Ronnie was held on homicide charges in 1967 in a South Jersey jail until one day he got hold of some white, "who-doo" powder from down south, and was told to spread it all over his face and arms before he goes in front of the judge, and he'd be set free. Ronnie did so and was released. Authorities had caught up with the man who actually did it.

I
The Family

My mother's father is Alonzo (Lonnie) Harris, born in 1883, the same year that the Brooklyn Bridge opened. He was born in North Carolina and his wife, my maternal grandmother, was born in South Carolina in 1896, and her maiden name is Emma Wright. She says her grandfather was a native American named Charlie Christmas, a Blackfoot slave bearing his owner's name. Ma sometimes mentions two of Grandma's brothers named Judge and Captain.

Captain Wright (Great Uncle Cap), Grandma's brother.

Me, Ed German IV, born 1950

Ed German I , my great grandfather, born circa 1845

Ma's parents are both firm, born-again Christians and members of the Church of God of Prophecy, and Granddad is a member of the Masons. We have a large extended family. My mother's siblings are Lonnie, Ellis, James, Jewel, Bill, Norman, Lewie, Mable, Evelyn and Sarah.

On Dad's side there's Lannie, Donald, Richard, Johnny, Ross, Ollie Lee, Willie Mae, Lillian, Ruby, Ola, and Lurine. Most of my father's brothers and sisters are in the south but he has numerous cousins who settled in Brooklyn and Long Island from his mother's side of the family, the Hendrix side. We are second cousins with the singer Nona Hendrix.

The German brothers, l to r, Richard, Dad, Johnny, Billy, Ross, Lanny

All of Ma's brothers and sisters and her parents settled in
South Jersey, then Newark, beginning in the late 1940s from
Georgia, so we got to know all of our aunts and uncles on
Ma's side from the beginning, but we don't meet Dad's
mother in Georgia until I'm 12. So besides having 20 aunts
and uncles, there are 5 of Dad's cousins in Brooklyn and 2 on
Long Island, and he has an uncle in Queens that we never get
to meet named John, who's my cousin Cedric's grandfather.
Cedric says that his grandfather, John Hendrix was nasty, and
kept a whore upstairs in his house that he shared with one of
his sons. He says that when he was about 12 he saw his

grandfather coming out of the whore's room and fixing his pants and said to him, "Boy, you better go on in there and gitchoo some of that pussy." Cedric and the singer Nona Hendrix are first cousins.

Dad's cousins Lizzie, Lottie, Gussie, Roosevelt and Shorty are all Hendrixes and live in Brooklyn, and Lillian and Bozo live on Long Island. We have about 100 first and second cousins in the New York/New Jersey area. My mother's parents are migrant sharecroppers who traveled north in the late 1940s and settled in the farmlands of the Jersey Pine Barrens in Bridgeton, New Jersey, where they worked in the fields and food-processing industries indigenous to the region. They picked string beans and tomatoes and peaches and blueberries and topped onions and they worked for Hunt's Tomato and Ritter's, 7UP, Seabrook Farms and Owens Glass. They all came north in an old army truck with a canvass-covered top that sheltered most of my aunts and uncles traveling in the back. There was no way to communicate with the driver and my grandparents traveling in the cabin, and the only way to signal if you had to stop and pee was to toss an empty bottle out the back towards the front of the truck and my uncle Buck, the driver, would stop.

Grandma and Granddad, Ma's parents, in an eggplant field, Florida, circa 1945.

Before we moved back to Brooklyn in 1953 we lived in a place called Lanning's Wharf off of Back Neck Road in the South Jersey Pine Barrens, in the town of Fairton. Lanning's Wharf is remotely deep in the farmlands and my grandfather lives in a large house that he leases from the Lanning Brothers who own the land. Granddad is also sharecropping for a local farmer named Dominick Sorrentino. Dominick's brother Harry Sorrentino owns a car dealership in Bridgeton, New Jersey.

The house is on the banks of the Cohansey River and we live there with my aunts, uncles and cousins and there are chickens in the yard and a rooster that terrorizes and attacks me. He flaps his wings and lands on top of my head going after the piece of bread in my hand. Granddad also has a pig pen with a few hogs slopping around. The house smells like kerosene and is bordered by farmland and the river, where they can fish and set crab traps. We kids play by the river unsupervised, throwing rocks in the water and waving at passing boats. Ma has a washing machine in the backyard with a wringer on it, and I remember standing next to her and holding on to her dress as a big boat passed and sounded its horn at us.

Before they lived here they lived in a large house near Lakehurst, New Jersey where they worked the cranberry farms. The house was so large that some people showed resentment and while they were in church one Sunday, the local Ku Klux Klan burned a cross on the property.

My cousin Charles, who is a year older than me, is always bad. There are cats around the house and a litter of kittens and one day Charles picks up 3 of the kittens and says "Let's throw 'em in the river." I shake my head and say no but he says "Yeah, let's do it." He tosses the kittens in the river and watches for a few seconds and then says "We better go git 'em." He wades into the river up to his waist after the kittens, grabs them up and takes them in the house and puts them in a chest of drawers right next to the front door. A couple of days later the dead kittens begin to smell and when my grandmother finds them she screams "Who did this?" I say "Charles" and he says "You did it too!" and we both get whippings.

View of the Cohansey River from the house at Lanning's Wharf

Dad gets a job in Brooklyn working at the Cascade Laundry on Myrtle Avenue. Cascade is a commercial laundry that services local hospitals and businesses. One day when Dad was working he found $138.00 inside a uniform pocket and he hired a man named Solomon Jones with the money, who moved us from Lanning's Wharf back to Brooklyn.

We visit Ma's parents many times in South Jersey and on one visit Charles and I are playing by the river and he reminds me of when we threw the kittens in the river and the whipping we got. He steps back behind me and when I'm not looking he kicks me in the groin so hard that I get a ruptured hernia. I'm so traumatized by this that I don't remember the kick when he does it, but Ma tells me later. When we get back home to Brooklyn Dad carries me up to Dr. Hitlin's house with my groin so swollen that it looks like an egg and I can't walk. They take me to the hospital where I was born, Kings County Hospital, and I have an operation and when I wake up in the recovery room I'm thirsty and the nurse gives me lukewarm water in a tea cup and I throw up.

There's our neighbor up the road from Granddad's house on Lanning's Wharf , a white man named Mr. Plummer, who lives in a one-room house and he has a white, plow horse and some chickens. He lets my brother Ronnie ride the plow horse around the premises and in the fields, and Ronnie likes Mr. Plummer and they're friends. There's a thick iron spike driven into a tree in our yard that Ronnie uses as a step to mount the horse. One day when Mr. Plummer is away, our cousins Stanley, Charles and Sonny, who are brothers, sneak into his yard and turn over his chicken coop, grab a bunch of eggs and smash them against his house. When Mr. Plummer gets home and sees his chicken coop ransacked and his house covered with smashed eggs he comes over to our house and the boys blame it on Ronnie, because they're jealous of Ronnie's relationship with Mr. Plummer and his riding the white horse. Ronnie gets a whipping from Granddad and from Ma. The next day as Ronnie and my cousin Jean get off the school bus they immediately smell blood and flesh in the air, like from a butcher. As they walk towards the house and past Mr. Plummer's, he and another man are loading the dead, white horse onto a truck. Mr. Plummer slit the horse's throat as punishment to Ronnie. He killed the plow horse that Ronnie loved to express his outrage and anger. It was the closest thing he could do next to killing Ronnie.

Mr. Plummer's House at Lanning's Wharf

One day Ronnie, Sonny and Stanley are playing in front of the house and decide to pick up sticks and chase the rooster around. They start chasing the mean old bird and laughing and throwing dirt at him and poking him with sticks and they don't let up. They chase the cackling bird all around the front of the house, all around the back and down to the edge of the river and it tries to fly and keeps running and dodging and ducking and this goes on until the rooster finally falls over dead. Now the boys feel shocked and trapped, and decide to hide the dead bird by throwing him in the river. Later on in the day just before dark, Granddad notices the rooster's absence because there had been no crowing for hours, and starts looking for him around the yard. After he can't find him he lines up the boys and sits them on the front porch. By this time the three of them are in quiet moods of ignorance and denial.

"What happened to that bird?" He demands. "That bird ain't gon just vanish like that, somebody did somethin!" They're all looking down at the ground, as innocent as they can until Stanley, the youngest, notices out of the corner of his eye, the big, white, dead bird being sent right back to them by the evening tide and says....... "Uh Ooooohh"...... and Granddad whips them all.

Where the school bus drops off Jean and Ronnie at Lanning's Wharf

II
Life in the Cellar

My first picture of urban life is when I'm 3. We're standing in the gutter between cars waiting to cross the street and a pile of dog doo-doo is under the tailpipe of Dad's car and I'm wondering if it came out of the tailpipe, because I've never seen doo-doo on the ground because even though I was born in Brooklyn we'd lived in the country, down in Jersey with my mother's parents, where there are dirt roads and no gutters and I don't even remember seeing a dog because we didn't have one. People in the farmlands don't walk dogs. Ma grabs my hand, looks down at me and says: "Stop looking at that mess and come on!"

It's 1953 and we're crossing Willoughby Avenue to our building where we'd just moved into the cellar, from the Pine Barrens in South Jersey, arriving in a truck late at night with our belongings and live chickens that Ma prepares the next day for our first meal in the bottom of this building.

671 Willoughby Avenue Brooklyn, 1940

671 Willoughby Ave. today

Dad becomes the super of a 20 unit apartment building at 671 Willoughby Avenue. We live in a two-bedroom apartment located at the rear of the cellar of the building, the super's apartment, and all our windows face the back, except for the bathroom window which faces the alley. There's a dumbwaiter in our kitchen and the building is heated by a coal-burning furnace and a hot-water boiler and the radiator in our apartment knocks and clanks when the steam comes up. The radiator knocks so loud that you can hear it from outside the house even when the windows are closed. Our telephone number is EVergreen 7-6033.

Ma cooks grits and eggs for breakfast, and sometimes a piece of bacon or sausage. We do everything with grits. We have it in the morning for breakfast, then we might have it for dinner. Grits and gravy, grits and butter, grits and crushed tomatoes, grits and sugar, milk and butter, fish and grits, rabbit and grits, smothered pork chops and grits and gravy. When the grits box is empty I stick my foot in it and wear it like a peg-legged pirate.

My brother Ronnie doesn't care for eggs much, and if he eats them they have to be cooked well done, with no yolk or egg whites running like snot. He remembers when he was a little boy back on Lanning's Wharf, that Granddad's chickens used to lay eggs in the outhouse. When Ronnie used the outhouse and saw soft, fresh-laid eggs, mixed with the smells of the outhouse and soiled toilet paper, his aversion to eggs started. He thought, "Chickens. Dumb, pigeon-toed *and* bowlegged, but being secretly and mysteriously smart at the same time, laying their eggs in places that stink the most, to make people not want to eat them."

The cellar is enormous to us. Besides our apartment there are 3 huge coal bins, a large storage area for the Jewish tenants who live upstairs, and there are stacks of trunks piled up 7 feet high and filled with their old belongings. For a bunch of kids the cellar seems endless with unlimited plundering opportunities. There's enough room in the cellar for us and a bunch of our friends to roller- skate on the concrete floor and there are 2 poles, one on each end of the huge room that we grab onto and whip ourselves around, propelling us even faster on our noisy, iron-wheel skates. We skate and scream and we can make all the noise we want. You can see all of the building's pipes and wires and the big fuse-box area for the tenants' apartments upstairs and plenty of areas where kids can get hurt, along with rats, water bugs, roaches and silverfish. The cellar has 3 tool and utility rooms that have photos of pin-up girls from the 1940s and other dark, dusty areas that we never bother with, places that Ma says, "The Booga Man is in there."

The building's hot-water pipes that run through the cellar are covered with asbestos that we peel off with our hands and poke holes into with sticks as we constantly plunder this big place. The entire furnace and the hot-water boiler are covered with asbestos as well. The upstairs tenants knock on the pipes to signal Dad when there's no heat or hot water.

At 4 years old I take my sister Sissy by the hand and walk down to the corner, cross Throop Avenue, a busy, two-way street, and go into Ben's grocery store and get potato chips, cup cakes and candy and take them up to the cash register and ask Ben for a bag to put them in. He puts the stuff in the bag and says, "35 cents!" I look at Sissy who's looking up at me and Ben says, "Do you have any money?" We nod our heads "no" and he says, "Well you gotta have money. Now go home and come back with money!" So I take her by the hand, cross the street and go home disappointed. We don't know what money is. I thought that when you wanted something the store was the place to go. What's money? I learned to go to Ben's by going there with Ma, and she gets what she wants and Ben puts the stuff in a bag and we go home. I didn't pay attention to any transactions between Ben and Ma. Later, when we learn about money and go to the store, my sister Linda always asks for change even when there *is* none. She grabs 25 cents worth of candy and pumpkin seeds, hands Mr. Sussman a quarter and asks for change.

One morning Dad finishes breakfast and puts on his coat and kisses Ma and I say "Where you goin Daddy?" Dad says, "I'm goin' to work." When he walks out the door I ask Ma what work is and she says it's Dad's job, but she doesn't say what he does so I imagine that he must be somewhere with his hand gripped on a cylinder that he pushes down and as he does, steam comes out of the side of it with a hissing sound. As I imagine this, I don't connect it in any way with what he's producing or earning, because I don't know what money is. He calls Ma "Monk". We don't know why he calls her Monk and we never ask.

Dad gives me and Ronnie haircuts in the cellar and sits us on a big green metal can that Ma uses as a dirty-clothes hamper, and he uses a pair of manual clippers with handles that he squeezes to clip the hair.   Whenever Dad and Ma aren't home, we have fun plundering through the cellar and in the house, all in their personal belongings, just to see what they have.

The cellar today. One of the poles we grabbed onto while we skated.

The entire block is Jewish and Catholic and all of the tenants upstairs are white, mostly Jewish. There's a synagogue on the northeast corner of Willoughby and Throop Avenue and a Yeshiva on the northwest corner. Directly next to our building is a Jewish catering hall called the Gold Manor where weddings and Bar Mitzvahs are held, and it has a canopy that extends to the curb of the sidewalk, where we spend many evenings waiting outside after a wedding reception amongst anxious guests and photographers to see the bride dressed in white like a princess, with her groom and the waiting car. There's an alley that separates our building from the Gold Manor and we hear the sounds of accordions playing and people stomping on the wooden floor, singing and dancing and clapping and shouting.

Jewish men dancing inside the Gold Manor 667 Willoughby Ave.

The next day we go to the side entrance near the kitchen and ask the Gold Manor dishwashers to give us leftover wedding cake, which we eat right there on the spot. We don't like the taste of the icing on the cake but we eat it anyway, just to have something sweet.

The former Gold Manor, now offices of Black Vets for Social Justice

We're the first black kids on the block and most of our friends are Jewish. My brother Ronnie, born in 1945, is the oldest. His friends are Jackie Levine, Stewie Schwartz, a red-haired kid named Sidney, and a tall kid named Michael Peltz, who wears huge, black, wing-tip Cordovans, and stands at the front of 660 Willoughby, shifting his weight from one foot to the other. They all wear yarmulkes. I'm friends with Hashie, Little Stewie, Howie, Lois and Susan Roth and Betty Kivens, whose older brother Robbie is also a friend of Ronnie's.

Sissy German, Howie, Lois Roth, Little Stewie, Susan Roth, facing 671
Willoughby Avenue, 1956

One day Ronnie is going to the movies with Stewie and Jackie
and he has to take me with him, but I don't know where we're
going because I don't know what the movies is. All I know is
that I'm going somewhere with the big boys. As we walk
down Throop Ave. they're talking and laughing and Ronnie
grabs my hand when it's time to cross the street and he keeps
saying we're going to see a monster picture but I don't know
what that is either. I don't know what a monster is because all
I ever watch are cartoons. I don't know how to read yet. We
turn down DeKalb Ave. and stop at the Kismet Theatre and
Ronnie and his friends buy tickets from a woman behind a
glass booth but I don't know what tickets are or what a
theatre is or where we're going. I just remember Ma saying
for Ronnie to be careful and come straight home. We go into
the lobby and I smell popcorn and hot dogs and mustard, and I

see people with hot dogs and popcorn and sodas in their hands going into big, wide doors. There's a lighted showcase filled with big boxes of candy and Ronnie gets popcorn and soda and we go in the doors where there are hundreds of chairs and it's full of people and the lights are on and there are three women in white dresses with flashlights walking up and down and showing people where to sit. We sit down and start eating the popcorn and Ronnie and Stewie and Jackie are goofing around and talking but no one's talking to me and soon the lights go off and it's the biggest television I've ever seen. There's music playing and writing on the screen but I can't read and I'm just eating popcorn and looking around, across the theatre and up at the ceiling and at the giant screen. The movie starts but I don't know what the people on the screen are talking about because I'm 4, so I'm not really paying attention to that. I'm just eating popcorn and soon my eyes get heavy and I fall asleep. Then, all the people sitting in the seats around me start screaming and I wake up and look at the screen and there's the giant face of a growling, horrible, black monster and the people on the screen are running and screaming and I think it's real and think it's going to break out of the screen and kill all of us. I start crying and screaming so loud that the women in the white dresses come with the flashlights and tell Ronnie that we have to leave. Ronnie grabs me by the hand and jerks me up the aisle and we leave Jackie and Stewie looking at The Creature from the Black Lagoon.

When we get back outside the warm sunshine hurts my eyes but I feel safe again in the comfort of daylight. Ronnie is mad at me all the way home.

The next monster I see is on television and it's King Kong, but he's not big like the one in the movies and I'm home in my own house. The next monster I see after that is another giant ape, Mighty Joe Young, and he's on the stage holding up a platform with a woman sitting at a grand piano playing Beautiful Dreamer.

Dad's watching Charlie Chan on the dim black and white television but I don't understand Charlie Chan's mustache and goatee so I think he's got chocolate all over his mouth, the way the white kids upstairs have when they're eating Fudgesicles.

On the next block going east is the huge Gothic cathedral, St. John The Baptist Roman Catholic Church, St. John's Prep School and St. Joseph Hall, a catholic orphanage for girls.

St. Joseph's is staffed by nuns and every day a parade of them dressed in their habits comes through our block while changing shifts at St Joseph's and after school at St. John's. The building is scary and threatening and the thought of it being full of catholic white girls with no mothers or fathers with a statue of St. Joseph at the entrance is alien to me and too big for me to try and think about. You can't go in and talk to them or see them but sometimes if you walk by on a warm afternoon when the windows are open you can hear them talking and laughing or somewhere deep in a chapel singing songs. One time I heard them up in their rooms singing the song Silhouette by the Rays. I don't know what goes on in there because it's guarded by nuns. You can only go into St. Joseph Hall when they're having a bazaar in the basement where they sell strange collectable stuff, used clothes and old 78 records and baked goods, toys and popcorn, and there are little arcade games set up, or you can go in on Sundays when they have Bingo.

St Joseph Hall, the Catholic orphanage-asylum for girls, Willoughby &
Sumner Aves, Demolished in 1964.

Former site of St. Joseph Hall today, public housing corner of Willoughby &
Sumner Ave. Sumner Ave. is now Marcus Garvey Blvd.

St. John's High School, Willoughby & Lewis Aves

St. John's Catholic High School corner Lewis Ave. & Hart St.

There are 5 candy stores within 1 block walking distance, and Doc's drug store on the corner also has a soda fountain with ice cream and candy, Sussman's on Throop Avenue, Ida's on the corner of Hart St. and Throop where teenagers hang out , Buddy's on Throop, but Buddy's candy sometimes has baby roaches in it so you only buy comics and tops and yo-yos, Sonny's on Willoughby near Sumner Avenue, also where teenagers hang out and Phil's on Sumner near Hart Street. They all serve seltzer and make chocolate and vanilla egg creams. There's a commercial on TV about Bonomo's Turkish Taffy that goes b-O, n-O, m-O, bono-MO, Oh, Oh, Oh, - It's Bonomo's......*Candeeeee.* We get our Bonomo's Turkish Taffy from Sussmans. When we walk into Sussman's he or his wife says, "Vaddah ya vont?", not "May I help you?" Or "Can I help you?", always, Vaddah ya vont?" Mr. Sussman's first name is Isidore and his wife, Mrs. Sussman, has numbers tattooed on her arm. We see Jewish people with numbers tattooed on their arms often while growing up in Brooklyn.

702-706 Willoughby Ave., 1940

It's simple to get spending money for candy by knocking on doors for empty soda and beer bottles for their generous deposit refunds, 5 cents for a quart size and 2 cents for the small bottles. Sometimes the bottles have dead roaches in them and we have to wash them out before taking them to the store.

Phil's Candy Store on Sumner bet. Willoughby and Hart, 1940

One day Ronnie and Stewie were playing in the courtyard and Ronnie was swinging a stickball bat and accidentally broke Stewie's nose. Stewie went back and forth to school and everywhere, with his nose bandaged for weeks, often clogged up with boogers and blood.

Jackie Levine's older brother Arty is tough, muscular, handsome, and wears his hair like Elvis Presley. He sings doo wop with his deep voice and puts cigarette packs in his shirt sleeve, and doesn't wear a yarmulke. He's tall and strapping and whenever he comes down the block he picks me and Sissy up and carries us down the street with us holding on to his muscles. Robbie and Betty's mother, Mrs. Kivens, is involved in civil rights and the democratic club, and there was an occasion when Ronnie and a group of people from Junior High School 57 went with Mrs. Kivens to Washington, D.C. for a rally.

699 Willoughby Ave., 1940

699 Willoughby Ave. today

Ronnie is my half brother but I don't discover that until I'm older. One day I hear Ma talking to him about his "father" coming over and I don't understand it because Dad is sitting in the living room. Even when I first see Ronnie's dad I don't understand how he's Ronnie's father because Ronnie calls my father Dad, too. But Daddy raised Ronnie since he was a baby, as long as Ronnie can remember. Ronnie's father is Abraham Jones and his wife's name is Lee Scott, and she's the twin sister of Freddie Scott, who made the hit record "Hey Girl". Ronnie's dad and his wife Lee and my mom and dad are friends and sometimes they all get dressed up and go out together. Ronnie was born in Pompano, Florida, before my parents moved up north, and Ma and Dad worked for a wealthy couple who had a home in Massachusetts and a home in Florida, and they'd summer in Massachusetts and winter in Florida. Ma cooks and cleans for them and Dad is their chauffeur. When the couple winter in Florida Ma and Dad spend their weekends partying in Havana, Cuba.

"Ma?..................Ma?...............I'm hungry !"

Little Stewie yells up to his mother on the third floor. A couple of minutes later she comes to the window and says, "Here..........catch!", and drops a sandwich down wrapped in wax paper, in a brown paper bag. Some kids' moms hang down a string with bags of snacks attached to it. Kids use the word "up" to describe where they are or where they're going. "I'm going up David's house" - because unless you live on the ground floor or in the cellar, your apartment is up. I say to David who lives next door, "Ask your mom if I can come up your house."

696 Willoughby Ave., 1940

696 Willoughby Avenue today

690 - 694 Willoughby Ave., 1940

678-694 Willoughby Ave. today

There are 2 doctors on our side of the street, Dr. Hitlen at 679 and Dr. Grenchlog on the parlor floor of the mansion at 691 where the Kivens live, with his office entrance on the side. Sometimes we knock on Dr. Grenchlog's door and he gives us lollipops. Then one day he says, "OK, enough with the candy, no more, too much candy is not good for you. It'll rot your teeth! You can't just eat candy candy candy candy candy."

This enormous house with its wrap-around balcony is the Willoughby Mansion, and there's a huge Horse-Chestnut tree in the backyard.

The Willoughby Mansion, where Dr. Grenchlog and Robby and Betty Kivens lived with their Mom, Mrs. Kivens.

There are other black families in our neighborhood bordering Bed-Stuy and Williamsburg but the three blocks of Willoughby Ave. from Throop to Stuyvesant Avenue are unique because of the immediate religious and cultural institutions and businesses, like the Gold Manor, the Synagogue and Yeshiva, and St. John's and St. Joseph with all the Jewish and Catholic traffic. The only black businesses are the barber shops - Aiken's on Sumner Avenue between Willoughby and Vernon, and Fat's on Sumner between DeKalb and Kosciuszko.

The first black person that we meet outside our family is the super of the twin building attached to ours, 675 Willoughby. He's real black and bony with sharp facial features, wears a gray, coal-saturated Apple Jack hat and he chomps on a fat cigar all the time, as he perches with one foot on the top step and the other below, leaning elbow to knee and peering up and down the block from the grimy concrete staircase leading to *his* cellar apartment. He lives alone, is about 40 and from Cuba. His name is Mr. Tippy. Whenever we play in the alley of 675 and his cellar door is open you can smell body musk and cigar smoke that soaks his apartment. You can smell it up and down the alley, and when you walk past 675, you can smell Mr. Tippy's house from out on the sidewalk . Sometimes he's across the street leaning against the fence of the Spanish house, talking to the Puerto Ricans with his cigar jumping up and down in his mouth.

Mr. Tippy's Alley, 675 Willoughby

There's a dark-skinned woman named Miss Bee, who goes all over the place and knows all the supers on Willoughby Ave. and Hart St. and she stays with us for a while, and you see her going in and out of Mr. Tippy's, day and night, and with another super Mr. Leroy, who lives around the corner on Hart St. Sometimes she comes walking down the street with Mr. Perry from Hart St., staggering drunk with her short, straightened hair combed simply straight back, her red lipstick and broken top tooth, clenching a long Pall Mall and drinking wine out of the bottle and "piffing" out pieces of tobacco from the unfiltered cigarette. She comes and drinks and smokes and watches us play in the cellar, with a Pall Mall that has red lipstick on its tip, held between long, black fingers with red polish on the nails. We always tease Linda by telling her that Miss Bee is her best friend, and that she just **LOVES** Miss Bee.

There's also a man named Reverend Jackson who wears blue overalls and needs a shave and has a bottle of wine in his pocket that he calls Old Betsy, and always smells like wine. Reverend Jackson sits on the ledge outside our apartment just like Miss Bee and drinks his wine and watches us play and sings songs to us, and every five minutes he says "Hold on......, I got to git Old Betsy." He reaches into the side pocket of his overalls and pulls out a pint of wine, turns it up to his mouth, takes a long guzzle and swallows with a "GhaaaaaaDUH!" and we laugh and he continues singing Brother Frog, replacing the lyric "pistol by his side" with "Old Betsy by his side". I always tease Cathy and tell her that Reverend Jackson is her boyfriend.

There's an old Jewish woman next door at 675 who drags her metal chair noisily on the grainy sidewalk down the block to sit, because the tall buildings directly across the street block the sun. She wears loose, opaque stockings over blue veins in her legs and black, old-lady shoes and lives alone on the first floor and her living-room window faces the front of the building and as the block becomes more crowded with kids she suffers from being tormented with noise from the sidewalk as kids play and skate and play Chinese against the wall under her window, and jump rope and scream and shoot firecrackers and build scooters and jump up and bang on her window to annoy her and she shouts from within the house

through her closed window, "GO AVAY FROM HERE - GO AVAY FROM MY VINDOW - I'M SICK." She has no telephone and desperately screams..........
"POLEEEEEEEEECE.......................PO-LEEEEEEEECE!"

There's a man who lives across the street on the ground floor of 666 named Oscar who lives alone, and he's old and white with white hair that looks yellow and he always has his door open in the summer when it's hot, and the sour smell of his house comes all the way out to the sidewalk, and Ronnie is always talking to him. They talk for hours, Oscar telling Ronnie about the days when he was a Jewish gangster. He's big, and tall and sick, and wears big dungarees. Sometimes Oscar comes over to the cellar and sits on the ledge outside our apartment just like Miss Bee and Rev. Jackson, and watches us skate and play, and then he takes his false teeth out of his mouth and scares us with them. When he comes over, he smells just like his house. Oscar eats leftover food from the Gold Manor almost every day for lunch and dinner. When I told Sissy that Oscar was her boyfriend, she told me that the old Jewish woman who drags her metal chair and yells PO-LEEEECE was my girlfriend.

The block is filled with kids and teenagers. The big boys and my brother Ronnie congregate across the street in front of 670 , 20-30 kids at a time, leaning and sitting on parked cars in front of the huge apartment building, talking loud and goofing and being macho with their muscles, cigarettes and bubble gum and nice hair and tight pants, listening to pocket-size radios, cat calling and whistling at the passing girls and singing doo wop. These are big, tough Jewish boys, 5-10 years older than me. As it gets dark, the street lamp directly above them abruptly comes on fully bright, and the big crowd of boys, all white and Ronnie the only colored, lets out a great "Yeaaaahyyy" as the scene is illuminated, and their sidewalk "stage" is set for the night.

There's a man for everything. The milkman, the garbage man, the rag man, the junk man, the White Horse bleach man, the ice cream man, the ices man, the knife-sharpening man, the watermelon man, the peanut man, the knish man, the seltzer man and the soda man, with Hoffman's and Fox's U-Bet brands. The watermelon man is black and drives a horse-drawn cart and hollers, *"Wardee Meh, Wardee Meh, Wardee Meh-lone."* When the bleach man comes through he only yells one word, *"BLEACH"*, and that's all. He goes all over Brooklyn. All he says is bleach. The seltzer man wears a yarmulke under an Applejack hat and when he comes through the block he just yells one word really loud from his truck, **"SELTZER"** and that's all. He doesn't ever say anything else. Just seltzer.

But the dirtiest man of all is the coal man. His fingernails are caked with coal dust, his clothes are stiff and sooty and coal is in the pores of his face and behind his black cigar and whiskers, as he hops out of the hissing dump truck with "Burns Bros" printed on its' side. He goes down the cellar and peeks into the coal bins, then comes back up and lets down a shaft that goes in the bottom windows, lifts the hatch on the truck and the fresh coal travels down below, forming small mountains in the bins. Sometimes he has to grab the shovel and hop up into the truck to guide the coal down the shaft. I watch the new, fresh, damp coal roll by imagining it's a train.

After the coal man leaves we go in the cellar and climb among the heaps and slide down the black slopes. One Sunday after church our friend Donna Hipp and some girls from upstairs get yelled at and spanked for sliding in the coal bins with us in their Sunday clothes, with their shoes, socks and dresses caked and soiled with coal dust.

The cellar is dusty with soot from the coal bins and ashes from the furnace. As we grow older and start school we're ashamed of living there, especially because the entrance is on the side of the building, down 7 steps through the alley. Parents tell their kids, "Don't go near those steps." If one of our schoolmates walks us home we enter the building through the main lobby as if we live upstairs, then go down the hall and turn right, down 3 steps to a door that leads to the court yard, turn left and down 6 more steps to the rear alley and go in the side door on the left into the cellar where we live. One day a classmate walks past my house as I'm coming out and his eyes get big and he says "You live down *THERE* ?" "No, I was just emptying the garbage" I tell him. But he just laughs and runs down the street with the look on his face like he's going to tell everybody.

The cellar smells like piles of black coal and the red-hot coal that's burning in the furnace. It smells like warm asbestos and heat and steam that comes from the huge boiler, and stuff that's old and not wanted anymore. It smells like iron and copper and puddles of dark, dusty water. Sometimes it smells like the hair of a dirty, wet dog, except when you get closer to our apartment in the back, then you can smell Ma's cooking and Dad's cigarettes. When you open the door to our place the bathroom is directly in front and Dad might be finishing up shaving, and rinsing out the shaving brush and putting it back in its cup, and you can smell his soapy, warm, clean face. If it's early evening Ma might be cooking tripe and you can smell the crushed, red pepper in it. Or maybe boiling freshly-killed chickens and you can smell their feathers as they loosen up in the hot water. Or she might have big fish heads simmering under salt and pepper and onions and gravy. Ma and Dad and Grandma get discarded fish heads from the fish market on DeKalb Ave. for little or sometimes nothing, and eat them with rice and they suck the eyes out of the fish-head sockets and chew all the juice and spices from the fish skulls. On an early Saturday afternoon you can smell peanuts being roasted in a pan. Dad buys them raw and roasts them in the oven and eats them while he's watching television.

Sometimes he buys green peanuts and boils them in salted water. Dad is from Savannah, where on a Friday or Saturday night you see men standing on the corners after work, eating peanuts and drinking liquor.

Coming up out of the cellar. When we lived there, the staircase leading up to the sidewalk was straight ahead. Now it's to the left.

Of all the occupants of 671 Willoughby we have a small silver lining. We have immediate access to the enormous concrete backyard that extends the width of the building and where our windows are all on the ground level. We kids have a private place to play with our friends and Ma and Dad occasionally have bar-b-cues and Ma prepares food and passes it right out the window and it's far from the noise and traffic of the front. We can go in the backyard by climbing out the window. There's a ledge at the end of the backyard that separates 671 from 675 that people call the hoover. It overflows with rain water when the sewers clog up in the backyard of 675. When this happens the water cascades like a waterfall. It's not until I'm much older that I figure out why all the Jewish people who lived in the building called this wall the hoover. Somebody named it the hoover because whenever it overflowed with water it reminded them of The Hoover Dam. When I got big enough to finally jump off the Hoover I thought that was a big accomplishment, and we boys used to get umbrellas and try to parachute off of it, and get yelled at for ruining the umbrellas.

The Hoover today. There was no staircase when we lived there.

THE FURNACE

I learn about hard and dirty labor when I start rolling coal to
feed the big furnace which heats the building, and my first
tools are a shovel and wheel barrel that I roll into one of the 3
coal bins, fill it up with coal and then roll and dump the coal
into a growing heap facing the front of the furnace with its big,
hot face waiting for me like a giant Jack O' lantern. Rolling
coal is a solitary chore that I begin at age 7 out of curiosity and
wanting to be strong, worthy and accomplished. It is daily,
dirty, heavy black work underground, below the sounds of kids
playing upstairs on the sidewalk, the voices of their parents
and the noise of busy traffic from downtown passing through
our block running west to east. The song "Sixteen Tons" is on
the radio, and I hum it in my head. Filling the wheel barrel in
the coal bins takes about 15 shovels full, heavy enough for me
to lift and roll to the furnace, then dump into a heap. This is
one of Ronnie's chores from age 8, and I catch on from
watching him and Dad. We're breathing in coal dust all the
time and after rolling barrels and barrels I blow my nose and
cough, and the mucus and spit are mixed with coal dust.

The furnace has to be fed constantly. When it's time to feed
the furnace you open its heavy doors to see a bed of red-hot
coals waiting to be covered with fresh, new black coal. After
covering the red hotbed with new coal you close the doors but
not fully - the doors have to be cracked so that the coal dust
embers have sufficient oxygen to safely burn off, and the red-
hot coals can breathe, otherwise the furnace can blow up. I
don't know this but Ronnie does and one day when we're

home alone he decides that he wants to see the furnace blow up - to see what it will do - to experience an actual explosion - since nobody's home. He rolls about 8 barrels in front of the furnace, fills it up with fresh coal and shuts the doors fully. He doesn't crack them. We sit on the stone ledge next to the furnace and wait. He doesn't reveal anything to me about his plan and I don't know what we're waiting for or even that we *are* waiting. I'm just sitting here, fumbling with some marbles in my hand. Then it explodes. The noise is loud enough to be heard upstairs on the sidewalk and throughout the building and when the furnace doors violently burst open, it hollers like a monster and coughs coal dust, ashes and soot into my face and eyes. I'm crying from the shock of the bang but I'm not hurt, just shocked and blind. Ronnie takes my hand and quickly walks me back through the cellar and into the kitchen, opens the refrigerator and grabs a container of milk, sits me down and pours milk into my eyes. "Why you pouring milk in my eyes?" I scream. "Shut up and be still!" He snaps. "Open your eyes." I let some of the cold milk in and it works. As the milk drips down my face I'm able to see. Ronnie reaches into the bathroom and grabs toilet paper and wipes my face. By this time Jewish tenants are coming into the cellar screaming "Vhat heppen ?" Ya vont I should call a doctor ?" Later I ask Ronnie how he knew about pouring the milk and he says "I don't know."

During the cold months Ronnie hangs out in front of the furnace and entertains his friends there, and reads his comics and roasts chestnuts that he gets from the market on DeKalb Avenue. He roasts them on a shovel filled with red-hot coals from the furnace and falls asleep on the ledge in front of its giant, burning face, reading Superman or Sgt. Rock comics. He loves Superman, The Lone Ranger, Hop-a-long Cassidy and we fight over the television because I want to watch cartoons - Farmer Gray, Popeye and Betty Boop, who makes me flush and whom I secretly love and want to kiss, while he wants to watch Tarzan and Ramah of the Jungle. Dad, Granddad and Grandma call cartoons film funnies.

The furnace is the heart of the building with its partner the boiler, that sometimes overflows spilling gallons of scalding-hot water flooding the area just in front of the furnace, ankle deep. Planks of wood are placed over the hot water as a bridge when this happens and you can walk on them to tend the furnace and the boiler. One day Ronnie slips off the planks into the boiling batch and gets third-degree burns on his feet and ankles that immediately peel his skin off. He twists and turns in pain and misses weeks in school, his feet and ankles wrapped in gauze and salve, covering the burnt, peeling skin and blisters. The festering smell of his painful, healing feet makes me sick and I don't hide holding my nose. As I walk past and hold my nose Ronnie looks at me like he wants to kill me if he can just reach me. Maybe he fell in the hot water because he let the furnace blow up in my face.

People don't watch their kids closely. Ma says "Go outside somewhere and play." Ronnie is in charge when Ma and Dad go away. He's the boss and makes sure we know it. He sometimes makes us kneel on the floor in front of him and say repeatedly, "Salami, Baloney, Ham, You are the King."

Even when my parents are home, we're regularly out of their sight - around the corner, down the block or up somebody's house, playing in elevators, ringing bells and running, in some cellar somewhere hiding with some girls or up on the roof with its views of the urban landscape. Going on the roof in the summertime is private and edgy, with the smell of the tar paper baking in the sun as soon as you open the roof door. No one down on the sidewalk knows you're there on the roof but the folks directly under you on the top floor do. They can hear you walking around. You can see other neighborhoods on the horizon. It's an escape. When the Drifters come out with the song Up on the Roof, I know exactly what they mean. People in the country can't feel the song like I can. I live in the city and we go on the roof. The roof is handy for spying, star gazing, making out, flying kites, raising pigeons and dropping water balloons or ambushing rival street gangs with broken bricks and bottles. Kids are warned by their parents to stay off the roofs, but it's a challenge to keep up with kids' whereabouts.

Sissy is the fastest of all of us kids. She talks the loudest and the quickest, imitates grownups and gets out of her place often, is the first of us after Ronnie to smoke, is the most flippant and boisterous. Ma sometimes calls her Toots, after Dad's sister whom we call Aunt Toots, because Sissy seems to get her ways from Aunt Toots. When the Jewish kids upstairs have temper tantrums on the sidewalk their mothers keep saying, "Look at him, he's screaming his *brains* out!" Sissy, after hearing them say this, sees Little Stewie hollering and crying over a fudgesicle and decides to imitate his mother by exclaiming, "Look at him, he's screaming his *GUTS* out!"

Deborah (Sissy) German

One day Ronnie takes me up to the P.A.L., the Police Athletic League at the 79th Precinct on Gates Avenue and Throop where they have games set up for kids to play after school. Ronnie sees some of his friends from school and they start playing table hockey but there's nothing for me to do and I don't know any of these kids because they're bigger and older than me. Ronnie's having fun playing table hockey so I go outside and sit on the steps of the precinct while cops are going in and out, then I decide to go home. Willoughby is 10 blocks away up Throop Avenue so I just walk all the way home because I know our house is in the direction of the big church at the end of Throop Avenue. Whenever you look down Throop Avenue you can always see the big church at the end. I'm proud to be independent and I know that Ronnie will be behind me soon. When Ronnie finally comes in the house 2 hours later, he's holding his head and almost crying because he has a Migraine headache from looking for me and worrying. I never considered or thought about him worrying. Ronnie says that the Migraine headache stayed with him for a week.

Northwest Corner of Throop and Willoughby Aves., 1940

Northwest corner Willoughby Ave. today

All Saints Church Columbus Day Parade   Brian Merlis Coll.

660 Willoughby Avenue, 1940

I start kindergarten in September, 1955 and sit in the classroom on the first day among a whole class of crying kids. One girl has a snot bubble come out of her nose. Our teacher's name is Mrs. Schryer.

P.S. 25 is 4 blocks away on Kosciusko St. and after a couple of weeks I'm going back and forth to school on my own and each day at 3 o'clock there are fights outside the school. You can always tell there's a fight down the street from the animated crowd of kids gathered in a fight circle. I see this each day, so one day after school I approach a kid and ask him if he wants to fight. He says "yeah" and punches me right in the eye. I grab my eye and start crying as he hits me over and over. Then I realize these fights I'm seeing are real. I should have asked him if he wanted to 'play' fight. I thought they were playing. I just wanted to gather a big crowd around me and be the focus of attention.

My reading level is always good so I'm placed in classes designated either 1 or 2 and attend school with kids who are clever, articulate and talented, and some of them live in houses owned by their parents. School is good and our teachers are interested in us. P.S. 25 is well kept, well furnished and well staffed, and they give us milk and cookies every morning at 10 o'clock. The milk monitors deliver the half-pint containers of milk, and our teacher keeps the cookies in a metal can that sends the smell of the cookies through the classroom when opened. We get hot school lunches every afternoon, and sometimes you can go back for seconds. We learn a song called "The Patriotic Wish" and sing it during assembly.

"I'd like to be the type of man the flag could boast about.

I'd like to be the type of man it cannot live without.

I'd like to be the type of man that really is American,

that is A-me-ri-can,

With head erect and shoulders square,

clean-minded fellow just and fair,

That all men picture when they see,

The Glorious Banner of The Free,

The Glorious Banner of The Free

P.S. 25 Kosciuszko Street entrance

I'm in the first grade and I see a twin for the first time. I don't know what a twin is. There are none on our block, none in my class, none in our family and none on TV and neither the subject nor the word has crossed into my vocabulary, nor even the image or idea. One day as school is letting out a classmate named Robert Wheeler goes to his waiting mother and his identical twin brother is with her. I guess Robert's brother's reading level is lower than ours, otherwise he'd be in our class. I'm shocked and speechless when I see this other Robert Wheeler. I walk home with nothing else on my mind except that there are two of them. I immediately tell Ma when I get home and she explains them to me and familiarizes me with the word. Twins.

Fats Domino has a record out that says "I'm gonna be a wheel someday, I'm gonna be somebody, I'm gonna be a real gone cat, then I won't want you." I don't know what he means by being a "gone" cat and I don't understand why he wants to be a wheel, so I ask Ronnie and he says "Gone man, cool, out of this world - can't catch him"! Then I ask him why he wants to be a wheel and Ronnie says, "A wheel, man, a big shot. A *big* wheel!" Every time I hear the record I think about Robert Wheeler and his twin.

Our block is between two major avenues, Throop and Sumner, that run north and south and are two-way streets with thick, black cables hanging above that the buses cling to with their long, black, mechanical arms stretching and crossing back and forth down the avenues under a canopy of wire. People shuffle and bop back and forth down both avenues to the market on DeKalb, P.S. 25 on Kosciuszko, and the elevated train on Myrtle Avenue. The sound of shoes with metal taps is constant. On a quiet night as you lay in bed you can hear people walking around the corner on Vernon Avenue with taps on their shoes. Boots called brogans become popular which are thick and black and strung up above the ankle with shoe-string hooks attached and they have large taps on the heels. All the poor kids on Willoughby get them because they last long. Having taps becomes cool in the city because they accentuate your walk and you create a cadence to bop to: TAP TAP TAP TAP *CH* TAP TAP TAP TAP.

I'm becoming kind of particular about my clothes and take care to keep my shoes shined and look neat. Sneakers come on the scene - P.F. Flyers and U.S. Keds. When kids come from down south we find it funny that they call sneakers "tennis". The reason sneakers are called sneakers is they're soft and quiet and you can "sneak" up on somebody. Before that, everybody had hard shoes and could be heard walking.

We and our white friends are close and share each other's ice cream. Betty Kivens sucks on a Fudgesicle, then sticks it in each of our mouths, all of us slurping on it, down to the wooden stick.

When the Black kids arrive from down south they're wild and rowdy, and menace the Jewish kids by snatching their Yarmulkes off and pulling the curls on the sides of the boys heads. The Jews begin walking differently now, less relaxed, faster, looking around and being careful. They look at people suspiciously.

The Yeshiva on the Northeast corner of Willoughby and Throop

Vacant lot today, where Yeshiva once stood.

There are bad kids and kids who aren't bad. The bad boys throw cats off roofs. There are lots of stray cats and dogs around, having litters here and there, and even in remote corners of our cellar, many kittens are born. On our way to school early in the morning we can hear the tiny mewing of newborn kittens off in a dark corner. There's one local stray cat named Bobtail, because most of its tail has been cut off by the wheel of a car. He never lets anyone touch him and the tail took about 3 weeks to heal but it healed itself, with Bobtail helping by licking it. He doesn't belong to anyone, and he sleeps somewhere in our cellar and sometimes in Mr. Tippy's cellar, and he goes across the street to the Puerto Rican house all the time, but now he knows how to cross the street and looks before he crosses, and he never walks, but always runs. He learned from getting his tail cut off.

My first black friend on Willoughby Ave. is Calvin Lewis who lives around the corner on Vernon Avenue with his mom and his brother Noel. Calvin's mother and Noel are light skinned and Calvin is very dark skinned and likes doing bad things. He's also Catholic and goes to St. John's Church and is a member of the Sea Cadets, who practice their routines and marching drills in the basement of St. Joseph Hall for orphaned girls. The Sea Cadets are like the Boy Scouts except that they're Navy cadets and they wear authentic, miniature Navy uniforms. They march crisply with precision and tightness. I envy Calvin in his Sea Cadet uniform and want to be a Sea Cadet and march in the Brooklyn Day Parade down Stuyvesant Ave. I meet Calvin when we're in the 2nd grade and he goes around saying,

"Listen motha-fucka let's git this straight, Yo mama got a pussy like a B-48. It don't burn much oil, it don't burn much gas, but listen motha-fucka, I'm gon kick yo ass."

I walk my sister Linda to school who's 5 and in Kindergarten. Each morning we go out of the way to Calvin's house and wait for him and the 3 of us walk to school together. This annoys Linda but I think Calvin is neat and cool. He has things I don't have, like the Sea Cadet uniform that my parents can't afford, and he also has a set of Lionel trains, neat clothes, and always has money for candy. But he's also strange for a kid because sometimes he doesn't spend his money on candy, instead, he'll buy a bottle of olives from the Spanish store and eat them out of the jar like they're peanuts or something. There are six kids in our family but in Calvin's it's only him and Noel, who's Ronnie's age. I notice that kids who don't have lots of brothers and sisters usually have more and better things, nicer clothes, more toys, go more places and sometimes go to private schools, just because there's only one or two of them in the family.

The first modern hi-fi I see is up Calvin's house, Christmas morning, 1957. The family has a new hi-fi and Calvin, Noel and one his friends all stand around the hi-fi as it's spinning, actually watching the record go round and round, fascinated by the technology of a disc with a handle that holds up to 8 records stacked one on another, automatically dropping one to be played at the end of each record. The 2nd modern hi-fi that I see is from Miss Hipp, Ma's friend who lives upstairs in 2D and she only has two kids, Donna and Leona.

There's something mean about Calvin. There seems to be something about his blackness that makes him different from his brother Noel and his mother, something that makes him vindictive and mischievous, almost like he's angry for being so black. He says, "Let's go play in the back alley so we can curse".

Susan and Lois Roth from up the block have a dog named "Gobby" who is pretty old, probably about 14. Gobby looks like a mixture of Beagle and something else. He's white, black and brown with large, long ears. He walks around slowly by himself, never on a leash, up and down the block and never into the street and never too far from his Brownstone home to be out of sight, and he never bothers or bites anyone. One day Calvin and I are walking up Willoughby towards Sumner and Gobby's walking ahead of us towards his house, with his toenails clicking on the sidewalk and his old groin hanging and swaying, when Calvin suddenly and unexpectedly kicks him in the balls. Gobby's scream sounds like the brakes of a car and he falls over to the side, yelping. I'm horrified. That's our neighbor's dog. Calvin runs up the block laughing and I never see him again.

679 Willoughby, former home of Susan and Lois Roth and their parents Birdie and Irving, and their dog Gobby.

Our first dog is named "Beauty", a little black and white, delicate long -haired Mutt who is Ronnie's pet and love. Ronnie watches television and Beauty jumps in his lap and licks him all on the chin and mouth, and follows him all over the cellar and everywhere he goes. Ma piles us in the car to go for a ride , all except Ronnie, and when she takes off Beauty chases behind the car trying to follow us and we watch her out the back window until Ma turns right on Sumner Avenue. When we get home that night the house is dark and

Ronnie is sick in bed, crying and holding his stomach. Beauty was killed by a car on Sumner Ave. The next day as we walk to school I ask him to show me where Beauty died and he points to the blood-stained spot in the gutter and he almost cries. Every day on the way to school I want him to show me the spot until he hollers and points: "Right there!! And don't ask me again!!" It's the most traumatic, tragic and hurtful moment in Ronnie's life, and he says he'll never cry over anyone like that again. Our next dog is Peaches, a rust-colored, long-haired Mutt who goes everywhere. Neither of these dogs ever had leashes or collars. They're wild and free and northerly urban, just like us kids. Our dogs eat Ken L Ration and Kadet dog food and sometimes Ma mixes leftover grits with the canned dog food to stretch out their meals. After two litters of puppies and 4 years of living with us, our dog Peaches simply disappears one day and we never see her again.

"This the way you Willoughby, Willoughby, Willoughby,

this the way you Willoughby all night long.

OH struttin' down the alley, alley, alley,

struttin' down the alley, all night long,

OH strut back Sally, Sally, Sally,

strut back Sally, all night long,

OH here comes another one just like the other one,

a little bit skinny but that's alright."

The girls sing and act out this little strut of a street dance
called The Willoughby and they form two lines and take turns
Struttin' Down The Alley.

In front of 666 Willoughby l to r top, Carmen, Sissy German, Ann , Betty-
Jean, Donna Hipp- middle, Don German, Joyce, Linda German-bottom,
Cathy German, Pop

The street games we play are Skelly, Chinese, Johnny-on-the-
Pony, Ring O' Livio, (which the Puerto Ricans call Coco Livio,)
Hot Peas and Butter, Crack Top, Punch Ball, Stick Ball, Box Ball,
Handball, Stoop Ball, Truth Dare Consequences Promise or

Repeat, and "Order in the Court Let the Monkey Speak, first one to speak is a monkey for a week", and everybody has roller skates. The heavy iron skates which come with skate keys are adjustable, plentiful, and affordable. These metal skates are also used to make scooters by nailing a wooden milk crate to a short beam of 2x4, then separating the skate and nailing each set of wheels to the ends of the beam, and finally nailing the milk crate to the 2x4 to lean on and steer. These homemade scooters are what later become skateboards.

We also make carpet guns, which use cut-up pieces of discarded linoleum for ammunition, and the gun is actually a rifle fashioned by using a 1x2 piece of wood about 3 feet long, 3-4 rubber bands knotted together and anchored on one end by some small, flathead tacks and a clothespin as the trigger, bound on the other end also by rubber bands. You cock the rifle by stretching the rubber band down to the clothespin, then squeeze the clothespin which bites down on the band and then you load a piece of linoleum between the rubber bands. When you squeeze the clothespin the bands snap loose, zipping and flying the half-dollar sized scrap of linoleum across the street. If you really want to be vicious, you load a piece of an old 78 record, which has the potential of really hurting someone. We pick old records out of the trash and fling them like flying saucers.

One day a girl is standing across the street from me and I'm about to throw a piece of a broken record and wondering about the odds of it hitting her if I fling it in her general direction. It hits her directly on her cheek and splits open her face under her eye. Ma whips me with a switch. I know the scar on the girl's face is permanent.

There's no playground or park nearby so we use the street for everything.

"Looka dat drunk man comin'."

He comes up the block in a short-sleeved white shirt tucked into his grey pants and has black suspenders and a dark grey hat. He's in a staggering stupor, stopping and swaying, his cigarette leading the way, and we harass and tease him, play with him, snatch his hat off, try to put our hands in his pockets and he stops, disoriented, and plays with us for a while. Sometimes we keep him for about an hour.

Dad works very hard. Besides being the super he also has a fulltime job. He works for a car dealership in Flatbush called Black Buick, where he details cars and preps them for sale, and he also Simonizes cars on the side. Dad's car is a black, 1949 Buick Dynaflow. I'm plundering and come across his business cards which read "Motorist-Wise with Simonize and be Surprised, says Eddie." There's a little picture on the cards showing a man wearing glasses and standing next to a car so I assume this is Dad. Dad is fair and nice, mindful and dignified.

He sweeps and mops the halls and staircase of the four-floor building, tends the furnace and lifts the extra-heavy ash cans one step at a time, full of ashes from the furnace, up to the sidewalk along with the garbage cans from the alley on collection days. He rolls wheel barrels full of coal from the coal bins to the furnace and he sweeps the sidewalk and the alley and whenever bad things happen in the building the results show up where we live in the cellar, so when the drains back up, the floors are flooded with toilet-paper and sewer water, and Dad and Ronnie have to wash down the concrete floor using hot water, scrub brushes and yellow industrial-soap powder that makes us sneeze.

One day while plundering I come across Dad's Army uniform hanging in a clothing bag in his closet and I unzip the bag and see all the shiny medals hanging on his jacket, and there's an inside pocket that has a brown leather folder, and inside the folder is a paper that says Honorable Discharge. I can see from all of this that he's been somewhere far away and done something important.

Ed German III, born 1916

"Boy, why you pee in the bed every night? Why cantchoo wake up and go to the bathroom? Aintchoo shame of yosef?"

My sanctified, born-again grandmother looks down at me with both hands on her hips, head held to one side, her long, grey hair divided into two braided pigtails hanging halfway down her back. "Whatchoo be doin ? Dreamin and peein ? Do you like the way it feel when you sleepin? And you just lay there and pee? You just peeeeeeeeeeeeeeeee!"

She looks up at the ceiling and closes her eyes like she's sleeping.

"You just peeeeeeeeeeeeeeeeeee!"

She says it in a funny, dreamy way and it makes me laugh so she says it even more and I laugh and make her say it over and over again, and she laughs with me, although I honestly bear the shame of peeing in the bed and can't explain why.

 She strips the bed and tosses the pissy sheets in the bath tub with warm water and lye soap.

"Now git in there and walk them sheets clean. When you eat supper tonight you ain't gon drink nothin. Um gon have to git some plastic and put it under them sheets on toppa dat mattress."

I'm walking the sheets and laughing in the bath tub, at the way she said peeeeeeeeeeeeeeeeee. There's a tall radio in the living room always playing on 77 WABC whenever the TV is off, and as I walk the sheets I start laughing again because they're playing a song called The Battle of New Orleans and they're singing about loading the cannon and they call it "powdering his behind". It's the first time I'm hearing someone say behind in a song on the radio.

Ma's parents come to live with us in 1958 when Granddad gets sick and has to give up the house they lived in on Shumaker Lane in Bridgeton, New Jersey, across the road from the freight-train track, sickle-pear trees and corn fields. Granddad had a chicken coop near the side of the house and a pig pen just inside the woods.

Grandma, born 1896

On hot summer days, Ronnie or some of the Puerto Rican kids open the fire hydrant, but we call it a "Johnny Pump", and with a tin can opened on both ends, create a powerful water cannon to shoot plumes 25 feet high and across the street, showering passing cars and flooding the gutters with flowing urban streams, hosing each other down and diminishing local water pressure until the cops come by and shut it off, only to be turned on again minutes later. Ma says that the Puerto Ricans turn on the Johnny pump because they come from a hot island and they're always surrounded by water.

The big boys buy firecrackers, ash cans and cherry bombs from Chinatown and Little Italy in Manhattan and we make homemade fireworks by tying steel wool to the end of a rope, light it with a match, and swing it around causing it to shoot flaming, sizzling sparks.

The Synagogue on the corner and the Yeshiva on the opposite corner are busy with Jewish men in their traditional, religious dress going in and out and the boys and girls in the Schul chanting their studies and prayers in the late spring and summer with the bare windows open for ventilation. Around the corner on Sumner Ave. is an underground bagel bakery, located in the cellar off the sidewalk. The smell of the fresh bagels comes out of the cellar from its sidewalk-iron doors which are usually open. When we peek down we see bagels floating and men wearing t-shirts, shorts and Yarmulkes, handling the bread and dough. We laugh at the bagel bakers because when we peek down there we can only see them from the waist down, their hips jerking back and forth in their short pants, high-top sneakers and white socks, running bagels. "Hey Mister!" We call down to the cellar bakery, and one of the young bearded bakers looks up and says "Vhat? Vhaddaya Vont?" "Can we have a bagel?" He gives us a crazy look then quickly reaches over and hands us a hot, fresh-baked bagel. "Here's von bagel, share it together." The bread is hot, chewy and soft, and we eat it immediately, feeling like we're Jewish and mock the bagel baker, saying to each other, "Vhaddaya Vont? Here's Von bagel!"

I'm always teasing my sisters and making up names for them. I call my sister Linda Jewish because she behaves more properly than the rest of us and more reserved, and soon we're all teasing her and calling her and accusing her of being Jewish, because she always tries to do everything correctly and perfectly and is very careful and thoughtful about everything, and she has money when no one else does, and when we've eaten all our candy and chewed all our bubble-gum, she has some hidden somewhere, and she's the neatest of my sisters with everything, so we say "Why are you so Jewish?" Whenever we eat meals with something special on the plate or something really good, Linda always has hers still on her plate after we'd eaten ours, saving it for last, knowing that she's taunting us because we're staring at it, and she knows we're staring at it, but doesn't let us know she knows. How could she leave something so delicious for last, teasing us with it, while all of ours is gone?

There's a jewelry store next to the bagel bakery on Sumner Avenue and there are all kinds of clocks, watches, and antique silverware in the windows and the man has a grandfather clock and a coo-coo clock in the back of the store that we discover one summer day as we walk by while the door is open and the clock is sounding. We ask the man if we can see the coo-coo clock and he takes us in the rear of the store and shows it to us, clicks a switch on the back of it and the bird comes out, coo-cooing. Then he says, "Alright, that's enough", and then ushers us out of the store. Cathy and Don begin going there regularly, pestering the man about the coo-coo clock almost every day, until one day Cathy comes home laughing and says that when they asked to see the coo-coo clock the man said okay. Then she said, "When he walked us the to the back of the store he was holding us by our pee-pees."

Synagogue on Southeast corner of Willoughby and Throop

Cornerstone of Synagogue, Willoughby & Throop Aves.

The former Synagogue, a day-care center today.

There are men selling fruits and vegetables from pushcarts on the corners and a black man selling hot-roasted peanuts from a contraption of a peanut roaster that has a steam whistle. The peanut man is very black and has a big nose with bumps all over it. He stands on the corner of Sumner and Willoughby Ave. all day, talking with folks passing, playing numbers and selling peanuts. Then later on after dark he comes cruising through the block in a brand-new yellow Cadillac.

The best knishes come from the knish man's silver-painted wagon on wheels that he pushes around the neighborhood and he sells round knishes that have pieces of onion in them and there are metal salt and pepper shakers attached to a chain.

Ruby Oshinsky, the knish man

There are 2 ice-cream trucks - The Good Humor man and the Bungalow man. It's a special treat if we get ice cream because most of the time Ma can't afford it for the 5 of us. Ma waits for the Ices Man, who has a horse-drawn, Italian-ices wagon painted red, white and green and he has 3 flavors-lemon, cherry and pineapple. They're homemade and delicious and refreshing and served in a generous-sized paper cup that fills your whole hand and costs 5 cents. He reaches up and rings a bell that hangs from the front of the carriage by hand, and you can hear him coming around the corner just when the more fortunate kids are finishing their ice cream bars and Ma says, "Oh yeah, here comes the good old Ices Man!" He drives through our neighborhood in his red, white and green horse-drawn wagon, ringing his bell with a cadence that goes Bing........Bing-Bing-da-Bing..........Bing Bing-da-Bing........He wears thick, black-framed glasses and black orthopedic shoes because one leg is shorter than the other. He's about 55 and hobbles back and forth from flavor to flavor, dispensing ices and collecting money and making change from the hand-operated change machine attached to his belt. The ice-cream men have these change machines too. The ices man has graying hair and short, gray whiskers, and no one ever complains about the sound of his bell. It's comforting and delightful. The smell of horse doodoo immediately reminds me of Italian ices, because the horse usually goes while you're waiting to be served and I smell a combination of cherry ices and horse doodoo. We also get a chance to pet the horse while he's there. I don't mind the smell of the horse doodoo. It's like a pleasant distraction.

Freezer Fresh, Carousel and Mister Softee start coming around selling soft ice cream with sprinkles, banana splits and milk shakes and playing loud clown music and things seem like they're changing. It's getting more crowded and louder. Two amusement-ride trucks come around. One of them is called the Whip and has cars that sit 2 kids each on an oval-shaped track and at each end of the track we get whipped around to the other side. The other truck ride is called the Half Moon and is hand operated with benches built inside and it swings back and forth, high into the air. The operator has a small transistor radio set on WABC and smokes a cigarette while he operates the ride, and Perry Como is on the radio singing Catch a Falling Star.

One of my childhood friends is David Duryea. He and his sister Donna live next door at 675 Willoughby with their Mom and Grandmother. They're Irish/Italian and Catholic and attend St. John's Church on the next block. I start going to church with David on Sundays and almost become Catholic. The huge, Gothic cathedral of St. John's is magnificently elaborate in design and dimensions and it overwhelms me to come out of the cellar and walk up the block and be in such an awesomely palatial cathedral, right down the street from my own house, watching the priests and the altar boys perform Catholic mass with all its mysterious rituals and incense, and speaking in Latin. One day we're walking from mass and we see some Jewish kids heading for the Talmudical-school-Yeshiva and David says, "You know the Jews killed Jesus, right?" I look at him in doubt and disbelief and he says, "Yeah, they really did. Them - (pointing at the boys in their Yarmulkes) They killed Jesus!" I tell him, "Nobody loves Jesus more than my Granddad and Grandma, and they don't have anything against the Jews." And David says, "Go down in the cellar and ask your grandfather. "THEY KILLED JESUS!" Late at night I turn over in my sleep and my grandparents are in their bed with the radio on and I catch a voice on the radio saying, "Have no fear, Big Joe is here." They fall asleep listening to Big Joe Rosenfeld on WABC who has a program called Big Joe's Happiness Exchange.

Interior of St. John's R.C. Church, Willoughby Ave.

St. John's R.C. Church 2011. Hart St. View

On another day David says, "Your mother yelled at God. I heard her." I ask him what he's talking about and say that my mother doesn't yell at God. He says, "I was walking by your windows in the backyard and I heard your mother yell, 'JESUS, WHO DID THIS'?" Then he starts laughing and says, "Why does your father call your mother Monk?"

I like going up David's house because he has a Lionel train set and a portable record player, and we run the train and play Chubby Checker's hit record, The Twist, over and over, and his grandmother gives us cheese sandwiches or spaghetti with Parmesan cheese sprinkled on it. David's Dad drives a tractor-trailer truck and is always away from home. We play in the living room and Donna is in the bedroom watching TV or doing homework. David and I are 7 and Donna is 9. They go to St. Ambrose Catholic School on DeKalb and Tompkins.

St. Ambrose Catholic School

One day David and I are playing in the alley of 675, surrounded by the odor of cigar smoke, musk, and the Flamingos singing I Only Have Eyes for You, coming out of *their* super's open cellar door. Their super is Mr. Tippy. Donna is wearing a yellow dress and walking on the ledge above the staircase and David and I are below her and David's peeking up her dress and laughing and he whispers to me, "I can see it. I can see it". And I whisper back, "Yeah? What does it look like?", and he looks up, laughs and says, "a piece of cheese", and he beckons and whispers "hurry up, hurry up, look". I go down the steps and peek up her dress and see what he's laughing at. He always talks about the Long Island Railroad and traveling out to his aunt's house in Massapequa.

The ledge Donna walked on when we peeked under her dress.

I like to draw and Ma buys me a set of oil paint-by-the-numbers and I isolate a little alcove under a light with a chair and a table in the cellar where I can work because the smell of the oils is too strong to use in the apartment and there's no room there, so I work for hours in this dimly-lit perch, using real oil paint, creating landscapes and seascapes by-the-numbers. Ma saw that I was interested in drawing when I was six and I got a piece of drawing paper and a brown crayon and drew a big circle for a head, two slits for eyes, two black dots for nostrils and a mouth showing teeth. I colored the rest of the head brown, presented it to Ma and said, "Look Ma, this is a colored man". She laughed and laughed and kept that drawing and showed it to people and repeated what I said and they laughed at it for a long time. While I'm painting Dad comes in the cellar from the alley on his way into our apartment, passes me and glances at what I'm doing but doesn't stop for long. One day I stop him to show him my progress because I want his approval and he bends over my work, looks and says, "Um Hm, Das good". It's serious work to me, requiring focus and control, and I feel like a real artist, enchanted by the aroma of the oils, and rinsing the brushes in turpentine, though it's only by the numbers.

Dad sometimes sends us to the barber shop with no money and says: "Tell Fats I said cutcho head" or "Tell Cookie I said cutcho head"! "I'll pay em when I come by." Dad is generous to us with money. He doesn't buy us clothes or gifts, only Ma does. We soon discover that the best time to ask Dad for money is when he's had a couple of highballs. If you ask Dad for a quarter when he's sober he'll give you a quarter. But if you wait till he's had a couple of drinks and ask him for a quarter he'll give you fifty cents.

Dad and Ma

I start playing records for people when I'm 8 at Dad and Ma's poker-game parties. In our 4-room flat in the cellar, the kitchen is the first room you enter, then the living room, our bedroom and my parents' bedroom in the back. Ma cooks and sells chicken and fish dinners and sandwiches with cold cans of beer and shots of whiskey and Dad is in the back room "cutting" the poker game. I'm in the living room playing the records and watching the grownups dance.

My Uncle Bill on Ma's side comes up from South Jersey to gamble, whether we're having a poker game or if the game is down in Brownsville somewhere. He drives 150 miles to gamble in someone's apartment on Osborn Street, because gambling is his thing and he can handle cards and dice expertly, and the bigger money is in New York, where men have good-paying jobs and there's plenty to choose from for a guy who's come to take people's money. He drives a 1949 dark-purple Dodge with a miniature, oscillating, rubber fan on the dashboard.

74 Osborne Street 1950s   Brian Merlis Coll.

39 Osbourne Street   Brian Merlis Collection

After gambling all night Uncle Bill comes over our house to sleep before driving home and we go through his pockets and steal quarters from his pants hanging on the bed pole. It's eerie and risky when we steal his quarters because he sleeps with his eye lids half open and it seems like he's looking at us. The poker parties at our house go on for over 20 years, wherever we live.

86 Osborn Street Brownsville, 1950s, Brian Merlis Collection

We don't have a record player or records but our upstairs neighbor, Ma's friend Juliette Hipp does. She brings her suitcase-hi-fi and a stack of records down for the party. Dakota Staton's album "The Late Late Show" and records by

Gloria Lynne, Ray Charles, and Nina Simone. The first time I heard Nina Simone singing I Loves you Porgy, I thought she was saying I Loves you Bucky. People are dancing the Madison, wearing Continental suits and doing the Continental Walk. There's an afternoon TV program called Jocko's Rocket Ship, with black teenagers dancing The Stroll and the Slop, then dancing slow to Tears on My Pillow, and one of Ronnie's favorite records is Dream Lover by Bobby Daren. Teenagers are wearing tight, high-water pants that show the color of your socks that match the color of your shirt with its shirt tail hanging out. Young men are wearing their hair straightened process style, or conked.

One cold winter after a snowstorm three of us boys go into the coal bins and get shovels and walk up the block and ring the bell of St. Joseph Hall and offer to shovel a path from Sumner Ave. to Lewis Avenue. The tall Sister comes to the side entrance and opens the large iron door and says, "Okay, ring the bell when you're finished." We shovel a walking path the entire block and our feet and hands are wet and cold. Halfway through the block I turn around to look back and see how far we've gotten, and the Sister is down the block checking our progress too. When we finish we ring the bell and the Sister says, "Okay, leave your shovels outside and come in. Hang your coats up over there and come with me." We hang up our coats and follow the Sister to the cafeteria while the delicious smell of lunch is pulling us in. They serve us spiced-ham sandwiches and split-pea soup and cake and milk. We're in the big cafeteria alone and don't see the girls who live there. Their lunch hour is probably over. We eat the food gratefully and the Sister says, "Do you want some more?" We get second helpings and follow her back upstairs, put on our coats and the Sister gives us $3.00 each, more than we ever expected. God and St. Joseph are friendly to us.

Main entrance to St. Joseph Hall

Ma mother gets a job cooking and cleaning for the actor Burl Ives and she comes home with autographed posters of the big, bearded man. He also gives Ma the record album West Side

Story which I play over and over memorizing each song from When You're a Jet to Maria.

One day I'm sitting in Aiken's barbershop waiting my turn in the chair and the jukebox is playing. There's a man singing in a West Indian accent saying, *"Oh my friend it's easy to tell, a white man's heaven is a black man's hell."* I'd never heard anything like that and I start looking around and feel relieved that there's no white people in here to hear this song because I would be embarrassed for them and ashamed for myself.

A family moves into apartment 1A called the Martins. The husband and wife are German and French, and very big people and somebody said they had been professional wrestlers. They're both kind of fat and Mr. Martin sometimes shows off his thigh muscles to other tenants, making them move up and down above his knee, under his brown pants. He has thinning, brown hair combed straight back, a large nose and he smokes cigars. He looks like a fat version of Bud Abbot of Abbot & Costello. Mrs. Martin has red hair and speaks with an accent and has high, fat cheekbones and her mouth looks like she's always eating something even though she isn't. We begin having problems as soon as they're settled in because they don't think we should be out front playing with the other kids because we're black. Dad operates the building and she moves in 5 years later and starts barking orders to my sisters. "Don't play over here. Get avay from here. Get back downstairs. Get out of the hallvay. No sitting on the front steps!" To her, my sisters Sissy, Linda and Cathy are the black super's kids who live in the cellar where the black coal bins are and the entrance to their house is down a flight of grimy, concrete steps, next to where the garbage cans are kept and their windows are at the bottom of the building and face the back of the house so that's where they're supposed to play.

Mr. Martin doesn't like Ronnie and when he has a chance he harasses and provokes him. One day Ronnie is walking home and approaching the corner of Throop and Willoughby, and Mr. Martin sees him coming and won't let him cross the street, so Ronnie goes to the other corner and Mr. Martin again blocks his way. They go back and forth like this for some time. Ronnie finally dodges his way around him and tells Dad what's happening and I remember Dad and Mr. Martin facing each other in the cellar near the coal bins looking like they're getting ready to fight. I'm ready to jump in if they do. I can't wait to hit him. I'll kick him in his mouth if he touches Dad.

The Martins have a son named Leo and soon Leo and I start playing together. Mrs. Martin doesn't care about me and Leo playing and I don't know why, but she won't let my sisters near her daughter Karen. Their oldest son Dennis has red hair and Ronnie and Dennis also soon become friends. It's funny and stupid. The Martins eventually start harassing their Jewish neighbors on the first floor and leave something in a brown paper bag hanging on the door knob of Ellen Levine's apartment across the hall from them. Ellen's mother, Mrs. Levine, is in the hall and says to me pointing to the bag on the door knob, "What kind of people are these?" I look at the bag and say "What is it?" "Who knows what it is?" she says, "I'm not gonna touch it." When the Martin's apartment door is open it seems like their house smells like spit.

Things finally come to a head one day when Mrs. Martin and Ma get into a fist fight in the lobby of our building because Mrs. Martin is harassing my sisters again. Ma is 7 months pregnant with my brother Don and there's much wrestling and hair pulling and scratching and banging each other against the lobby door. Ma punches Mrs. Martin in the head several times. The fight happens real fast and Mrs. Martin calls the police and presses charges against Ma but when they go to court and the judge sees that Ma is 7 months pregnant he dismisses everything.

There is an elderly Jewish woman who lives across the street at 670 on the 5th floor who shouts down to me from her window, "Sonnyeee" and she waves her hand beckoning and says "Come up! It's 5B". I cross the street, enter the lobby and take the elevator to the 5th floor and she's at her door waiting. "Come in, come in." Her apartment smells like moth balls and she ushers me into the kitchen where a stove burner is on. She points to it and says, "Turn that off for me like a good boy." Then I follow her into the living room to a light switch. " Turn this off for me like a good boy." After I turn off the various switches in the house she gives me a nickel and some candy and says "Thank You, you're a nice boy. Your father's the super across the street.......... I knowwwww!" On certain Saturdays I simply look up to her window and she's there waving me up.

670 Willoughby with 666 Willoughby on right, 1940

There 's also a man in our building named Mr. Zimmerman who pays me to do the same things in his apartment. Mr. Zimmerman's legs are somewhat crooked and he walks funny with a cane and works at one of the Kosher bakeries on Lee Avenue in Wiliamsburg, and he comes home waddling down the street with a bag full of Pumpernickel and Challah bread and gives it to my mother. We kids like the Challah bread but not the Pumpernickel. There are lots of old Jewish people on the block and they congregate on their folding chairs and sit in front of the buildings and talk. Even on cold days in the winter they bundle up, the women in their babushkas, and come outside to find a place in the sun to sit and get fresh air. They sit on our side of the street which faces south with the most sun. In the spring and summer I pass them sitting there and I see tattooed numbers on their arms. In the fall I see Jewish men making their fire escapes look like little houses. Ronnie's friend Stewie explains to me that it's for Sukkot, and that when the Jews roamed the desert for 40 years they had to build little houses to make shelter. The corner of Throop and Willoughby is busy with Jewish men and boys dressed in their Orthodox clothing, and on Holidays, many of the men wearing fur hats called Schtrimels.

An Orthodox man wearing a Schtrimel on Sabbath

We wear clothes handed down from the tenants upstairs and down the block. My sisters wear dresses given to us by the Roth family for whom Ma cleans house. Ma scrubs the Ross' floors and waxes them with thick, pungent, Dandee brand floor wax on her hands and knees. Ma is always working. She cooks and cleans for others and cooks and cleans at home. Their two daughters, Susan and Lois play with Sissy and Linda and give them a life-sized doll named Suzabelle, who used to belong to Susan Roth. She's about 3 feet tall and wears a dress and shoes. She has blue eyes and dark brown hair and comes to live with us in the cellar. She sleeps in the bed with my sisters and sits up and watches cartoons with us. We all sleep in one bedroom - the girls in one big bed by the window and me and Ronnie in another bed opposite them. Suzabelle sits propped up at the kitchen table while we eat grits and eggs, and stares at the oatmeal in our bowls and stares at the TV, watching the silent, musical cartoons of Farmer Gray. I play with her eyelashes with my fingers, brushing the thick, stiff lashes and opening and closing her eyes. One day she's sitting in a chair naked and I ask "Where's her clothes?" "Ma put 'em in the washing machine", the girls say. There's a washing machine in the cellar with a cylinder that wrings out the clothes before you hang them on the line. My arm got caught in the wringer once because I was playing with it, and Ma had to wrestle it loose. Ma uses Oxydol detergent in the washing machine and there are commercials on TV about Duz Soap Powder. My baby sister Cathy drags Suzabelle around the house by one arm and crushes cookies on her little red lips and pours milk onto her closed mouth. Ma wipes the grime off her pink and white face with a dish cloth. She's like having a little white sister in the house.

Suzabelle becomes a victim of Hurricane Donna , which comes through our block and also takes down the big tree in front of the Roth's house. She gets left out in the backyard and drowns during the hurricane. We don't know she's been left out until we open the window curtains and see the concrete yard flooded with about 3 feet of water and Suzabelle floating face down amongst the debris. When the water recedes I lift her up and water comes out of her eyes like tears and her plastic body is heavy with liquid and she has to be put in the garbage.

Our block becomes more crowded and noisy. We never see people moving in or out because this is always done at night, and since we live in the cellar in the back, we never see the new arrivals until the next day, when suddenly there are more kids. As the whites move, many new arrivals are blacks moving from the tenements on DeKalb Ave. between Sumner and Lewis which have been condemned to make room for the new DeKalb Avenue housing projects. Ma wishes we could have a "nice, decent apartment in the projects because they're clean and neat and everyone is equal and we wouldn't be the super and might even live on one of the top floors and have a nice view from our windows."

The New projects. DeKalb Ave. looking west towards Sumner Ave.

Brian Merlis Coll.

Our block is unique for the area because it has 10 apartment buildings totaling over 450 apartments, plus 16 two and three-family buildings. The population potential for the block is huge. Dr. Grenchlog is moving and early one evening a crowd gathers in front of the Willoughby Mansion and he and his wife are bidding farewell to their neighbors near the waiting moving truck. Many neighbors are former patients of his and one man says, "Thank you Dr. Grenchlog for saving my life." Then he shakes the bald Doctor's hand, the crowd applauds and they get in their car and the moving truck follows them away.

Across the street from P.S. 25 is the Annex, an addition to the school, a red, brownstone building dated 1879 whose interior is all wood and there are tall, sliding doors between the classrooms. I attend 3rd and 4th grade there before resuming in the main building for 5th and 6th grade, and the Annex is where I find out about Green-Leaf Day. Each spring, when the leaves return to the trees, Green-Leaf Day comes and you have to carry a green leaf or else get beat up by the big boys. They'll stop you and say, "Show me your green leaf or ummo bust yo ass." So we put green leaves in all our pockets. The meanest teacher in the school teaches in the Annex and her name is Mrs. Hayes, a short, bent over, bowlegged black woman with gray and black hair and a slight hunch in her back who walks with a jerk and whose wet lips are perpetually formed into a fish mouth. She teaches at the Annex and is always yelling at kids and sending them to the principal's office and walking boys down the hall by the ear. She hates kids. I make sure I never give her a reason to say anything to me, but Sissy has her for her 2nd grade teacher and hates her because Mrs. Hayes beat her with a yard stick one day.

We line up in the Annex school yard each morning before class and in the afternoons after lunch and my teacher, Mrs. Troolis, rounds up all the kids by ringing a bell that she calls a Glockenschpiel. During Christmas break 1958 Mrs. Troolis goes to Hawaii and comes back all dreamy eyed and teaches the class a Hawaiian song, then for Easter recess 1959 she goes to Greece and comes back marveling and telling the class all about Greece. When I started 25 the principal was Mr. Gershbein but he soon retired and Mr. Weintraub took his place. I remember Mr. Gershbein addressing the assembly on his last day there, and crying on the stage during his speech. When he was crying he reminded me of Lou Costello.

My fifth- grade teacher is Mr. Kaplan, who wears two suits, one brown, one blue, alternating each day. The pants on both of his suits are shiny in the back. Mr. Kaplan hits us if we get out of line, but he doesn't hit the girls. Just like Dad does. But he slaps the boys on the back of the head or lays us down on top of his desk and whacks us on the behind, which is both painful and embarrassing, and he says to us boys, "If you don't behave I'm gonna kick you right in the pants." In the afternoons he pulls down a map of the world and illustrates what he thinks the United States will do if the Russians decide to attack us, and points to all of our geographical military advantages and where he thinks the United States will have its nuclear missiles on the ready. He teaches us the song, When the Caissons go Rolling Along, and The Sidewalks of New York.

Down in front of Casey's old, brown, wooden stoop, on a summer's evening we would form a little group, boys and girls

together, me and Mamie O'Rourke, would hit the light fantastic on the sidewalks of New York

The Annex of P.S. 25 on Kosciuszko Street bet. Throop and Sumner

Looking northeast to residential bldg on Kosciuzsko St. where P.S. 25 annex
once stood.

DeKalb projects in background

One day a boy enrolls in our school who was severely burnt in
a fire. He's dark skinned and his face has been terribly burned
with his skin melted into a severely disfigured, grotesque and
distorted, life-long impairment. When I first see him I'm
horrified and I can't believe what I'm seeing. To me, it's like
looking at a monster. At the end of the day when school lets
out there are girls literally screaming, crying and running down
the street from him, simply because his appearance is so
disturbingly hideous and shocking. They've never seen
anything like it, none of us have, not even in a monster
picture. I feel sorry for the boy immediately, but can't look at
him for more than a glance. I continue to see this kid years
later as we move from neighborhood to neighborhood and

imagine what kinds of things make him feel good and what he hopes for.

There's a witch on Kosciuzsko Street just a few doors down from the school. At least, she's our witch. Everybody says she's a witch. She lives on the ground floor and her kitchen window faces the street and she's old and pale with long gray hair and there's a constant stream of us kids walking by her window every day on our way to and from school and she's cooking something on the stove and yells to us, "What are you looking at? Get away from here." She has a long, sharp nose and looks like the wicked witch on the Wizard of Oz. She's irritated from living so close to the school with all its kids and it shows on her face. Plus, her building is right next to the school yard so even when school is out there's always kids playing in the school yard to irritate her. If we catch her eye she leers back at us and since she's old and white with long hair and a sharp nose and always stirring something on the stove and hates kids, she's the witch. We look forward to walking past her house to and from school every day, especially in the Spring when her window is open. In the winter we bang on her window and run.

One day I change my last name from German to Germain because I'm tired of kids teasing me about my last name and saying Heil Hitler and then laughing. It's stupid. Ma checks my homework one night and sees that I've changed my name and makes me change it back. But my teacher, Mrs. Fenderson, calls me Edwin Germain for a couple of months. I'd never thought about my last name much. I know that all the Jewish and white kids tease me about it . Dad served in Burma,

France and Germany during the war and had people in Europe puzzled about his name tag. The Jewish people in our building always address Ma like a question: "Hello, Mrs. German?"

It bothers me that my name is German because I'm a kid and don't know how to handle it. When everyone's laughing and looking and focused on me I don't get it and don't want it. I don't want to be different. I want to be neat and not teased. I don't want to be weak or small or ugly. I want to be applauded, not laughed at. In school I'm teased about my last name but back on the block I'm teased about my nickname *and* my last name. Bucky German. German is bad enough but "Bucky Beaver", the animated buck-tooth beaver is selling Ipana Toothpaste on TV commercials. If the kids in school ever find out my nickname is Bucky and that I pee-the-bed and live in a cellar I'll never return. I get the nickname from Ma's brother Ellis, whose nickname is Buck.

Ellis (Buck) Harris

Lonnie (Preacher) Harris

Ronnie constantly teases and criticizes me because he's my older brother and feels it's part of the deal. He teases me about peeing in the bed, not knowing how to catch a ball, and he follows me around the cellar and the backyard rubbing it in and provoking me by singing "Anything you can do I can do

Better." One winter afternoon I come home from school and take off my coat and get ready to change my clothes and look in the mirror and like the way I look because we'd had assembly that day and had to wear a white shirt and tie and when I see myself in the mirror still looking sharp and crisp I decide not to change my clothes. I feel important, middle class and worthy. All the important men on television have white shirts and ties, and lots of people on television sit down at the dinner table in a white shirt and tie. I'm sitting in the cellar dressed up and looking at television and Ma's cooking dinner when Ronnie walks in the door.

It's about 5pm and already dark outside and he comes in to get something and go back out with his friends. I'm 9 and he's 14. On his way out the door I catch his eye and he stops, looks at me with surprise and disdain, and speaks properly: "Why haven't you changed your clothes?......... Why are you sitting there in a white shirt and tie?..... Who do you think you are?........You mean to tell me you have the **AUDACITY** to sit there in a white shirt and tie like you're somebody?.......... I can't answer him because I'm stunned and unprepared for his attack. I'm so self absorbed, and beginning to get comfortable being neat and clean and dressed up after school, that I *do* feel like I'm somebody. I feel as important as the people on television. What's audacity?

Edwin (Bucky) German

We speak in a language that combines what we're taught at
home and what we hear on the sidewalk. We're forbidden to
curse but we can't even use the words lie or liar. A lie is a story
and a liar is a story teller. We learn this from Grandma. We
refer to our private parts as our pee pees and behinds and
doo-doo is also called mess. Our Jewish friends call it doody,
and so do their parents. Going to the toilet is either peeing or
messing and it's funny to us whenever the landlord comes
around because his name is Herb Messing. But we have to call

him *Mr.* Messing. We laugh out loud in front of him as he looks at us puzzled. One day in school a staff member says to my teacher, "Come out and see my new car." And the teacher said "I can't right now, cause I'm on duty." I instantly look down at her feet, expecting to see doody under her shoe.

We're growing up in an environment of hustling, gambling and drinking . There is certainly drinking, smoking and gambling during the countless poker and crap games held at the house. By the time Ronnie is 15, he's already cutting the poker game for Dad at these gambling sessions. When we wake up the following morning the smell of cigarettes and empty beer cans fills the house. There are lots of people running numbers and playing numbers and the Number Man makes his rounds all over the neighborhood with two pockets full of money, one with bills and one with coins that jingle as he walks, and as he fondles them when he stops and talks. Number players are keeping their eye on the "handle", which appears in the Daily News each day, and getting hints of numbers to play from the Chinese- cartoon character in the newspaper, Ching Chow.

Our number man is Mr. Bob. He dresses sharp and is good looking with a neatly trimmed mustache and drives a white, 1958 Cadillac Eldorado with red leather interior. He wears Panama hats, Ban-Lon shirts, pleated Gabardine trousers with an alligator belt, and 1 and 1/2" cuffs over biscuit-toe, brown Kangaroo shoes with white stitches along the soles, or sometimes in the summer he wears brown and white Spectators.

Daddy has a cousin named Jimmy Blunt but everybody calls
him Blunt but we have to call him Uncle Blunt or Mr. Blunt.
He's dresses sharp and is peculiarly funny and says "I like my
whiskey straight and my women crooked!", and "There's 2
things I can't stand, a dirty car and a ugly woman!" And if
somebody says: "Hey Blunt, you look nice", he says "And I
smell good too." or, "Well hell, Um gon' live till I die!" He says
the funniest things with a straight face and when he laughs,
he breaks out in a broad, hearty laugh and then stops
abruptly, switching to a serious glance. He keeps a bottle of
whiskey in his inside jacket pocket. He does tricks with his
fingers and a routine that he does with an empty paper bag,
throwing imaginary items in the air and catching them in the
empty bag with a "thump" that he makes with one of his
hidden fingers. One day Dad comes in the house with Blunt
staggering behind him singing Que Sera, Sera, by Doris Day,
and walks in the kitchen singing and laughing and tells my
mother the following story:

"Heyyyyy Ollie Dear Darlin, Listen to what just happen roun
the corner. Me and Ed was drivin up Sumner Ave. and I was
sittin there relaxin wid the winda down and Ed was gittin
ready to turn left on Hart Street and one o'them black-ass
jitterbug niggas was standin in the street cuttin'-the-fool and
ain't payin attention to traffic and I was watchin' him............
so when Ed turned the corner........ I reached out........ and
hauled off...... and slapped that nigga right upside his head
and we kept goin. I slapped that niggah so hard it hurt my
hand and he stumbled back on the sidewalk. I liked to broke
my arm reachin out and slappin that niggah. I swear.....

Ed....Tell Ollie what happened!" Ma is laughing and so am I, and Daddy confirms his story, laughs and calls Blunt a damn fool. Blunt gives my brother Don the nickname Thumb, because he's the baby of the family and the littlest, and Tom Thumb is playing in the movies.

When the TV series Peter Gunn comes out, a dance comes out with it called The Peter Gunn, where you hold your hands on the sides of your waist pointing your forefingers like you have two pistols, and jerk your pelvis front and back. Don learns to do the Peter Gunn when he's 3, and whenever my Uncle Jewel comes over he pays Don to do the Peter Gunn, and laughs until his eyes are wet. Later, Uncle Jewel nicknames himself Pete, then finally he calls himself, The Peter. He's the smallest of Ma's brothers, and the loudest. When he comes over, he walks in the door and loudly announces: "Have no fear, The Peter is Here." It all started with Peter Gunn.

Dad never plays with us or takes us anywhere, unless it's all of us going to see Ma's family down in South Jersey. Whenever we take these trips Dad and Ma cap them off with a shot of bourbon once we hit the turnpike. Ma reaches in the glove compartment and pulls out the pint of Ancient Age and pours Dad a shot. Dad drinks the shot, then lights a Marlboro that smells good when it's first lit, kind of toasty. One day we're getting ready to go down to South Jersey and we're packed in the car and Dad is behind the wheel with an uncomfortable look on his face and he puts his hand on his stomach and Ma says to him, "What's wrong?" Dad says "gas", and shakes his head, and I say "Daddy, there's a gas station right around the corner", and they look at each other and laugh.

Ma is the one who piles us in the car on a Sunday afternoon and says "Let's go get lost." She drives us all up in Harlem, down in Sheepshead Bay, touring the mansions on Bedford Avenue, and she takes us into Forest Hills and up in Jamaica Estates and through President Street in Crown Heights where some of the rich Brooklyn Jews live. Dad comes to Coney Island with us once. He knows how to swim but we don't, and my mother doesn't allow us to go swimming because when she was young she and her sisters were swimming in a pond in Georgia and her sister Mable drowned and Ma tried to help her but couldn't save her and it bothered her all of her life. But dad is in the ocean at Coney Island, floating on his back with his big toe sticking up as we watch from the shore. He never tosses a baseball to me and doesn't teach me to ride a bike. He doesn't do these things. He's always working on his job or around the building and in the cellar or trying to make some extra money by having a poker game.

He grew up in the south on farms and his dad didn't play with him either. He said he left home at age 14 when one day in the middle of plowing the field he had enough of being behind the mule. It was burning hot and he said he couldn't do it anymore, and had also had a taste of the big city, Savannah. He dropped the plow and headed for the house. "Whatchoo doin' boy?" His father said, "Git back in that field!" Dad said he was drinking water from the pump at the well, and told his father he didn't want to do that anymore and was going to the city, Savannah, to find a job. He said that as he was leaving, his father fired a shotgun at him and the buckshot hit the side of the house, and he was gone, out on his own, never to live with his dad and ma anymore. Dad's father committed suicide by drowning in the Savannah River. He had stolen money from the church to buy a Model A Ford.

Ed German II, Dad's Father, born 1876

The first Puerto Ricans I meet are these two boys who live at 679 Willoughby, on the ground floor in the Roth's house with their mother and grandmother. I don't know where their dad is. They only live here for a few months but we play together in the neighboring backyards and alleys. One day around 5pm their grandmother calls them in and the older boy says "We gotta go in now, my mother's coming home and we're gonna get a beating." "Why? What did you do?" I ask. And the boy says "We didn't do nothing. We get a beating every day when my mother comes home just in case we did something bad." They go into the house. I listen later by their window as their mother yells at them in Spanish and hits them with a belt.

More and more Puerto Ricans are moving in and we see little Puerto Rican boys in tenement building windows, walking on the window ledge, playing naked among the sheets that hang for curtains, in full view, not caring that we can see their pee pees. We hear people using the word Spic, because Spanish people who can't speak English say "I no espic'...... I no espic English." The Puerto Ricans we get to know are Georgie, Sammy, Tito, Raoul, Rafael, Gilberto, Diego, and Ronnie is friends with Mike and another kid named Willie Camacho.

The first U.S. Marine I ever see is a Puerto Rican kid named Rafael, standing in front of 666 Willoughby in full Dress Blues on a sunny Saturday afternoon , surrounded by Spanish people, telling them about boot camp. The dress blue uniform stops me where I am, standing in front of the Gold Manor and I stare at him from across the street, enchanted as the sun glistens on his shiny brass buttons and the Marine Corps emblem against the white cover on his head, and he's standing there with white gloves on at Parade Rest, his proudest moment ever.

Georgie Garcia lives across the street in a private house that always has Spanish people living in it and he's always getting into trouble. One day I'm in the courtyard playing with some darts because Ma can't see me there and she forbids us to play with darts and I'm there alone and think about the odds, wondering to myself, "If I throw this dart straight up in the air and not move, will it land on my head?" Without another thought I fling the dart into the air and stand there waiting. It strikes me straight on the top of my head and I run in the house crying and bleeding and Ma screams "What happened?" I'm scared to tell her I had a dart so I blame it on Georgie and she grabs me by the hand and takes me across the street to Georgie's mom and screams, "Look what Georgie did!" Poor Georgie's mouth hangs open and he's confused and defensive, nodding his head "no" and pleading, "I didn't do it Mrs. German, I swear, I didn't do nuthin." Georgie's mom smacks him on the back of the head and he runs through the house crying. I didn't expect Ma to confront him so quickly, and I never tell her that it wasn't Georgie.

The House that Georgie's and other Spanish families lived in at 676 Willoughby Ave.

The courtyard is a place where I injure my head twice. One day I'm playing with a boy named Lennel, and Dad's friend Mr. Leroy walks through and we say "Hi Mr. Leroy, could you swing us around?" He often grabs us boys by the wrists and swings us around and around. But this time he says "Lemmy hold you by the ankles." So Lennel goes first. He gets on the ground like he's going to do a push up, and Mr. Leroy takes him by the ankles and swings him in the air and he's flying in a circle with his arms stretched out. Then he says "OK you next." I think about the odds again, of him dropping me. Somehow I know he's going to drop me and he does, right on my head, and I'm hurt and bleeding and he carries me in the house to my mother. It seems like the courtyard is cursed because I hurt my head there twice and Ronnie broke Stewie's nose there by mistake.

Another Puerto Rican boy is named Sammy who lives around the corner on Vernon Ave. and comes around and knocks on our door and Ma lets him eat grits and tomatoes with us. "How you get these tomatoes like this Mrs. German?" Sammy asks ma. "They come crushed in a can Sammy, and you just heat 'em up and add a little sugar and black pepper and some butter, and serve 'em on top of the grits with some melted cheese." "Ummm, these are good....I'm gonna tell my ma!" Sammy has a unique kind of urban-jungle call, a high-pitch, alternating yodel, sort of like Tarzan, and on quiet summer nights while lying in bed I can hear his holler from around the corner, across the roofs and backyards.

Two more Puerto Rican boys on Willoughby are Gilbert and Diego, brothers who live across the street at 666. Gilbert is my age and Diego is Ronnie's age. Diego was born in Puerto Rico, but Gilbert was born in New York. Gilbert shows me how to make a shoe-shine box and teaches me to sing,

I've got sixpence, jolly jolly Sixpence

I've got sixpence, to last me all my life.

I've got sixpence to spend, and sixpence to lend, and sixpence to take home to my wife.

A Spanish couple moves into our building upstairs on the top floor with windows facing the street and also the courtyard. Their names are Dominick and Angie. Dominick is an auto mechanic and likes to drink beer and his eyes are always red and they fight a lot. When they fight, most of the noise seems to come out of the courtyard windows when I'm standing there looking up at the sky as I often do, or just crossing from one building to the other and suddenly the most violent and frightening sounds come from Dominick and Angie's apartment. Deep and horrible screams that make me jump, stacks of dishes crashing, mirrors breaking and kids screaming. I stand frozen in the courtyard, astonished and horrified with my heart beating, because I've never witnessed violence this emotional, not even on television. It's immediately real and I'm afraid that Angie will come flying out the window any moment, with lamps, radios and television following her down to the concrete and her head will hit the ground and crack open. I don't know what it is about the courtyard.

To escape from the concrete sidewalks and have a little adventure we go climbing in the connecting backyards, treading on fences 7 feet high, plucking the scuppernong grapes that line some of the neighbor's fences and dodge around the barking dogs. It feels a little like being in the country when we escape into the connecting backyards in the summer when the trees are full and you can smell honeysuckle and flowers and see pear trees in the middle of the city and eat mulberries from the mulberry trees so plentiful in Brooklyn.

There's a man who lives around the corner on Vernon Avenue on the top floor whose back windows face ours and he smokes cigars and takes early-evening naps on his fire escape on a narrow beach chair. He lays there facing west, watching the sun sinking over Bedford Avenue. He looks Italian, with his dark hair combed straight back and his white, sleeveless undershirt. He sleeps on the fire escape until the sun sets, then he brings the set-up in the house. I name him The Booga man. Our white friends say Boogie Man, but we learn the name from our southern parents and grandparents, and people from down south who say Booga Man. I tell all my cousins who live in the country that the Booga man sleeps up on a fire escape, and when my cousins come from South Jersey to visit we take them in the backyard and point to the fire escape and tell them that he sleeps there, which they think is nonsense, and they've never seen fire escapes because they're from the country. But as the sun retreats over the rooftops , he steps out of his window and sets up his beach chair, lights a cigar and lays down. This is the strangest thing they've ever seen and they accept him as the Booga Man, because who would sleep on the side of a building with a lit cigar in his hand? My little cousins go back down in the Jersey Pine Barrens and tell their friends that the Booga man lives in Brooklyn.

But down in the Pine Barrens where they live there's Raw-Head Bloody Bones, a character that Ma told us about when we were very little, on our way back to New York from Bridgeton on a dark night traveling north on rural Route 77. In the dark car she turned off the radio and started talking about and describing Raw-Head Bloody Bones in detail and we were mesmerized not just by the detail but also by his mere name. Then Ma pulled the car off the side of the road near a corn field and turned off the headlights and ignition to show us how dark and quiet it was. It was black blindness and quiet terror and we screamed and she laughed and started the car and headed for the brand-new, New Jersey Turnpike. We'd never seen darkness and stillness like that in our New York, urban lives, and had never heard of anybody called Raw-Head Bloody Bones.

Ma is notoriously mischievous and always ready to do something different. She tells us the story of how one night she and my Aunt Evelyn and my Aunt Sarah were driving home to Lanning's Wharf on Back Neck Road, a dark, country road, and they were being tailgated by a tractor-trailer truck who seemed to be in a hurry but couldn't pass them because the road was so narrow. When they pulled over to let the truck pass it disappeared and wasn't there. There was nowhere for it to turn off and Ma and my aunts were baffled about it and talked about it for years as being a ghost truck.

Some of my cousins who've never been to our house and never go anywhere have the notion that we're rich just because we live in New York. My cousin Charles ridiculously says, " I betchall eat steaks for dinner every night , dontcha."

The building where the Booga Man slept, but his fire escape has been replaced by this smaller one.

There are these 2 men, Al and Jimmy. It's 1960 and they both have 1960 Chrysler Imperials with telephones in the cars. Jimmy's Imperial is black and Al's is white. Al's telephone is real but Jimmy's is fake. They both wear processes and have their heads wrapped in scarves. Jimmy is black and has the black car and Al is light-skinned and has the white car, is very good looking with green eyes and gold-capped teeth and always dresses very well. Jimmy's Imperial is severely damaged on the passenger side but the driver's side is OK, and passengers have to use the driver's side to get in and out of the car. Jimmy works for Al, who owns a pocketbook factory downtown Brooklyn on the corner of South Elliot St. and Fulton, where he makes cheap, vinyl, ladies handbags and sells them to variety stores and Jimmy and I peddle them on the sidewalks of Manhattan, mostly up on 115th Street and Park Ave. under the railroad tracks in Spanish Harlem. We ride uptown on the FDR in Jimmy's car, and if a pretty girl passes him on the driver's side of his car he picks up the fake phone and acts like he's talking on it, and Ben E. King is on the radio singing A Rose in Spanish Harlem, and Jimmy leans over to me and says "See? That's where WE goin baby!" He does the same thing if he sees a pretty girl on the sidewalk on his side of the car. He grabs the fake phone and pretends to be talking. If a girl looks at him from the damaged side of the car where I sit, he acts like he doesn't see her.

I don't how I got here with these guys or who said I could go with them. I never see them talk to Ma or Dad or Ronnie. I just know that I'm across the street from our house one day playing with two boys named Ronald and Dennis and we're playing in the elevator of 670, going up and down and pressing all the buttons when these grown-ups catch us and yell at us and tell us to go outside and the next thing I know Jimmy's driving me downtown to the factory where I meet Al and the girls, and Lloyd Price is on the radio singing Stagger Lee. The factory is 1 flight up off the street, and as we approach the workroom the smell of fresh-cut vinyl fills my nose combined with the smell of cuchifritos from the Spanish restaurant downstairs. There are 8 women in the workshop cutting patterns and operating sewing machines and foot presses and folding machines. There's a foot press used for attaching the brass rings on the ends of the straps for the handbags and I learn to load the machine with rivets and take the strap and insert it through a ring, then fold the strap and place it under the press, push the foot pedal down and the brass rivet secures the ring, which is then attached to the pocketbook. Al walks around yelling, "I want mass production dammit !" I want mass production you know?"

My senses are saturated by the intoxicating environment of this sharp guy who owns a pocket book factory and drives a brand-new car with a telephone in it, making money and distributing goods. The factory is filled with wholesale, colorful vinyl and brass accessories, stylish young women operating sewing machines and adoring me, singing along with the radio in the corner playing all the hit songs. I'm 10 and each time one of them passes me at the foot press they either stroke my chin or pat my head and give me a kiss on the cheek. These cheap pocketbooks are apparently popular because he makes and sells a lot of them in about 5 or 6 different styles, and one style is called the "Twist", named after the dance. I work in Al's factory and at the end of the day he gives me $5.00 and I arrive home smelling like plastic, perfume and Spanish food.

The phone in Al's car has an 18" tubular antenna attached to the rear quarter panel and the telephone is under the dashboard, situated over the hump in the middle, and has a rotary dial. Jimmy got hold of a regular house phone and placed it over the hump in his car and secured the wire under the dashboard with black tape. Sometimes if he makes a sharp turn the fake phone slips off the hump and he gets mad and says "SHIT! Grab that damn phone for me Eddie and slide it back up there". We're up in the factory and Al calls in from his car phone and one of the girls answers it and starts complaining: "Al, I can't hear you.......your voice is breaking up Al, speak sss....slower!" Everywhere we go people watch us because of the cars and when Jimmy takes us up to Harlem to peddle on the sidewalk the police sometimes chase us away. Jimmy spreads out a blanket and we quickly unload the handbags from the trunk and line them up in rows, while Jimmy is calling out: "CLOSE OUT GIRLS, A DOLLAR! SELL 'EM OUT LATEST STYLE BAGS GIRLS, CLOSE OUT GIRLS, A DOLLAR - "SELL'EM OUT A DOLLAR HERE, SELL 'EM OUT A DOLLAR....WAYVAB, WAYVAB.........." I don't know what wayvab means and don't ask, but try to imitate Jimmy up on the street, hawking like he does, and saying wayvab, but he looks at me and laughs so I stop saying it because I'm embarrassed. One day we spread the blanket and lined the handbags up on 14th Street and when the cops came to chase us away there was a small crowd gathered on the sidewalk, on

Jimmy's "good side" of the car, and a well dressed, rich looking white guy remarked, as he's watching us throw the bags back into the trunk, "Yeah, but look what he's *driving !* ", and then I instantly wonder what he would have said had he been on the *damaged* side of Jimmy's car.

Al and Jimmy seem to have lots of girls and Jimmy and his friends talk about having sex with them in front of me, describing how he moves and how she moans, from behind the wheel of his car, wiggling his waist and imitating the girl saying " Oooohhh stop it baby, stop it baby, you're gonna make me pregnant!"

On Saturday mornings I'm outside playing skelly and Al swings by in his white Imperial, talking on the phone with its white coil wrapped around his wrist, red, Paisley doo rag on, pulls over and says "Hey Eddie, whatcha doin?" Wanna go downtown"? I hop in the car and my friends say "wow" and we're off. Al and Jimmy and the girls in the factory downtown are the first people to call me Eddie. Al uses the expression "You KNOW thaaat!" to signify "yes" or that he agrees with you.

One night after closing the factory 5 of the girls get into Al's car and 3 of them get into Jimmy's car and we go up into Crown Heights to Al's house and Al and all the girls go in and Jimmy drops me off to my house. It seems now that all the girls live with Al, who lives in a 3 story brownstone. A couple of weeks later up in the factory there are words between Al and the girls and he slaps a girl named Wyona in the face and punches a girl named Phyllis in the stomach. Phyllis is wearing a yellow skirt and bends over clutching her stomach. I've never seen a grown woman get hit. The radio is playing "Kookie, Kookie, lend me your comb".

III
A Step Up

I don't see the Martins when they move out of apt. 1A but soon after the wrestling match between Ma and Mrs. Martin in the lobby, they're gone. They'd reminded me of people who work in the circus.

The vacant apartment is being freshly painted a pleasant grey with pink, flower-like patterns applied to the walls. The floors are stripped and scrubbed and waxed, then new linoleum is installed throughout. Brand new modern furniture is put in the living room and a coffee table with a Lazy Susan on top of it, and pretty, matching lamps and new bedroom furniture for the two bedrooms, and a table and chairs for the kitchen. Then Dad, Ma, my 3 sisters and my baby brother Don move in. Ronnie and I remain in the cellar to live with Granddad and Grandma. Moving into 1A is our family's proudest and sweetest moment on Willoughby Avenue. Everything is new, and it's actually beautiful and up-to-date, and even the new telephones have that fresh, coconut smell of the plastic. Our new phone number is HYacinth 7-6033.

We're finally happy to invite our friends in and show off our new home.

Ronnie and I do live in the cellar with Grandma and Granddad but I spend most of my days in our new apartment with its pleasant freshness and go down to the cellar at the end of the day where my grandparents are finishing dinner and getting ready to watch the news, then wrestling. They send me to Sussman's to get peppermint barrel candy, and they suck on these and watch the news, then all the wrestling stars, Haystack Calhoun, Killer Kowalski, Happy Humphrey, Pretty Boy George, the Midgets and Skull Murphy. They're watching television with peppermint barrels rolling around in their mouths and I lay on the floor beneath them flipping through a Life Magazine. It's December, 1959 and the new 1960 cars fill up several centerfolds. I'm particularly enchanted with the new 1960 Pontiac because Dad has a 1952 Pontiac Chief. The new cars are long and sleek and look like rocket ships. As I flip through the pages I'm saying , Wow, the 1960 Buick !.......... The 1960 Oldsmobile!........ The 1960 Chevrolet! But when I get to the Pontiac I keep repeating, "Wow the 1960 Pontiac", over and over, until Granddad finally shouts "HUSH"! "Stop saying Pontiac! It AINT Pontiac, IT'S PONYAC!" And he means it. Then he begins mocking me saying *"Pontiac!.............. Pontiac!"* Then he scours me with his eyes. In the deep south the old people do say Ponyac because that's how they pronounce it. But I'm young and from Brooklyn and pronounce things the way they're spelled. I'm only 9 but I know he's wrong but I don't dare challenge him or correct him. I conclude that he thinks the car is named after a pony. He's an ultimately rustic and simple man.

Lonnie Harris, Ma's Father, born 1883

I'm walking through the alley one day and passing near our bathroom window, when the wooden spool that goes inside the toilet- paper roll comes flying out the window. I pick it up and look up into the window and Granddad is in the bathroom, pulling the chain and flushing the toilet. I go in the house as he's leaving the bathroom and have the spool hidden in my pocket so he won't see it. I go into the bathroom and the toilet paper is just hanging by the two metal hooks where you attach the spool, so I put the spool back into the roll of toilet paper and back onto its' metal hooks and go back outside. I'm afraid to explain to Granddad that you're not supposed to throw away the wooden spool because I'm scared he'll holler at me for knowing something that he doesn't, then pull me to him and quietly grind his knuckles into my head, the way he does with all the boys in the family. I laugh to myself, imagining him in the bathroom with the toilet paper in one hand, looking at the wooden spool in the other hand, trying to figure out how they're supposed to hook up, then giving up and flinging the spool out the window. He's never lived where the toilet paper hangs from an attachment on the wall.

Home was a shack with no paint ,quality, four-cornered quaint.

When you gotta live there, it ain't .I didn't LEAVE home, I was driven',

Please........ excuse me for livin' - Oscar Brown, Jr.

The now sealed-up alley window where Granddad threw the toilet-paper spool out.

Our neighborhood market in Brooklyn is on DeKalb Ave between Throop and Sumner, a busy place where you can buy everything you need in the house. There are meat markets, Kosher and non-Kosher, fruit and vegetable stands, bakeries, a big fish market and appetizing stores, Waldbaum's supermarket, a hardware store, and there are barrels filled with pickled tomatoes and cucumbers. When you walk down the street you get hit with all the smells of the market. The pickles, the smoked fish, the bacalao, the butcher, the bakery, even the smells of fresh linens done in the big laundry across the street from Hymie who runs a fruit and vegetable market and he also has pickle barrels.

Crystal Steam laundry building across from Hymie's on DeKalb Ave.

Hymie is a tall Jewish man with sunken cheeks and hands large enough to palm a basketball. He has a large head covered with an old, grey Applejack hat and you can see his Yarmulke under his hat, and he wears a long apron. Granddad walks the four blocks to the market and sits on a chair in front of Hymie's with his black, wrinkled hands folded over his cane. We walk through DeKalb Ave. or stop by there on the way home from school to get a pickle and there's Granddad talking with Hymie. He looks up from the brim of his hat. "Whatchall doin down here? Go on and git away from here now." Nothing I can say seems to interest Granddad. He has too many grandchildren to even remember their names and never calls me by my name. When he calls me he says "Now see here - Boy!" Later on he comes walking down Throop Ave. with a bag of okra and tomatoes. Granddad and Hymie are probably talking about farming and growing and harvesting, and Big Joe Rosenfeld and the Happiness Exchange. I bet Granddad found out about Big Joe from Hymie. The only time I see Granddad laugh is when he and Grandma are watching wrestling. Otherwise, my grandparents purpose is to be grim faced and keep us minding them and God and saying Yes Sir and Yes Mam.

My cousins down in South Jersey answer "Yessum" to my grandmother for yes, and when they answer no they say "Nome".

The Market on DeKalb Avenue between Throop and Sumner

Brian Merlis Collection

During a thunderstorm we sit on the floor looking up at Grandma sitting in her chair. She makes us turn off the TV, lights and radio and says to be quiet because God is talking. Then she reveals to us that the world is going to end one day and she calls it Dooms Day. By the time she finishes describing the event we're all crying, because this is the first time we're hearing this. She talks about how the clouds will part and enormous bells will appear bigger than the Empire State Building and their ringing will shake the world and there'll be giant wheels turning in the sky that will make buildings fall and how waterfalls of fire will stream from the sky and set everything on fire and the streets will be filled with blood up to our necks, and the Chinese will be cutting off people's heads. As she's talking it's thundering and lightning outside. She never says you're going to hell, she says you're going to The Devil, which is scarier to me because the Devil is on the hot sauce bottle and sticking a pitch fork into hot peppers. Ma comes in the house loaded with grocery bags and sees all of us crying in front of Grandma, and she immediately knows what took place and says "Mama, whatchoo been tellin these kids?" Granddad often walks through the apartment and suddenly turns around like somebody's behind him and says, "Satan, git offa my back!"

In the summer Ma takes us to Coney Island every Tuesday night, not for the amusement rides because she can't afford them, but to see the free fireworks presented by Schaefer Beer from barges in the Atlantic, and we watch them from the beach. Sometimes Ma buys us tickets for the Carousel ride on the north side of Surf Avenue, and we ride the merry-go-round horses while the carousel music plays the song, The Poor People of Paree.

On this Tuesday night my cousin Larry is visiting us from South Jersey and he's never been to Coney Island and doesn't know what fireworks are. When Ma announces that we're going to Coney Island I conspire with my sisters. "Don't tell Larry about the fireworks - I'm gonna fool him when we get on the beach." The ride to Coney Island is long to us, about an hour, and when we get there and park the car and get on the beach Larry is astonished because he's never been in an amusement

park in his life and we pass the Cyclone, the laughing lady at
the spook house and we look up at the tall parachute jump
ride and smell the hot dogs and mustard and ketchup and
french fries on the boardwalk and Larry's never seen the
ocean and he's never been on the beach and is awe-struck by
the enormous ocean and the crashing waves and all the
people and all the deep sand and he's only 5. It's almost dark
and we're playing in the sand on the beach but Larry doesn't
know that we're here to see fireworks and doesn't know what
they are. He's grinning and looking all around. "Larry - The
world is gonna end tonight." I tell him and he looks at me
suspiciously, and the grin turns serious. He's only 5 but even
he's heard Grandma's stories about the end of the world.
"That's why everybody's here on the beach, 'cause God is
coming tonight." - "No he ain't!" He says. By this time Ma is
in on the joke and I take Larry by the hand over to Ma and I
wink my eye at her and say "Ma, tell Larry - the world is gonna
end tonight. That's why we're here, right?" Ma's forcing back
a laugh but tells us to be quiet because she thinks she hears
something. "You better start praying boy." I tell Larry. Soon
the neon lights on the barge light up announcing, *SCHAEFER
BEER PRESENTS*..... but Larry can't read and not only is it the
first time that he's on the beach with all the people, sand and
ocean waves crashing, but it's dark, and suddenly neon lights
appear on the black ocean. The fireworks explode and burst
into the dark sky above us and I scream "Oh Jesus Please" and
Larry is stunned and crying and trying to run and he's hiding
behind Ma and she's laughing and all the white people are
looking at us and I tell Larry "Look - here comes the Devil" and
BANG! And he screams and snot comes out of his nose and

Ma says "Alright, that's enough", but it's too late. Larry hides and cries through the entire display and Ma has to take us a few feet away from the big crowd so she won't be so ashamed of him and he's happy to finally get in the car and go home, and as we ride up Ocean Parkway his eyes get heavy and before falling asleep he says, "I'm gonna tell Grandma on you."

When Halloween approaches we fill old socks with pieces of large multi-colored chalk bought from the candy/toy store, then smash them all over the block on the sidewalk and against buildings until the chalk inside turns to powder, then smash the powder-filled socks against each other's arms and backs, and we're covered in chalk powder and the cheap makeup and lipstick and wax vampire teeth and Halloween masks bought in the variety stores and go trick-or-treating with big shopping bags and at the end of the night they're heavy with too much candy. We're not escorted by our parents. Trick or treating is a real adventure. We're on our own and free. One Halloween Ronnie and I go into 701 Willoughby, a 6 story apartment building more exclusive than ours which has a canopy in front and a bell system where you have to be buzzed in. We ring bells until the buzzer sounds and we take the elevator up to the 6th floor and plan to work our way down, ringing bells and trick or treating. The first two bells we ring, nothing. The building is still all Jewish and people open their doors with surprised looks on their faces, like they don't know what Halloween is. We ring the 3rd bell and a man opens the door and we say "Trick or Treat".........he has dark hair and thick, dark eyebrows and his hair hangs down over his forehead and he has big eyes and sunken cheeks and needs a shave and he says"OH.........OH............SUUURRRRE!" And makes a sweeping, welcoming gesture, holds the door wide open and says "Come Innnnnnnnn!" He looks like Zachary, the horror host on TV and Ronnie and I run down all 6 flights and out of the building. When we finally get out on the sidewalk we run down the block screaming and laughing hysterically and glad to be out of there.

701 Willoughby Avenue bet. Sumner and Throop

As soon as my grandparents come to live with us Grandma
finds a store-front, Pentecostal church on Tompkins Avenue
between Macon and Halsey for us to attend. We walk down
to Tompkins and take the B47 bus and get off at Halsey, but
soon we start saving the carfare and spending it on candy and
walking to Sunday school, often arriving late, to the indignant
grimace of the West Indian Pastor, Reverend Burris, but by the
end of service he's smiling after the collection. We make fun
of his West Indian accent and that of his wife, Sister Burris,
and the way they say Thank You Jesus: "Tonk Ya Jesus-ah!
Tonk Ya, Jesus-ah! - Praise De Lard-ah, Praise De Lard-ah."
Rev. Burris makes up this song and sings it to us.

Come to Sunday school, Come to Sunday school.

Hevery Sunday MAR-ning, come to Sunday school,

Bring someone wid you, bring a friend wid you.

Hevery Sunday MAR-ning, come to Sunday school

After Sunday school they serve us cookies and Kool-aid which
we don't like, because cookies are supposed to go with milk.
We attend Sunday School at this Church for a while until
Grandma meets this woman named Sister Haven who has a
store-front Church of God of Prophecy on Gates Avenue and a
drum & bugle corps that Sissy and I join called The Haven
Cadets, whose uniforms are black and pink. The corps consists
of a horn line, drum line and twirlers. Sissy marches and twirls

a baton and I carry and beat the big bass drum during parades, and my enchantment with drums begins. I'm proud to be in a uniform, like when I wanted to be a Sea Cadet, and I'm part of a musical group and learning how to march.

One night at P.S. 25 there's a competition between the Haven Cadets and another drum & bugle corps called Jackson, whose uniforms are green, black and white. Jackson's horn and drum line and their twirlers are distinctly sharper than Haven Cadets. Their uniforms are nicer, their instruments are newer and their routine is crisp and tight. The twirlers are wearing very short skirts. But when it's their turn to do their routine the twirlers include a step in their dance that has them jerking their pelvises in a sexual manner, and Sister Haven and the judges start looking at each other, and Jackson Corps is automatically disqualified. At the end they're absolutely shocked when Haven Cadets win, and they stand there with their mouths open in disbelief, as the Haven Cadets cheer and revel in victory. It's almost like Sister Haven had some influence over the judges.

Sister Haven is very strict and dead serious about Jesus. She's just like Grandma. One day all the Haven Cadets meet at this big church on Fulton St. and Hopkinson Ave. and Sister Haven makes us sit in the pews and say "Thank You Jesus" over and over for more than an hour. All you can hear is everybody repeating it over and over, and Sister Haven acting like a movie matron, walking around and chanting and making sure your lips are moving and saying thank you Jesus and your eyes are closed. She is a large woman, plain faced and stern, and I feel like she's trying to hypnotize us. I've never seen her smile.

It seems like everybody who says they're going to Heaven is kind of mean and serious and don't tell jokes and you don't want them to catch you laughing, and they're all old and don't seem to *really* like us kids because they're always screaming at us, and I'm not sure I want to spend eternity with all these people in my face looking at me and hollering and telling me what to do. Can we ride bikes and play baseball in heaven?

IV
The Gangs

By the time Ronnie is 14 he's a member of a gang called The Renegade Buccaneers and his gang name is Rock, and he loves the record Lavender Blue by Sammy Turner, and runs around with guys named Spade, Blade and Shotgun. The boys I hang around with call ourselves the Baby Buccaneers and I take the name Li'l Rock. There are many gangs in Brooklyn. The Buccaneers, The Stompers, The Bishops, The Ellery Bops, The Baldies, The Mau Maus, The Corsair Lords, The Spanish Lords, The Gay Lords, The Roman Lords, The Jesters, The John Quells, The Dragons and The Chaplains. Ronnie goes to the new Junior High School 57 on Stuyvesant Avenue, where there are Buccaneers *and* Stompers.

JHS 57, Stuyvesant Ave.

The Chaplains is the largest gang in Brooklyn, and they have several divisions, most of them located in the surrounding projects. The Marcy Chaplains, The Fort Green Chaplains, The DeKalb Chaplains, The Albany Chaplains, The Brevoort Chaplains, and the Red Hook Chaplains. We see graffiti on walls with gang names and the letters D.T.K.L.A.M.F. (Down To kill Like A Motha-Fucka).

The Ft. Greene Projects, Park Ave. view

The Marcy Projects

These are all juvenile gangs and no one has cars. They get around by walking and hitching on the backs of buses. The Baldies, who wear their heads shaved and no eyebrows, are carrying scissors around and terrorizing school girls by catching them and cutting off their hair.

When a gang moves through, it's intimidating because they move in large numbers. When they move it's called rolling. I see and eventually participate in movements of 60-80 boys, rolling on another neighborhood. A roll is like an invasion. The traffic of these movements stretches out to 4-5 city blocks of teenage boys bopping down the street. The bop becomes a distinct style of walking stiff with a dip, because the baddest guy in the gang has a rifle down the leg of his pants that prevents him from bending his leg as he walks. He's the one to watch out for, and the bad walk widely catches on. Being a gang member is known as being a Jitterbug. We also call them Bebops. I learn that from my friend David Duryea. We imitate and exaggerate the way the gangsters walk and one day his Italian grandmother sees us and says, "Stop walkin' like that! Youz ain't none o'them Bebops."

When you roll down the street with a gang you feel tough and protected, exhilarated and entitled because everyone stops what they're doing and watches and says nothing. Some of the gangs chant songs when they roll, with the president or war counselor leading the chant, and the other gang members singing a response, the way a drill instructor leads his platoon. One such song is called Hi-Lo.

Hi-LO,........... LO-HI,

THE BUCANEERS WILL NEVER DIE,

BUCANEERS COMIN, CHAPLAINS RUNNIN,

CAN'T FIND A HOLSTER FOR MY .45.

SAW A BUNCH O' CHAPLAINS IN TOMPKINS PARK,

TOLD HIM NOT TO BE HERE WHEN IT GIT DARK,

LISTEN MUTHA FUCKA LEMMY MAKE IT REAL CLEAR,

I'M A MIGHTY, MIGHTY, MUTHA FUCKIN BUCANEER.

HI-LO,......... LO-HI

UMMO' MAKE YOUR LITTLE SISTER AND YOUR MAMA CRY,

LO-HI, HI-LO

YO PEOPLE BE BEHIND YOU, WALKIN SLOW

The chants also remind me of native African men working and chanting. I'm sitting on the bottom step of our lobby with some boys and a gang comes rolling past from Stuyvesant Ave. I think they're the Stompers. As they pass the word punk comes out of my mouth and I say something smart and a guy turns around, bends over me and puts a knife to my throat and says, "Whatchoo Say? Whatchoo say?" "Nothing" I tell him, and he says "you better not!" He was pricking my throat with the blade and it made my eyes burn with water, then he let go and kept walking.

One evening Ronnie is hanging out in Ida's Soda Fountain on Hart Street with his back to the door when a Puerto Rican boy quietly walks in and lunges at him and tries to stab him. Ronnie's wearing a thick leather jacket and when the kid hits Ronnie in the back the blade of the knife breaks and falls on the floor. The kid runs out the door and down Throop Avenue.

Where Ida's corner-soda fountain was located, Throop & Hart

The first dead person I see is a teenage boy who's been killed in a gang fight. The story makes The Daily News and on the day of his funeral he's laid out in his casket at the funeral parlor on Kosciuszko Street and Throop Ave. in a white shirt and black tie. He's a dark skinned boy about 13 and his hair is high in the front and slopes down closer towards the back in a haircut called a Hi-Lo. Ma tells me to stay away from gangs and she walks me down to Kosciuszko St. that evening specifically so that I can see the young victim as a warning of what can happen in gangs. It's a summer evening and a crowd of people stand outside the funeral home and Ma makes sure that I get a good look at a dead kid who doesn't listen to his mother. With the funeral parlor door open, you can see the young man lying in his casket from outside on the sidewalk.

Former funeral parlor now a church, corner Throop Ave. & Kosciuszko Street

"Man, imagine if you was a fat, black, hammer-toed, bow legged, buck tooth, big nosed, on the welfare, snagger- tooth woman that can't read..... Don't laugh mutha fucka, it's plenty o' people out here like that."

Junior, who lives upstairs in 3A moves in from DeKalb Avenue with his two brothers and 2 sisters and his mother and they share a two bedroom apartment. He's fat and 14 and always talking dirty and singing songs about sex, playing hooky and breaking into people's apartments through their fire escape windows, and brags that he's a peeping Tom and that he once peeked in on my sisters through the backyard windows when they were getting undressed. He says, "I'm the only kid on this whole block who ever had any pussy," and then he says, "Niggah, you ain't had no pussy since pussy had you!" He also says, "I get more pussy on accident than you get on purpose." It seems like the nastiest boys are the fat boys.

One day I'm playing in front of 670 across the street and some new kids are hanging around and one of the boys, whose about 14 starts talking to me but he talks like a girl, then he finally says, "Well, you know I'm a faggot don't you?" I shrug my shoulders and shake my head because I'm surprised that he calls himself a faggot, because the word seems like it's something he should try to avoid.

Some kids are bad influences like Junior upstairs, who one day convinces me and another boy named Bobby to play hooky and come with him to his secret hideout. We go down to Bainbridge Street and Sumner Ave to an apartment building on the corner that's suffered smoke damage from a fire next door, but you can't tell from the outside. We go on the roof and down a fire escape through a window, into a completely furnished apartment that's been abandoned because of smoke saturation. The eeriness of it is immediately striking because everything is still here. Furniture, drapes, dishes, rugs, appliances. It's very neat and each item is in its place but everything smells like smoke. The electricity is off and the kitchen curtains are yellowed and blackened with soot but nothing is burnt. It's just unlivable. I wonder how David found out about this place. It's 11 am and sunny outside and I wish I were back in school because now I feel like I'm in a forbidden place and I'd like to get out of here before it's too late. We

leave there and follow him to burglarize an apartment from
the fire escape window but the people on McDonough Street
see us from their backyard windows and call the police, and
when the cops appear on the roof David is first to climb down
the fire-escape ladder which he dislodges on the way down
and Bobby and I are trapped on the roof with the cops, with
nowhere to run. They take us to the 79th precinct on Gates
Ave. where we squeal on David, telling the police where he
lives. They look up his name and see that he has an arrest
record and now they keep calling him the ring leader. It's my
first time in a police station and what's that smell? Maybe it's
the ink they use to make fingerprints. Since we got caught
way up on McDonough Street they take us to the closest
police station, because there's a police station right around
the corner from us on Vernon Avenue and Tompkins that
looks like a little castle.

Old precinct house on Vernon Ave. and Tompkins Ave.

Being country in the city is another thing to be ridiculed about and people are made fun of as they arrive from down south . When kids come from the Carolinas and Georgia calling sneakers tennis and calling a bike a wheel and instead of saying "they", they say "dee", and having names like Betty Jean and eating collard-green sandwiches, they're country. Some have problems pronouncing and they call drawers "grawers", they call the street the "screet", and drugs "grugs". They're ridiculing, laughing at and harassing the Jews with their curls and yarmulkes. They're wild, and start snatching yarmulkes off Jewish boys' heads and running off down the street with them. They don't know what pizza is, they don't know about knishes and salami, and chocolate egg creams or bagels, and they never had Chinese food and they're seeing

Chinese, Spanish and Jewish people for the first time, and now, instead of having to wait for a chance to go to the store in someone's car, there are five candy stores within one square block, in any direction. And they're going to school with white kids for the first time.

Tompkins Park, early 1950s, looking north to Lafayette Ave.

Brian Merlis Collection

The country kids talk about eating red clay from the ground down in Georgia, and people from down south are eating starch. Fat, black women are eating Argo Starch out of the box and rinsing it down with Pepsi Cola.

Being Dark skinned is a strike against you and there are lines and lines of jokes and riddles about being black that kids hurl about daily. Junior says "Aintcha Mama black on the pancake box?" And he says, "I went downtown to see Miss Lucy and paid two cents to see her pussy - the pussy was so black, you couldn't see the crack - Goddamn gimme my two cents back!" In school, kids say, "Yo mama so black they gotta turn the lights on when she come in the house." "Yo mama so black she don't git no light bill." - "Yo mama so black it git cloudy when she come outside." - "Yo mama so black I can't even see!"

When the 1960s come and black replaces negro, older people immediately reject it. Black is something to be ashamed of and avoided. "If you're white you're right, if you're brown stick around, if you're black, get back." Joanne Alston , who lives in 666 is called black a lot and says, "The blacker the berry, the sweeter the juice, when it comes to you it ain't no use."

Nappy hair is also something to be avoided. In black homes the smell of hair being straightened with straightening combs heated on the stove burner combined with Dixie Peach hair pomade is regular. Whenever you smell that, you know some special occasion is coming up. There's smells of food cooking, cigarettes smoking and hair frying on Friday and Saturday nights, with music playing and kids running in and out of the house and folks drinking beer. My mother routinely washes and straightens my 3 sisters' hair and before straightening, they frolic around the house with bushes of hair that will be called Afros in a few years. Girls don't leave the house until their hair is straightened and presentable. You don't permit your nappy hair to be seen by anyone outside the family and we never see girls on the street with their hair nappy until we see Miss Walker.

Miss Walker is a young woman about 20 who has an apartment in our building and she attends college and wears her hair natural. To see her come and go is a shock at first, because she doesn't straighten her hair. She just washes it. That's all. She never wears lipstick or makeup. She seems intellectual and wears round, wire- frame eyeglasses and always carries books and minds her business. We only see her come and go and never pause for casual conversation. We're puzzled because she's not ashamed to be seen out on the street with her hair like that. She looks odd and homely and plain.

There's a man who walks through our block with a long beard and his hair covered in a burlap sack that hangs to one side, halfway down his back over his left shoulder. The sack is filled with his hair which you can never see, but only the bulge of it under the sack as it bounces when he walks. He walks up our block across the street, usually from Throop Ave east towards Sumner, seemingly on a mission. One day he comes down the block drinking a dark bottle of beer and talking to himself in a West Indian accent.

There's a tall woman who wears her hair plaited in braids and walks all over town balancing a full, 16 oz. bottle of Pepsi-Cola on her head. She's tall, light skinned and usually half high with a smile and catching everyone's attention wherever she goes, causing people to point fingers and jeer at her, and she seems to like it. She comes down the street and we stop her and she talks to us. She stands still in front of our building with the Pepsi on top of her head, babbling and dipping and weaving to keep up with the full soda bottle, and expertly catching it in one hand when it tips over. "Whas yall's names?" She says with her wet lips clutching a long cigarette. "Look..........I got worms crawling in my hands! Look! Under my skin....Look." She shows the back of her hand with the veins extending from her fingers. She wiggles her index finger and when the vein running from it up to her knuckles begins to curl we grimace and wince at first but immediately know it's a trick and we look at her funny. One day she comes down in the cellar with us, just like Rev. Jackson and Miss Bee and Oscar from across the street do, just outside the door to our kitchen, sitting on the ledge, drinking wine and smoking and wiggling the worms in her hands and laughing as the full 16 oz. Pepsi sits on the ground next to her. When she's had enough of us kids she stamps her cigarette out on the concrete floor and picks up the soda, and heads towards the front, up to the sidewalk where she then situates the bottle on her head and continues her walk all over Bed Stuy and Brownsville.

280 Stone Avenue, 1953 Brian Merlis Collection

My sister Cathy is enchanted by her and walks her all the way up to Sumner Avenue, talking, then turning the corner, and I run up the block after her and bring her back because I think Cathy might follow her out of the neighborhood. Cathy always likes people who seem down and out, or just weird.

The kitchen-door entrance to our apartment in the cellar is an extension of the sidewalk and visitors use this as an "in" to our premises. The sidewalk- alley door that leads to the coal bins and the furnace and the general cellar area isn't locked, and the front door leading into the kitchen doesn't have a key lock, only a latch on the inside, and is old and wooden with cracked green paint, and long, grimy splinters jagging out at the bottom of it, that brush against the concrete ground when opened and closed, like an old, dirty broom.

Ronnie starts playing hooky from school and going to work at B. Cohen Food Products around the corner on Vernon Avenue. He does this occasionally, then more frequently when the money he's making becomes more and more irresistible and depended on, not only by him, but our family as well. By this time Ronnie is making as much money as Dad and he's listening to the jazz of Symphony Sid on station WJZ. He sings along at the beginning of each show while King Pleasure sings the theme: Jumpin With Symphony Sid.

Jumpin with my boy Sid in the City,

Jumpin with my Boy Sid in the City

Mr. President of the DJ committe,

We're gonna be up all night gettin with it.

B. Cohen Food Distributors is run by the Cohen family of Mill Basin, and is called COBROS, which stands for Cohen Brothers, Norman, Bobby and Benny Cohen and the Patriarch, Bernard Cohen, the father and founder. They're wholesale distributors of meat and dairy products and make deliveries to retail grocery stores all over Brooklyn. I eventually start working for Normie and Bobby during the summers, even before I get my working papers. Normie doesn't like of the idea of me working without working papers but I hang around so much and I'm pretty handy and the work relationship is informal and I'm paid in cash. It's here that I find out about Gouda and Baby Gouda cheese, Mortadella, fancy and market cuts of pork loins and beef, beef shells, pot cheese, various hams and salami and Souse meat, and we have to be at work at 6:00am to meet the various tractor-trailer trucks delivering cases of fresh, whole chickens under ice in wooden crates, cases of lard, butter and margarine, cream cheese, yoo hoos, chocolate cows, orange drinks and most food products including dairy and eggs found in neighborhood grocery stores and delis.

Normie Cohen is big, tall and fat and probably weighs over 300 lbs. He loves to eat, drive fast and listen to all the hit songs on WMCA and sing along with them. He likes the song by Shirley Ellis' "The Nitty Gritty". Ronnie and his friend Clifford sing the song by the Coasters that says, "Oh don't you know I'm bound-I'm bound, to my job, My boss-my boss is a big fat slob." I think he's singing about Normie. I overhear Normie say to someone on the phone one day, "You're so full o' shit you make *my* ass run ice water!" One day I heard Bobbie Cohen yell to somebody on the phone,"Tell Bob Havemeyer to pay his bill or I'm gonna come over there and kick him right in his fuckin' pants, or my brother Normie's gonna fuckin' sue him. Which way does he want it?" Working at Cohen's is where I learn about a "Schmear", cream cheese spread on a bagel or a roll. One of the drivers for Cohen is a short, bald,

older guy who wears thick black glasses named Willie
Klinkowitz, but they call him Klinky and he doesn't like it.

By 1960 most of the white families on the block are gone and
one of the last Jewish families to leave is the Halperins at 660
Willoughby, and Mark Halperin and I are in the same class. Mr.
Kaplan, our 5th grade teacher, hits Mark at least once every
two weeks. He calls him to the front of the room and lays him
on his stomach atop his desk and whacks him on the behind
once. Mark returns to his seat with his face red, takes off his
glasses and cries into his folded arms across his desk. He never
plays with us out on the street and I only see him at class in
school, and his mother waits for him each day at 3 o'clock to
walk him home.

Dad becomes friends with a bunch of his peers who came up
from the south and they congregate and play cards and keep
up with the daily numbers and all the talk and news and
business and they sing gospel. Dad and Big Mickey and Bo
Weaver and Simon and Mr. Leroy have become an informal
gospel group and they have five-part harmony, singing in the
old style of 1940s spirituals, rooted deep in the south. Their
harmony is crisp, tight and soulful, and they sit five-in-the-car
with a pint of bourbon going around, swinging harmony about
sweet Jesus. Big Mickey's Oldsmobile is parked across the
street with Dad sitting in the back, in the middle, singing
baritone with his head poking back and forth as he sings his
background vocal part. They're disciplined about their vocal
assignments and their sound is correct and makes people stop
and listen. This is how they gather on a cloudy, winter
Saturday afternoon. I watch them across the street in the car

singing, then I go down in the cellar and get the shovel and wheel barrel and start rolling coal, cause when Dad finishes singing and having a drink with the fellas and he comes in the cellar and sees the big pile of coal in front of the furnace he might give me fifty cents or even a dollar. I'm in the coal bin shoveling coal into the wheel barrel and I can hear them singing upstairs, across the street in the car, and I hear Dad's baritone through it all, even the passing traffic, and between each shovel of black coal that I hurl. Ma comes past the coal bin on her way outside and before she goes up the steps I call "Ma", she turns around and says "Ha", and I say to her, "Aren't you glad we're colored ?"

"Buckyeeeeeee!" Miss Hipp calls to me, "Go over to Sussman's and get me a pack of Pall Mall. Here's a quarter and here's a dime for you. Be careful crossing the street now."

It puzzles me about the Pall Mall cigarette commercials because on TV and on the radio they don't pronounce it Pall Mall, they say Pell Mell. But on the package it's spelled Pall Mall. Miss Hipp doesn't say Pell Mell, she says Pall Mall, and so does everyone else. It's common for adults to send kids to the store for cigarettes and store owners sell them openly. Cheap candy stores like buddies are selling loose cigarettes for 3 cents a piece and two for a nickel, and teenagers call them loosies, and go to the store with a quarter and buy a handful of candy along with a couple of loosies. Bubble gum and cigarettes, comic books and cigarettes, chocolate egg creams and chocolate-covered marshmallow twists, then cigarettes. And there are the peppermint-candy cigarettes.

Miss Hipp comes over to our house and hangs out in the kitchen while Ma's cooking, and she sits at the kitchen table smoking Pall Malls, drinking beer and chewing Doublemint gum. She's very light skinned and her husband is very dark. They kind of look alike except that she's light and he's dark.

Late one summer night I'm sitting outside on the bottom step of our lobby and looking straight up at the dark, clear sky when I see a thick, white, rocket-like beam of light silently and rapidly zip across the sky traveling south to north. It's like a comet. It's a wide, quick and quiet beam of light and it crosses above me in a fraction of a second. "WOW - DID YOU SEE THAT ?" No one else sees it because they're not looking up at the sky. But I don't care. I saw a comet.

I start 6th grade at P.S. 25 and I'm the teacher's pet. Our 6th grade teacher is Mrs. Jackson, an elderly black woman who is cultured, dignified and elegant, and she always wears black. She teaches us the song Bless This House. She's the oldest teacher at the school and has a daughter, Miss Jackson, who teaches 3rd grade, leads the glee club and plays concert piano. Miss Jackson takes to the piano during assembly and plays Rustle of Spring.

There's a boy who sits next to me in class named Hubert who has really bad breath. When he talks he forces me to turn my face a little so his breath won't hit me directly. One day I can't find my pencil and Hubert says, "I gotta extra one." He fishes in his book bag and comes out with a pencil that's very old, and the eraser on it has dried up and hardened. When I try to use the eraser it's so hard that it rips my paper. I stick the eraser in my mouth to try and wet it and make it softer and Hubert says, "I already tried that, it won't work." Now I feel like spitting but I can't because I'm in the classroom. What was I thinking? How could I put his bad-breath pencil eraser in my mouth?

Each day during class at 11:50 am just before lunch, Mrs. Jackson sends me to the store to get her a plain or vanilla Dannon Yogurt. By the time I return with the yogurt the rest of the class is at lunch in the cafeteria where I eventually join them or sometimes I walk home for lunch and see Ma. I quickly walk the 4 blocks and join her in the kitchen of our new apartment where she'll be reading the paper and drinking coffee.

Ma Petting a cat with Miss Hipp in Apt. 1A, and a bottle of Ancient Age, 1961

It's a clear, fall day that I walk home for lunch and I'm in the kitchen eating a peanut butter sandwich and talking to Ma and my baby brother Don is meddling around the house barefoot when Ma tells him to go and find his shoes and put them on. He's 3. The next thing we hear is him screaming from the bedroom. I jump up and run into the bedroom and he's kneeling down in front of the clothes closet which is on fire and all my sisters' dresses are ablaze. He'd gotten hold of some matches and was searching for his shoes in the dark closet. I grab him up and run shouting to Ma that the closet's on fire. By the time we look in the room the flames have spread to the bed and Ma shoves me and Don out the door and into the hall. I pull him outside and we run down to the corner and pull the fire alarm. We run back up to the house and Ma's shouting out of the window with smoke billowing up

from behind her "Somebody please call the fire department!"
The fire truck arrives and everything we have is burning up
quickly and the firemen begin tearing up the rest. Our entire
apartment, after finally being upstairs and out of the cellar, is
gone. We cry and cry. I cry until my eyes are dry. I'm also
crying because it's the first time that I see Ma crying. All that's
left is the little table where we were sitting in the kitchen, and
the pungent smell of burned hopes. My 3 sisters, Sissy, Linda
and Cathy are still at school and have no idea of the fire. They
always walk home together, down Throop Avenue.

As I see 3 o'clock approaching I start walking up Throop Ave to
meet them and prepare them for the disastrous news. I meet
the three of them near the corner of Hart St.

"Listen, stop. I gotta tell you something. The house burned up
today. Don set the house on fire. "

They react exactly the way I thought they would. They don't
believe me. They look at me and dismiss what I say as
nonsense and keep walking.

"No really, the house burned down today and everything is
gone. "

"Aw, get outta here" they say, rolling their eyes and sucking
their teeth and turning their heads. But once we turn the
corner and they look up the block their faces change. There is
still a fire truck parked out front and our windows are busted
out and surrounded with soot, and there is fire debris and
broken and burnt furniture covering the sidewalk. My sisters'
mouths drop open and their eyes bulge and all 3 of them fall

down on the sidewalk crying. That night we have to pile up in the cellar downstairs with Grandma and Granddad, back down again, traumatized and heartbroken, where we remain for the next 3 months until we finally move out of the neighborhood. Ma goes downtown to try to get help from the welfare but they deny her because Dad has a job as a super and also a full-time job. Sometimes we're able to get government food though. Big cans of Spam, the big can of peanut butter, blocks of cheese, powdered milk and powdered eggs, all with the government writing on the packages. We're embarrassed to open our fridge in front of our friends because they might see the government labels on all the food.

I was the handyman's child,

I grew up half hungry, half wild,

Way out where the refuse is piled,

and summer breezes ain't for sniffin,

Please, excuse me for livin.   - Oscar Brown, Jr.

On a cold winter night in February of 1962 with Ma sitting behind the wheel of her 1952 Plymouth and wheezing with asthma, and Miss Hipp sitting next to her with a lit cigarette, we're packed in and moving to our new house at 477 Halsey Street, out of the neighborhood. "Does this cigarette bother you, Ollie ?" Ma can hardly talk so she nods her head "yes" and Miss Hipp takes a final drag, tosses the butt out the window and we take off.

We're moving to the heart of Bedford Stuyvesant, the black pride of Brooklyn, with its private Brownstone houses and middle-class blacks who own their homes, many, for generations. Ma occasionally suffers with asthma, especially when it's real cold, and with all the work of packing and the kicking up of coal dust as we move out of the cellar, her breathing is particularly difficult. I glare at Miss Hipp from my vantage point in the dark, back seat of the car because my mother is struggling to breathe and she should know better than to smoke now. Miss Hipp doesn't drive and I know that later tonight after we're settled in, Ma has to drive her back home to Willoughby Avenue.

V
Halsey Street

By this time Dad has a floor-cleaning business and contracts with Lenox and Harlem Lanes, bowling alleys in Harlem, and also the Apollo Theatre to do floor maintenance. He recruits a crew of his friends from around Willoughby to work for him, including Ronnie. He's driving a clean, black, 1954 Ninety-Eight Oldsmobile.

We move into a two-family house on Halsey between Lewis and Stuyvesant on the north side of the street again, right in the middle of the block, and we occupy the ground floor and the parlor floor. Our landlady is an old, light-skinned woman named Mrs. Robinson, who lives across the street at 522, the house we lived in when I was born. Our kitchen, living room and den are on the ground floor and the bedrooms are upstairs. There are two bathrooms, one on the ground floor and one on the parlor floor and we have a backyard and a small front yard that has sunflowers in it. Our new phone number is GLenmore 7-6033.

Dad's older sister, Toots, has a daughter named Alma who's our first cousin but she's older than we are, and when we meet her she already has two daughters, Sherri and Leatha, who are kids like us. So we can't call Alma Alma, we have to call her Cousin Alma, because she's older. Sometimes we call her "Aunt Alma". She acts more like an aunt than a cousin to us, and she hollers at us and threatens us just like she's our mother or big sister. So one day when Ma and Dad aren't home, Sissy, Linda and Cathy decide to "prank call" Alma. They dial her number and when she answers the phone they commence to cussing her out in language they'd never use around grownups. After they'd had enough of calling Alma "you goddamn fuckin' bitch", they hang up and laugh hysterically. Alma shows up at the house about an hour later and beats them with a belt and promptly leaves, calls Ma later, and Ma whips them again.

Shortly after we move in we get a German Shepherd and name him Toy. I feel proud walking the big, handsome dog around the block on a leash and proud that we're living what we kids learn to call "decent". Toy is with us only briefly. One late-spring day after school I'm in the kitchen looking forward to some bread & butter & cocoa, and the song Johnny Angel is playing on the radio, when I hear the thump and brakes of a large truck outside, and my sisters screaming. I run out to the front yard. Toy had jumped the fence, run into the street and got hit by a tractor-trailer truck and he's crawling his way back to us, dragging his rear legs behind him and bleeding out of his mouth. I never ate the after-school snack, but cried all afternoon.

Dad and Ma are patriotic Americans and take pride in the way they carry themselves, how they dress and what they represent. Ma says, "I don't believe when somebody says, 'Do you think you're better than me' that you should say no. When somebody low down asks me if I think I'm better than them I say you're damn right I'm better than you. And if they say 'do you think your kids are better than mine' I say you're damn right they're better!"

Ma is practical and logical and flies the American flag. She thinks Cassious Clay is too "biggedy" and boisterous and she doesn't want to hear about black power and doesn't accept the description of being "black". She becomes involved in the local democratic club and helps with voter registration. She and Dad grew up in the segregated, Jim-Crow south and are grateful and proud to be hard-working New Yorkers.

I make friends quickly with a boy across the street at 512 Halsey named Tommy Bailey. He doesn't have brothers and sisters and they own their own house. I also make friends with Wally across the street at 506, Wayne, two doors down at 473, and Conrad, two doors up at 481. Wally's a year older than the rest of us and keeps up with all the trends, and he was born in the house that he lives in. There's a new-style sneaker out called Tracks, and Wally is the first to get a pair on our block, then Tommy, then Wayne, then Conrad, then me. We go to Jack's Army & Navy on Fulton and Sumner to buy sneakers, sweat socks and khakis.

Wally's always looking for a way to do something adventurous and different so he becomes interested in archery and gets a fiberglass bow and arrow with real arrows. We all follow suit and soon the 4 of us have bows and arrows and we shoot the arrows high into the air and they sometimes land as far as

Jefferson Avenue. We can actually aim an arrow from the middle of our block between Lewis and Stuyvesant and it'll travel all the way to Reid Avenue. Wally finally gets a bee-bee gun and one cloudy day when I'm walking past his house across the street, he shoots me in the foot, hiding from me behind the curtains in his living-room window.

There's a hamburger joint on Broadway between Woodbine and Palmetto called Greasy Louis, but some people call it Sloppy Louis, and they sell root-beer sodas and franks and hamburgers. The huge mug of root beer is 5 cents and the franks and burgers are 10 cents each. Wally, Tommy, Wayne and I scrape up 50 cents each, then walk the 5 long blocks and 4 short blocks to Greasy Louis and eat our fill and still have 15 or 20 cents left.

There's a bully in my 6th grade class named Mark who's taller than most of us and has a bad attitude and a big mouth. One day after lunch he threatens to beat me up after school at 3 o'clock, by showing me his clenched fist and then holding up three fingers. My mind goes blank for the rest of the afternoon except for the thought of what's going to happen at 3. The bell finally rings and my heart starts thumping and we're dismissed. I haven't had a fight after school since kindergarten but I had a fight back on Willoughby with a tough boy named Robert when I was talking about the comet and he called me a square-headed stupid ass. Robert also punched me in the eye that day because he could box better than I could.

By the time I make it down to the schoolyard Mark's talking with some boys and seems like he forgot about his appointment to beat me up, and I can't take the anxiety of this threat hanging over me because I'm scared and can't think and I want to get it over with no matter the outcome. I really can't take it so I walk up to him. "Hey Mark, remember what you said?" He shoots a glance at me and says "Oh yeah!" He gives somebody his books and we put up our fists and circle around, throw punches and grab each other and I get him in a headlock and punch him over and over on the head and kick him in the stomach and someone breaks us up and he's crying, actually bawling, as if I'd picked on *him* and threatened to beat *him* up. I never expected him to cry the way he did. I didn't expect to beat him. He's the bully of the class and taller than us and it's near the end of the year and I beat the bully and have a whole crowd of witnesses who saw him crying like a little boy. I walk home down Sumner Ave. afterwards feeling like a king and know that I'll sleep good tonight. It was the opposite from back in Kindergarten. I'd finally got my big crowd around me. The next day in school, Mark actually offers his hand and apologizes.

Tommy and Wally have known each other all their lives. Wally comes from a big family with 5 brothers and sisters like me, and his parents are from Barbados. Lots of Blacks own their own homes, especially West Indians, and many kids go to private schools like Holy Rosary, Bishop Loughlin and Our Lady Of Victory. We take pride and comfort in being native-New Yorkers and we speak like kids from Brooklyn. New York has a brand-new baseball team, The Mets, and their home field is

The Polo Grounds, but ground is being broken for their New
Home, Shea Stadium and The Worlds' Fair in Flushing, Queens.
By the time the weather gets warm in the late Spring of 1962,
I'm finishing up public school at P.S. 25 walking the 3/4 mile
each day back and forth, because I was getting ready to
graduate when we moved and asked not to be transferred and
offered to walk the extra distance. My 3 sisters are
transferred to P.S. 129 on Gates Avenue. I'm approaching
puberty, ready to graduate and start Junior High School in
September. A girl named Joann lives upstairs on the top floor
and she's pretty and has green eyes and I like her so I consider
her my girlfriend. I start spreading jazz in the summer of '62
by turning up the volume on the hi-fi so that the sounds can
be heard from the stoop and sidewalk through the open living
room windows. I sit listening to the album "Groovin with Jug"
by Richard Groove Holmes and Gene Ammons, and the album
"Here "Tis" by Lou Donaldson, and I still pee in the bed
sometimes, and Sissy's the one who's always ready to
announce it in front of my friends, even my girlfriend, if we get
into an argument. All the "cool" older people walk by, stop,
listen and say, "Who's that playing?" And I proudly announce
"Gene Ammons". These people look like intellectuals and I
admire them. Dad and Ma still have Poker parties to make
extra money and I'm playing the records and watching people
dance. They're doing the Wobble and the Mashed Potatoes
and The Dog.

Ma and Miss Hipp are in love with the record "Release Me" by
Esther Phillips. I don't think Ma is happily married. I think she
feels trapped with 6 kids and wants to be free. Sometimes we

aggravate her to the point where she shakes her head in frustration, and says "You know, I wish I could just run away. I wish I could just take my pocketbook and run away."

Ma and Dad do argue, sometimes late at night when they're having highballs together, but I can never tell what they're arguing about because I don't stay long enough to listen.

There's a guy named Johnny next door at 479 who always sits on his stoop sleeping. Johnny is about 20 and dresses nice wearing alligator shoes, nylon socks and herring bone pants, knit shirts and a Velour hat, and in the summer he wears a stingy-brim Panama. Every day, he sits on the stoop dressed up, sleeping. People stop and talk to Johnny and he scratches and smokes while they talk, and when they walk away, he goes back to sleep. One day I put on a Gene Ammons record and sit on my stoop and Johnny says, "That sounds like Gene Ammons. Is that Jug ?" I say "Yeah, Johnny, how did you know?" He says, " I just know his sound man", and he falls asleep in front of me, but he keeps waking up if he hears something good, or loud, then falls asleep again. One day he comes outside, sits on the stoop and crosses his legs and lights a cigarette and falls asleep with the lit cigarette between his fingers and a couple of minutes later it burns him and he yells "Aw FUCK! - You see that ?"

Easter Sunday, 1962. 477 Halsey Street. From top l to r Rickey Maxwell, Me,
Cathy, Linda, Sissy, Don. Johnny's stoop is to the right, at 479.

Joanne, our neighbor upstairs whom I "considered" my girlfriend.

Uncle James, Ma's brother, comes over one day and I play these records for him and he's surprised that I'm listening to this music at such a young age. The next time he comes over he brings me an old Encyclopedia of Jazz with the front cover missing, but the contents intact, and I read and keep this book for years, and I sit on the stoop on Halsey looking at the book as the music plays inside, feeling like a jazz scholar. None of my friends on Halsey relate to this music. Uncle James is kind of odd for an uncle and sort of a beatnik, whose eyes bulge and he talks to himself. I first caught Uncle James talking to

himself when I was 7 and it really scared me. He wears a
goatee, sometimes plays around with the trumpet, and often
sits with his legs gapped open and one leg cocked over the
arm of the chair, wearing short pants with no drawers and his
big nuts hanging out the side of his pants. He likes making up
stories and hanging out in Philadelphia. If you keep asking
him, he'll tell a story that he made up, about a bar-room fight
on a rainy night in Philly. There's a big bottle of cheap gin on
the floor beside him and a Lucky Strike between his fingers. He
takes a swig of gin and inhales a puff from the Lucky and
begins the yarn:

" I was in a bar down on 6th Street and there was a nasty,
mean man, big like a damn giant. He worked in the steel mills
in Pittsburg and hated everybody, and the more he drank, the
meaner and nastier he got, and he was sittin' at the bar
drinking and talkin' out loud to hisself, and eatin pickled eggs.
It was a Saturday evening, early, about 6 O'Clock, and there
was a dark, hot summer rain outside. It was rainin so hard
you could hardly hear the piccolo . I never seen rain like that
in my life, not even in Florida, and the rain was leaking
through the roof in 9 places.   I was just sittin at a card table
tryin to play a friendly game of Tonk with all the water leakin,
looking at this big, mean rascal down the bar talkin to hisself,
drinkin Jack Daniels and eatin pickled eggs right out the jar,
but soon as he looked my way I looked somewhere else. He
was goin back and forth to the piccolo playin that record Big
Bad John, over and over. I was scared of him. I didn't want
nothin to do with him I was trying to avoid him but I couldn't
keep my eyes off him......... He saw me looking once and I

thought he was gittin ready to git up so I turned my head real fast. Then he caught me lookin again and snapped and hollered way cross the room, 'WHATCHOO LOOKIN AT NIGGAAAAAAH ?"

"There was pickled eggs all in the corners of his mouth and he slammed his drink down and slid off the bar stool comin at me and I jumped right up from the table and was goin' out the door and he grabbed me by the back o' my jacket coat collar and pulled it so hard I was chokin'. I tried to grab roun' the front of my neck to stop chokin but the zipper on the jacket cut my hand and it started bleedin and he slammed me to the wall and was beatin me down and bangin my head on the floor and I jumped up and we fell out the door fightin' in the pourin rain. A police car came by and saw us fightin and wouldn't even stop, it was rainin so bad. The bar was situated on a steep hill and we started slidin and fallin and rollin down the hill all the way to the next corner, all the time he got me by the back o'my jacket. He wouldn't let me go and I was tryin to hit him but he was so big I couldn't reach him. I started callin on Jesus and somehow I finally managed to kick him in the nuts and he bent over and I grabbed him roun' the neck and got him in a head lock and we fell in the gutter. By this time I wasn't scared of him no mo. Then I reached down and I had him like this here, but we was so wet his head started slippin outta my grip and I grabbed him under his chin but my hand slipped in his mouth and he bit down on my fingers but somehow I got his big, wide head between my knees like this here, and squeezed until he started gagging, and I took my other hand and reached down and grabbed on to his top lip and I managed to git a good fist full of that top lip and I pulled up as hard as I could with his teeth bitin down on my other hand and I yanked up, and tore off his lip.......... his nose.......... and finally yanked real hard and snatched his whole face off and threw it on the ground and it floated down the street in the gutter and the rain water washed it down in the sewer."

After I stopped laughing I said, "What happened to the man after you tore his face off Uncle James?" His eyes got big and he said, "Shit, I left that niggah hollerin' in the pouring rain like a hit dog. The last time I saw him he was on third street with his head wrapped up like a mummy. Somebody said he in the crazy house."

Uncle James rescued me and saved my life when I was a toddler in a place called Cowtown in South Jersey where they have Saturday fairs and rodeos and where they sell everything you'd find in a 1950s rural flea market, everything from horse saddles to Bowie knives. You can even buy cows and bulls. I somehow got away from my mother while she was busy with my aunts and uncles at the fair and wandered off and got lost. When they saw I was missing everyone went in different directions trying to find me and Uncle James found me in a bull pen surrounded by curious and snorting bulls. He calmly and immediately walked in the pen and scooped me up and left the bulls there looking at him, and he delivered me to Ma's grateful and nervous arms. He forgot all about danger and acted from the instinct that directed him to save a baby.

Uncle James Harris, Ma's Brother

When we move to Halsey St. Grandma and Granddad move to Newark to live with my Aunt Sarah and her children. Tommy and I have baseball gloves and we throw a softball back and forth across Halsey Street to each other for hours. Halsey is a two-way street with a bus route running back and forth from downtown Brooklyn to Ridgewood, the B26 Putnam. There are pretty, teenage girls all over the place. Wally's older sister Gail is pretty and popular and always parades up and down the block with a group of her girlfriends, who think Tommy and I are cute and give us kisses whenever they pass and we always look forward to them. One of Gail's friends is a very pretty girl named Regina who's about 15 and lives on the next block between Stuyvesant and Reid, in a walk-up apartment on the 2nd floor. She's beautiful and petite and looks like a Native American, and every time she passes through she gives me and Tommy warm kisses on the cheek and smiles and we love her. The song Playboy by the Marvelettes is on the radio.

One morning I come outside and see a crowd of people in front of Wally's house and some girls are crying. Regina was stabbed to death in the lobby of her building the night before. It is unbelievable, tragic and unforgettable. I wonder who was mad at her enough to stab her to death, as pretty and delicate as she was, and why she had to die. She was so nice and shy and gorgeous. I don't know her family or parents of even if she has sisters and brothers. I just know that she lived on the next block and gave me and Tommy a kiss every day.

There are black businesses in the area like McDonald's Dining Room on Stuyvesant and Macon, well-established black cultural institutions and prominent black churches like Concord and Cornerstone, and Brooklyn A.M.E.

Rev. Billy Graham addressing a crowd outside Cornerstone Church on Madison Street Brian Merlis Coll.

A man named Mr. Hogan opens up a small Grocery Store on Lewis Ave. between Halsey and Hancock and names it The Stupid Market. The big window in the front is labeled THE STUPID MARKET and underneath is the caption: " *We must be stupid, because we sell so cheap !*" Mr. Hogan is tall and light skinned with hazel eyes and a mustache and fast talking and always has two pockets full of money and he drives a green, 1962 Cadillac Fleetwood. I start working in the store when it first opens, helping to stock the shelves and there's a boy also working named Glenwood. One day he makes a mistake labeling some cans of food and Mr. Hogan says, "Glenwood? You so dumb you stink!" I can't help but laugh out loud and when I get home and tell my sisters what Mr. Hogan said they all laugh hard and we joke about it for years.

169 Lewis Avenue, Brian Merlis Collection

There's a luncheonette down the block named Ruth's Burger Haven, owned by a black woman named Ruth whose boyfriend is a white man named Marty who owns a meat market on the corner of Lewis and Halsey, right across the street from Ruth's. Ruth serves burgers and fries and sandwiches, breakfast and coffee and ice cream, desserts and sodas and has a jukebox with a record in it called "Rat Race", and a record by Don Gardner called I Need Your Lovin, which is the funniest record I've ever heard. A man named Norman comes in every day, pops a dime in the jukebox and plays Rat Race, hops up on the stool at the counter and says, "Um out here in this rat race, man!" I get a job there working behind the counter and washing dishes, making ice cream cones and malteds, and working in the back kitchen preparing hamburger patties for freezing. Marty comes over from the meat market with a big bag of ground beef and takes it into the back kitchen and I peek in from behind the counter and he and Ruth are kissing and she has her fingers in his dark, curly hair and his hands are on her behind. I think Marty's probably married with kids and Ruth is his girl on the side, making her money conveniently across the street from where he makes his. And I imagine that he doesn't charge Ruth for the ground beef.

Halsey Street looking west towards Sumner Avenue, circa 1959,

Brian Merlis Coll.

By the summer of 1962 Ronnie is married with a son and living in his own apartment on Willoughby Avenue. His first son is named after him, Ronald, but Dad starts calling him Junebug, which eventually gets shortened to June, and that becomes his nickname. Ray Charles is singing I can't stop Loving You, and Dad's floor cleaning business is doing well, so he packs up the whole family and we drive to his home, Savannah, Georgia to see his mother and his family. This is our first time seeing Dad's mother and our first time down south. On a hot, August morning we hit the road in Dad's 1954, Ninety-Eight Olds, my three sisters and I in the back and Ma, Dad and Don in the front. The hit song The Locomotion is playing on the radio. We hear a lot of country music on the radio while on the road, and there's a hit-country song called Wolverton Mountain that plays a lot during this, our first long ride to the exotic and mysterious south. As we approach Savannah around 3am the next morning the nauseating, alien smell of the pulp mills where they turn wood into paper hits us kids for the first time, and after 2 days we all feel like we're poisoned down to our taste buds by this rank blanket of breath. The combined smells of the pulp mill and the stale sweetness of my grandmother's house and our mysterious, new relatives are overwhelming. One of our Aunts, Ruby, has cerebral palsy and can't talk but she tries, and it's the first time we're seeing a retarded person, and she stays in the bed and her room smells like sour milk. After we meet Aunt Ruby we nickname Cathy after her, teasing her for years, calling her "Ruby Junior". Dion has a record out called Ruby Baby, and we sing it to Cathy, replacing Ruby Baby with "Ruby Junior". We never meet our paternal grandfather who died way before we were born. His body was found where he'd drowned, in the Savannah River.

Our grandmother is mysterious to us, and reserved. She's even older than Granddad. We don't call her Grandma, we call her Big Mama. The inside of her house is hot and still, and we never see her smile.

Levenia Hendrix-German, Dad's Mother, born 1880

We're gone for about 6 days and when we return Ronnie is there to meet us with bad news. Dad's cleaning contracts in Harlem have been cancelled. He'd actually been a sub-contractor and had assignments to various businesses. At first Dad and Ma can't understand but after Ronnie explains how things went for the past few days they figure out the straw that changed everything and the line that had been crossed.

A few weeks earlier Dad's cousin Roosevelt (Rose Hendrix) had gotten a brand-new 1962, light-blue Cadillac Sedan de Ville. One day Dad's on his way uptown to pick up the payroll for his crew and Rose lets him borrow his Caddy and Dad leaves the 98 Olds with Rose. Dad puts on a suit and buys a cigar and shows up in Harlem in a brand-new Caddy. When the Jewish guys who run the business see this they decide to teach him a lesson for trying to be a big shot. They're not driving Caddys and wearing suits and smoking cigars. "Maybe Ed German's making too much money. So he shows up to pick up payroll like this?" Tommy and I were playing catch when Dad pulled up in Rose's car with a cigar in his jaw. I'd never seen him with a cigar and didn't know whose car this was and I stopped and watched as he parked, got out and went into the house briefly. Ronnie also explains that he thinks the contractors tried to set them up one night by entrapment. They'd showed up to clean a night club and when they arrived there were 3 or 4 piles of money around the bar and in the office and everyone's eyes bulged but Ronnie made sure nobody touched anything and he immediately locked up the club and left. When they arrived at the next place they were scheduled to clean, all the locks had been changed. All this happened while we were in Georgia and Ma was furiously outraged at Dad for having such bad judgment and leaving Ronnie, a teenager, in charge, and for being immature and showing off like a big shot in front of those white men with Rose's car and the big cigar.

But despite this setback, Dad decides to treat himself before things get too bad, while he has the chance. Dad never took me anywhere, just the two of us, except when he carried me down to Dr. Hitlen's house when I had the hernia. But one day we leave the house and walk down Stuyvesant Avenue to the Utica Avenue train station at Fulton, and take the "A" train to

Harlem and get off on 125th Street. We walk over to a car dealership and Dad signs all kinds of papers and we drive home in a 1959, white Oldsmobile Ninety-Eight, with a blue top.

I start Decatur Junior High School 35 in September 1962 and I'm in class 7-2. My intellectual world is expanding. Our academic schedule includes French and I feel special, although it's pretty complicated grammatically. Our French teacher's name is Mr. Fein. Our Hygiene teacher is a black man, Mr. Ashby. Another popular black teacher is Mr. Vann (Al Vann) who later enters politics.

JHS 35, Decatur Street & Lewis Avenue

Our math teacher is a young, white man named Mr. Sherman who does something very peculiar every day that I can't figure out. Our first class after lunch is math and Mr. Sherman begins class by writing some math problems on the board for us to solve and then he starts pacing around the perimeter of the classroom. I sit on one of the end rows near the door and I watch Mr. Sherman whose eyes are always very red after lunch, and during those quiet minutes that he paces around he's laughing on the inside and I catch him several times suppressing an inner laugh and sometimes he has to go out in the hall so he can laugh at whatever it is he's thinking about, then he comes back in the room wiping his eyes, clenching his lips and clearing his throat.

My favorite teacher is Mr. Goldberg, our social studies teacher who, in the winter of 1963, takes us on a class trip to

see the Mona Lisa on exhibit at the Metropolitan Museum of
Art. We travel to the city on a school bus, the first time I'd
ever ridden a school bus, and one of the kids has a transistor
radio and the song playing is Mama Didn't Lie, and Mr.
Goldberg is singing along with us. Some of the hip talk in class
includes "Shut your face", and soon Mr. Goldberg is saying it
back to us. Everybody likes him. By the end of the term I have
a crush on my classmate Sandra Ancrum and carry her books
for her down Lewis Avenue and sometimes hold her hand, and
Ruby & The Romantics have the hit song, Summer Love.

One hot summer day in August of 1963 I'm working behind
the counter at Ruth's, and Our Day Will Come by Ruby and The
Romantics is playing on the jukebox, and Daddy comes in. He
looks at me kind of awkwardly and says, "Come outside, I
wanna tell you somethin'." He walks out the door and I go
around the counter and outside where he looks down at me
and his eyes begin to tear, his lips tremble and his voice breaks
and he says, "Daddy died." It's the first time I'm seeing my
father cry and I cry with him, because he's crying.

Granddad wasn't particularly close to me because he had so
many grandchildren and there was only one of him to go
around, and when I lived with him and Grandma in the cellar
he never really said much to me, but one evening when I came
from Sussman's with some peppermint barrels and handed
him the bag he gave me one and put one in his mouth and
told me about when he worked in a candy factory somewhere
down in Alabama, where, after the men ate their lunch they'd
take naps on huge piles of sugar, and how one day after they'd

gotten paid the men were nagging him to stop in a saloon with them and have a drink.

"So finally I told em OK, I'll go in but I'm not gonna drink. And they kept on trying to make me taste some beer and when I finally took a swallow it liked to made me gag. It was so nasty I couldn't stand it, and all them fellas was standin' 'roun laughin."

Grandad never drank but the story goes that it was my mother who stopped him from gambling when she was a young girl, and she found him deep in the woods in Georgia gambling with some men. He said to himself then, "If my oldest daughter can find me in the woods gambling it's time for me to stop."

When I get home later that day I find out that Ma had dropped to the floor when she got the news on the phone from Newark, that her father had died. They'd been each other's favorites, since she was his first-born girl.

Granddad dies in the Summer of 1963 and my mother gets a part- time job on the Lower East Side renting rooms and making beds in a small, cheap hotel owned by a man named Ben Guberman, and she always brings home Hostess fruit pies whose dates have expired. "The Hotel", as it's called, is at 175 East Houston Street on the corner of Allen, in the heart of the Lower East Side. The name of it is Houston Studios.

I start 8th grade in the fall of 1963 and once again have Mr. Goldberg for social studies and most of my classmates from the 7th grade. By the middle of October our family gets the

news that we have to move out of our apartment. There have
been problems with rent because of the final failure of Dad's
floor-cleaning business. We're moving out of the
neighborhood and this time we're not moving up, we're
moving down again, almost like losing apartment 1A to the
fire, then having to move back down in the cellar, but I don't
feel dismayed because I'm a kid and just have to make the
best of it. But I *am* disappointed because I like my school and
my classmates and teachers. Mr. Goldberg has already
planned a class trip in a couple of weeks to go see the movie,
How the West Was Won.

VI
Ralph Avenue

We move into a 3 bedroom apartment above a store front at 524 Ralph Avenue between Park and Sterling Place. Our new phone number is SLocum 6-0035. Sissy and I start school at JHS 178 on Dean Street and Linda, Cathy and Don go to P.S. 191 around the corner on Park Place.

P.S. 191 Park Place bet. Ralph and Buffalo Aves.

178 is on Dean between Saratoga and Hopkinson, just down the street from another Catholic orphanage for girls called The House of The Good Shepherd, now abandoned, standing like a ghostly, foreboding monstrosity, and kids throw rocks at its' remaining windows, breaking out the last glass panes of the now-condemned structure. The alternate Junior High School for us is J.H.S. 210 on Rochester Avenue but I'm glad we don't go there because 210 is notoriously bad, containing students who are Corsairs *and* students who are Chaplains, and the Principal of 210, George Goldfarb, committed suicide by jumping off the school roof on January 29th 1958.

JHS 210 Rochester Ave. Jan. 31, 1958, two days after the suicide of the school's principal. NYPD Patrolman Percival Noles. Brian Merlis Coll.

JHS 178, Dean St. bet. Saratoga and Hopkinson Aves (Pacific Street View)

Another Catholic orphanage for girls, House of The Good Shepherd on Hopkinson Ave. between Dean and Pacific Sts. (Pacific St. View) Demolished 1964. Replaced by The Atlantic Towers.

The Atlantic Towers on Hopkinson Ave. Pacific St. View

As I say goodbye to Mr. Goldberg I shake his hand and he says "Well, sorry you have to leave but good luck, and if you ever get the chance, stop by and say hi." I enroll at 178 but privately I have a plan devised. I know that the class trip with Mr. Goldberg is Friday so I cut school at 178 and show up for school at 35, just to go on the trip. It's a brisk and sunny autumn morning and I get up extra early for school that day because I have to travel to Decatur Street and I'm excited and leave the house smiling, with an adventure before me. I take the B#24 Ralph bus down to Decatur Street, get off and walk the 4 long blocks to Lewis Avenue and show up at Mr. Goldberg's class for school, ready to go on the trip. "I thought you moved." He says. "I did." I tell him. "So what are you doing

here?" "I didn't wanna miss the trip." I say . "Yeah but............
Oh alright, C'Mon." He shakes his head and waves me into the
school bus and we go to a theatre in Times Square and see the
film, How the West Was Won, and I'm enchanted with the
melody of the song Greensleeves, but the lyric goes "Oh come,
Oh come, fly away with me and I'll build you a home in the
meadow."

After the movie Mr. Goldberg gathers the class in the lobby to
wait for the school bus to arrive and there's commotion and
rushing about and people saying that the President has been
shot. At first we think it's phony 42nd Street gag news but
when Mr. Goldberg finds out it's true, he stands before us in
his cashmere coat, thick-framed black eyeglasses, yellow shirt
and brown tie, and announces to us that President Kennedy is
dead, crying as he speaks, and we all cry with him because
he's crying. The President of The United States is assassinated
in the western city of Dallas, just after we'd seen "How The
West Was Won."

Many whites still live in Ocean-Hill Brownsville in 1963, and
there are lots of elderly Jewish people who sit outside in chairs
around the corner from our house, and many white-owned
businesses in the area, including Rockford Moving and Storage
on the corner of Park Place and Ralph, The Blue Sky
Commercial Laundry on Ralph between Park and Prospect,
Krasner's Drugs on Ralph and Park, and Tony & 7 Sons bike
shop on Buffalo Avenue. Tony is an Italian widower with 7
sons. He wears thick-framed, black glasses and looks a little
like Jimmy Durante. Tony's specialty is converting. He can turn
a three speed into a ten speed and convert a free wheel into a

fixed wheel. There's a candy/toy store across the street called Hoola-Ka-Boola, Sperling hardware is on Howard Avenue & St. John's, and there's a shoe-repair and shine shop on St. John's and Ralph, where we spend many Friday and Saturday nights getting our "Kangs" polished after "gittin' clean", and the guy that shines our shoes is white.

Eastern Parkway looking west to Saratoga Ave. Brian Merlis coll.

Lincoln Terrace Park is set within the borders of Eastern Parkway and East New York Avenue, and Buffalo and Rochester Avenues, and is where we play handball and ride our bikes and tease the prostitutes that walk around it. We avoid going across the border of East New York Ave. because of the white boys in Pigtown. "Yo man, don't fuck around down in Pigtown, them mau-fuckin' white boys'll run yo black ass right back up this hill", a kid named Jimmy Kelly says. He also says, "Man I hang out in the Pinkhouses - 'das where I be at. Boy, you should see all the pussy walkin 'roun the Pinkhouses."

The Pink Houses Projects in East New York

My academic schedule at 178 still includes French, and we're able to choose either art or music. I choose music and attend band class, play snare drum and learn to read percussion music.

Our school is located in the gang territory of the Corsair Lords of the Kingsborough Projects, and there are members of the gang in our band class, and we go to school with the president of the Corsairs, Michael Snow, who is very black and good looking like Miles Davis. The War Counselor of the Corsairs is a guy named Stink, who always wears black Velour hats and Applejacks, and another gang member is a guy named Touch. The ruling body of the Corsair Lords is located in the 7th walk of the Kingsboro Projects, near the top of Ocean Hill.

The notorious 7th Walk of the Kingsboro Projects

So the main enemies of the Corsairs are just blocks away, the Albany Chaplains to the west, and the Brevoort Chaplains to the north, which border Fulton St., Ralph Ave., Patchen Ave. and Bainbridge Street.

The Brevoort, Patchen Ave. and Bainbridge bldg.

The prettiest girl in school is Josie Whitfield, who lives on Bergen Street and Howard, who is a stunning black beauty, so pretty that other girls want to beat her up, and she has to be walked to school by members of the Corsairs.   There are two Gym teachers for the boys, Mr. Berger and Mr. Saks, and there's graffiti on the school yard walls near the basketball court that says," *Faget Saks*".

"Man, will you look at them crazy mau- fuckas?" Artis is
pointing at the B40 Ralph Avenue bus as it's shooting down
Ralph towards St. John's Place. It's Friday night and Snow,
Boozie, Fish, Stink and Touch are all hanging on the back of
the bus dressed in Aqua Scutem and cashmere coats,
kangaroo and lizard shoes and sharkskin suits, going to a party
in Brownsville. When we're not hitching the bus and riding on
the inside we like to sit in the last seat in the back by the open
window, and there's often a hand there, belonging to the guy
on the outside hitching on the back. Sometimes you're sitting
there and the window is closed because it's cold, and it'll
suddenly slide open from the outside, by a guy on the outside,
needing to hold on. Years later they design buses so that
there's nothing to hold onto and no way to step onto the back.

One day Artis, me and Michael Black are hitching on the back
of the B65 Bergen, coming from downtown and it's raining.
We're standing on the steel back bumper which is wet and
slippery. As the bus heads up Dean Street it hits a dip in the
road and I fall off the back of the bus and hurt my right foot so
bad that I limp for weeks but never tell Ma because I'm scared
to tell her so I never go to the doctor. I'm lucky there wasn't a
car behind me when I fell off. I'm also lucky I didn't fall off the
bus three blocks back because I might have gotten jumped by
the Albany Chaplains. But I fell off in Corsair territory.

The Kingsboro Projects, east from Rochester Avenue & Bergen St.

One day the Corsairs are heading west down Pacific Street and Stink is leading the chant with the gang singing the refrain.

"Well I went to a party but I didn't wanna stay,

(Gang)   Yeah, I didn't wanna stay,

But some pretty girls came so I stayed anyway,

(Gang)   Yeah, I stayed anyway,

Movin and a groovin,

Movin and a groovin

Rockin and a rollin

Rockin and a rollin,

Hitchin on the bus

Hitchin on the bus,

With the Corsair Lords,

With the Corsair Lords,

Meetin Chaplains on the court,

Chaplains on the court

Rollin down in Brevoort,

Down in Brevoort,

Gonna Take "P" Street,

Take "P" Street,

Down to Albany,

Albany.

And we movin and a groovin like a

HI-LO

Slippin and a slidin like a

HI-LO

Gonna bust yo head like a

HI-LO

Gonna fill you fulla lead like a

HI-LO

Gonna whip you till you dead like a

HI-LO.

I'm a mighty Corsair like a

HI-LO.

We live on Ralph Avenue but most of our friends live around the corners on Park Place and Sterling Place, so we're aligned with Park Place. Though the Corsairs are the main uptown gang, most blocks also have their own clicks, and there are "sham battles" frequently, especially in the summer. The first sham battle I get in is in the summer of 1964, when word comes through the block that the St. Marks Ave. boys are coming through. It was arranged that Park Place and St. Marks would meet in the school yard of 191. It was about 4 o'clock on a hot summer day when 30 boys come rolling around the corner of Buffalo Avenue. There are no sticks or bottles or zip guns, this will be just with the hands. I was scared but as we clash in the school yard I face a kid with our fists curled and he throws punches at me which I block, then I catch him square in the stomach and his elbows go towards his stomach as he bends down with a sick look on his face. The two gangs back off of each other and later that same night, St. Marks, Prospect, and Corsairs from Bergen and Dean unite with Park Place as one uptown gang and about 70 of us roll down Ralph Avenue across Eastern Parkway and down the hill across East New York Ave. and invade Tapscott Street, but there are so many of us that the Tapscott boys just run, heading towards Sutter Avenue. It was Ocean Hill invading Brownsville. Since that day, St. Marks and Park Place are "boys".

P.S. 191 school yard, Park Place bet. Ralph and Buffalo Aves., where Park Place and St. Marks clashed in the summer of 1964.

One of the gang members in our class is Phillip Townsend aka "Fish" who plays alto saxophone. One day we're rehearsing Deep River Rhapsody and Fish and another alto player named Ike are going over their parts and Fish says to Ike, "Don't this sound like I'll Remember April ?" I'm in the 8th grade and impressed at his reference to an American popular classic, and yet he's rolling with the Corsairs, hitching buses, playing hooky and drinking wine. The Italian brothers Joseph and John Touma are in our class and Joseph plays tenor and his brother John plays trombone. Bobby Williams also plays trombone, Paulette Tabb and Eleanor Williams play clarinet. Our band teacher is Hyman Kletzyl, who plays tenor saxophone, and one day he's tuning up and I ask him if he could play Moonglow. I'm 14 and have no idea how I know anything about Moonglow. Probably from hearing it on WNEW playing in Ma and Dad's bedroom. When Mr. Kletzyl takes daily attendance and notices Fish missing he says "Where's Fish?" and the class responds..... "On the hook !"

We have the same group of friends in both the 8th and 9th grades at 178 because we're in the same class both years. There's me, Mike King, Mike Young, Robert Robreno and Eric, "the brain", who carries his books in a suitcase. Sometimes in late spring we play hooky and crawl under the turnstile gate at the "A" train on Ralph and Fulton saving enough carfare to come back home, and we take the train and go to Coney Island with just enough money to ride the Cyclone once. We take the "A" to Franklin Avenue, go upstairs and take the shuttle to Prospect Park, then transfer for the "D" train, singing, laughing and joking all the way.

After we ride the Cyclone once and get off, that regretfully familiar, deep feeling of being broke and hungry overcomes me because we have to walk past Nathan's and all the delicious smells of hot dogs and mustard and French fries and ketchup and shrimp frying, and past all the people with money in their pockets and nice cars parked at the curb, biting on fried shrimp with tartar sauce dripping from the corners of their mouths and licking ketchup and mustard off their fingers and smacking their lips and gurgling down beers and root beers with their pretty girls and their pretty kids, and here we are, walking past with the "white mouth", and only a tiny token to get home. We never have enough money when we play hooky.

Brian Merlis Collection

Our home room and French teacher is Mrs. Gluestein, our science teacher is Mr. Fishbein. Our 8th grade English teacher is Mr. Fletcher, a light-skinned, young Black man who Is

friendly and cool like Mr. Goldberg and he looks like Malcolm
X. I learn this poem while in Mr. Fletcher's class:

> *Hey man, you got a cigarette?*
>
> *Yeah, man that's all I got*
>
> *Go away, I ain't even got that, a cigarette's a lot.*
>
> *I had a wife, a home, a kid,*
>
> *and I was ridin high.*
>
> *But along came White Jim down the hill,*
>
> *and said I had to die.*
>
> *He told the law his poor, white wife had suffered by my gain,*
>
> *and when the man came to tip me off,*
>
> *he said, "Skip town or hang".*
>
> *I left my wife, my home, my kid,*
>
> *at 19 Cherry Street,*
>
> *And in the moonless, Georgia night I moved my weary feet.*
>
> *When I remember Cherry Street it hurts me to the bone,*
>
> *But hell I'm here up north, alive, although alone.*
>
> *Ain't got no job, no fine blue suit, no new ten-gallon hat,*
>
> *All I got's one cigarette, you might as well take that.*

I'm among tough, talented, flippant and artistic schoolmates, dressing neatly and stylishly and wearing cologne and talking to the girls. There's a boy named Barry in our class who hangs around the girls exclusively and walks, talks and carries his books like a girl, is simply effeminate, and during lunch he jumps double-dutch expertly with the girls, walks to and from school with them and never uses profanity. He looks like a young picture of Herbie Hancock with his black, thick-framed glasses. One day a wild, rattle-mouth country kid named Butch from North Carolina calls Barry a punk-ass faggot and Barry responds, "You're an unclean, inferior vagrant and you're infested with flies. My ears do not decipher your imbecilic, abhorrent, primitive uttering." And all Butch can say in his buzz-sounding voice is, "Yo Mama don't wear no *graws.*"

My friend Michael Young plays clarinet and picks up the instrument and plays Sonny Rollins' St. Thomas like a professional. He's only 15 and has a beard and is fat and always carries a little brown-glass bottle of Spanish Fly and a pack of Trojans, and every time he sees a pretty girl he sucks wind between his teeth making a hissing sound.

One day a bunch of us are at Artis' house after his family moved to Queens, which we called Long Island, and we're sitting downstairs in the living room listening to records while Artis' sister Iris is upstairs in her room. So Mike sneaks up to Iris' room and comes downstairs about 15 minutes later grinning and whispering urgently to me and Mike King and Michael Black, "I fucked Iris, I fucked Iris, I fucked Iris." Later that evening when we're all back in Brooklyn hanging out, Iris walks up to Michael Young, in front of about ten of us and says, "Hey Michael, I heard you fucked me." He turned red and put his hand over his mouth.

Another kid in our class named Livingston Harris also has a beard, and he's over six feet tall and weighs over 200 pounds.

He sits in the back of the class and using a squeaky voice he goes Oooooo......Aaaaaaah....... making sounds like a woman having sex, and always says, "Big-leg women is good to me", and "There ain't nothin' like a BLWW - a big leg white woman."

All the houses on Ralph Avenue between Park and Sterling are connected, and you have to climb up a ladder to get on the roofs but once you're up there you can walk down the whole block on the roofs, which are covered with gravel on top of tar. Ralph Avenue is a busy two-way street with buses running in each direction, north and south, and when people get off the buses during rush hour and walk across the street past our house, we shower them with handfuls of gravel from the roof and have time to duck back before they can look up. In the hot summer we "bomb" the passing buses with their windows open with water balloons.

One day six of us ambush the watermelon man as he's coming down Park Place. He comes around on a horse-drawn cart that he gets from the market in Canarsie, and we each snatch a watermelon. He can't chase after us and leave all his watermelons so he just yells and curses, "Ummo gitcho black asses next time, you watch"! We run around the corner to Ralph, take the watermelons on the roof and eat our fill. Then we take what's left and throw chunks of it on people walking below, getting off the buses on their way home from work.

The first time I drink is over Ronnie's house during Christmas, 1964 when Sissy and Artie and I sit around the Christmas tree drinking gin and wine and listening to Nancy Wilson singing Guess Who I Saw Today, and Jimmy Smith's new album Christmas '64. On the way home I sit in the last seat on the B#10 New Lots Bus, throwing up out the window as we speed down Sumner Avenue. I'm sick from the combination of gin and wine and the strong smell of pine from the Christmas tree which itself begins to smell like gin.

I lose my virginity when I'm 14 with a girl named Gloria who's 17 and 6 months pregnant. Sissy's boyfriend used to go with her but she's not pregnant with his baby. Her family's southern-country and we sit in her living room and she loves the record by Joe Tex, "Hold On To What You Got". We start off kissing and she pulls me on top of her one day when her mother is out and she reaches into my pants and takes control of everything and soon I'm feeling a sensation I've never felt, but I can't hold it back and afterwards I want to leave. When I start going around with her in the neighborhood I'm made to feel ashamed because of her stomach sticking way out, pregnant with a boy named Wardell's baby, and when Rosemary, Ronnie's wife sees her, she says Gloria looks like something the flies picked over. When I call it quits with her we're in my sisters' bedroom and it's raining outside and she's crying to Marvin Gaye singing Forever and the song is making her cry harder, but I'm glad that I finally quit her and glad she's not pregnant with *my* baby.

I kiss a lot of girls on Ralph Avenue. The first girl I ever kissed was back on Willoughby, and her name was Altermese, who lived across the street at 666 on the top floor, and her living-room windows faced the south, and on the warm and sunny Easter Sunday in 1960, when Jackie McLean was recording the album Capuchin Swing in Englewood Cliffs at Rudy Van Gelder's home studio, I was up in Altermese's house dressed in my new suit, dancing slow with her. The record playing was the Platters singing Smoke Gets in Your Eyes. I could distinctly feel her two nostrils breathing on the left side of my neck as we danced on the sixth floor, looking through her living-room windows at the Albany Projects on the southern horizon, a mile away on Bergen Street. Then I kissed Betty Jean, then her sister Ann, and Donna Hipp. When we moved to Halsey I kissed Joanne Belton. But when we moved to Ralph when I was 13, I kissed Gloria, Iris, Diane, Felicia, Joyce, Cora, Jill, Yvette, Charlene, and Paula. Paula's brother Freddie always kept a close eye on his sister, two years younger, and when I was kissing Paula in my sisters' bedroom on a rainy spring day, Freddie sat on the radiator near the side of the bed looking out the window at the falling rain, making sure that I went no further than kissing. It was okay with Freddie if we were just kissing. He wore black eyeglasses and an imitation-leather coat. Whenever someone was wearing a real leather guys would say, "Yo man, that's a bad leather", as a compliment. But when the boys remarked about Freddie's coat, which was imitation, they'd say, "Yo Freddie, that's a *bad* rubber you got on." So when I was kissing Paula during the rain I was feeling her and when I popped the snap to unbuckle her dungarees

Freddie heard it and instantly looked over at us, on guard. So we started calling him "Cock-Blocking Freddie".

Yvette Davis was the most intellectual and conservative and lived on Lincoln Place in a brick house owned by her family, and she played classical music on the piano. She used to call me on the phone and when I answered "Hello?", she'd put on the record by Shep and The Limelites, *I want someone.*

I leave Gloria for a very pretty girl a year younger than me, Diane, who is a virgin and soon tells me, "I hate jazz and I hate your fuckin' bicycle." She hates my bicycle because it's my car and I even ride it to work. There's a gang of us on Ralph Ave. and Park Place and we're experts on urban mobility and improvisation, and good bike riders and mechanics who steal bikes and paint them and exchange parts and convert them into practical and dependable vehicles that we ride all the way to Coney Island and across the bridges into Manhattan and we're gone all day sometimes, flying around the city, alternately crossing the Williamsburgh and Brooklyn Bridges, and in the summer of 65 we form a group of about 15 and call ourselves the "Night Riders", and on hot summer nights we find ourselves deep in southeast Brooklyn, eating hot dogs at the Canarsie Bay Pier.

Diane hates jazz for the same reason that all people who hate jazz hate it. She's the first girl who kisses me the way she does. The first time I kiss her she wraps her mouth entirely around mine, with a bubble-gum/cigarette kiss. Diane lives on Prospect Place with her Mom and Stepfather, Leon. She comes from a family of all girls and she has three sisters,

Brenda, Sharon and Patsy. Her best friends are Linda and her sister Janice who live across the street, two houses down from Shirley and Michael Taylor, also friends of ours, and a girl named Maria from Panama.

Diane teaches me how to smoke cigarettes and we have a routine of sneaking into the cellar of my house at 524 Ralph Avenue and there, on top of an old door placed on two wooden milk crates, in the dark among the boiler and the fuse boxes and the rubble, and Mister Softee playing ice-cream music upstairs, we undress halfway and behave recklessly like we can't help it. She comes looking for me daily but never rings the bell and asks for me. Instead, she yells for me from the sidewalk underneath my bedroom window. That's why my mother doesn't like her. One day I'm sitting in the chair at Blues' Barber shop right across the street from my house and Diane shows up under my window and starts calling me. I jump out of the chair with the apron on and yell across the street to her that I'm in the barber shop and when I go back to the chair, Junior, who is cutting my hair says, "Dontchoo make that girl pregnant boy." And I do just the opposite.

One day after an argument she threatens to tell my mother she's pregnant. She never speaks to my mother and usually avoids her. Later that evening when Ma is home the bell rings and I go downstairs to answer the door and when I open it Diane walks in past me and up the stairs, and I walk out, with just my tee-shirt on, and it's October. I run away from home and spend the night at Sissy's boyfriend's dad's house. Arty's mother and father are separated and sometimes he spends the night there and he has his own keys. Sometimes we play hooky there and watch his dad's silent French films on a projector. The next day I stop in Lincoln Terrace Park and win $5.00 playing handball against a girl named Charlene. I sneak home, get some clothes and get on the Long Island Railroad and go to my cousins' house in Amityville, because I'm ashamed to face my parents, especially my mother. When I finally get home after three days my mother knocks me in the head and hollers for about two hours. Diane had missed her period several times and we often bought quinine tablets from Krasner's Drugs on Ralph and Park because they were supposed to bring the period on if it was missed. But the quinine didn't work this time and I was in denial about her being pregnant and felt totally lost.

While I'm away in Amityville, Sissy catches Diane on Park Place and beats her up for doing what she did - getting pregnant and then coming over to the house to tell Ma. Sissy had gotten pregnant by Artis a few months ago and had an illegal abortion, and will never be able to have children.

Things happen very quickly on Ralph Avenue. Kids are "fast", and anxious to do adult things. We're paying attention to clothes and keeping up with the latest styles, wearing leather coats, Aqua Scutems, Kangaroo, Snake, Lizard and Alligator shoes, Italian knit shirts, wide-leg Herring Bone hustler pants with 1 and 1/2" cuffs, short and long-hair beaver hats and splashing Jade East, English Leather, Canoe and Hai Karate Cologne, driving our parents crazy, throwing hooky parties, smoking and drinking. When we dress casual, it's a pair of Khakis and some "Cons" with sweat socks turned over the top of the sneakers and a white handkerchief hanging out of the back pocket. Sometimes when we get clean we get a nice walking cane as an added embellishment to accentuate "The Hustle". We wear our hair too thick with too much Nu Nile or Murray's Pomade in it, and we sleep in stocking caps that press the greased hair down to make waves. When Afro hair styles become popular there are times when Dad reaches into his wallet without saying a word and hands me a five-dollar bill. "What's this for Dad?"

"Go over to Blues' and get a haircut!" He snaps.

Arty has a step brother named Junior who's from Jacksonville, Florida and talks country. One time he said, "Man, you shoulda went to that party downtown last night - there was some *fat* girls in there, man. I mean, them girls was *fat*. I said, "Man?.....What?......Sheeeit - I don't like no fat girls"! Junior said, "I ain't talkin bout fat, Um talkin bout *Fine-Fat*. **Fat IS fine, man.**" It's 1965.

Don learns to smoke when he's 7. I catch Don in the cellar smoking with my friend Mickey's brother Berto, and they're both smoking and saying,

"Listen Mutha Fucka let's get this straight,

Yo mama got a pussy like a B-48.

Yo daddy got a dick like a B-49,

I done talked about 'cho people,

dontchoo talk about mine."

"Who taught you how to smoke? Who started you smoking?"
"Bobby", Don says. "What Bobby?" I yell.

"Bobby from around the corner on Sterling, upstairs."

"Who - *My* friend Bobby?" "Yeah".

Bobby is my age and lives in the big apartment building on
Sterling and Ralph with his mother. He introduces me to the
music of Cal Tjader, from his mother's records. She has the
album, "Soul Bird", and he and I go up his house just to listen
to that album. It's the first time I'm hearing vibes. I'm
enchanted by the Latin-Jazz sound and the titles of the songs
and the sharp and crisp percussion, and Cal Tjader's articulate
handling of the vibraphone. Bobby is cool, dark skin and good
looking and dresses nice and is smart. But when I find out that
he teaches Don to smoke I ring his bell and he comes
downstairs and I confront him about it and beat him up.
While I'm hitting him he's apologizing and I'm even sorry that
I'm hitting him because of the musical moments of discovery
that we shared, but I hit him till he runs down the block crying
and I'm really regretful when he runs away from me because I
know that I just lost a friend so quickly, and even now, at the
age of fifteen, I understand that he's just a product of his
environment and a victim, because if he can appreciate the
music of Cal Tjader at 15, in Ocean-Hill Brownsville, he and his
mother are my kind of people. I never see him again and don't
know his last name.

By this time Ronnie's been married for 2 years, has 3 kids and
a well furnished, up-to-date apartment at 666 Willoughby

Avenue. He's a cool, well dressed, young Brooklyn hustler wearing suede and leather coats, continental sharkskin suits, alpaca sweaters and knit shirts and Russian hats, and buying his clothes at The Blye Shop, Phil Kronfeld and Leighton's in the city, and selling and smoking reefer. One day we're on the roof of 666 and Ronnie is getting his kite ready to fly. He attaches the rolls of string and gets the kite airborne and once the kite is steady in the air, he reaches into his shirt pocket and gets a real skinny cigarette and lights it and inhales with a hissing sound and when he exhales the smoke blows in my face and I've never smelled anything like it, and I get very scared and say to myself, "Oh no, Ronnie's taking dope".

He's hip to the jazz and club scene and hangs out at the Copa Cabana and the Palm Cafes and the jazz clubs on 52nd Street, and keeps plenty of money in his pockets. If somebody is stingy Ronnie says "He's tight as Dick's Hatband", and instead of saying "Payback is a bitch", he says "Retribution is a female canine!" He married his high-school sweetheart when they were still in high school who lives across the street at 666, Rosemary Maxwell. She and her brothers Clifford and Rickey are from Savannah, and I'm good friends with Rickey, and Ronnie and Clifford are good friends. Rickey gets killed years later, stabbed to death playing basketball in the park.

I got a Playboy Penthouse stuck in the sky,

A brand-new sports car and a fine hi-fi,

A bar full of booze that can keep me high,

And all of the true love that money can buy, Lucky Guy.

I got a bed of roses on which I lie,

in my custom suit and my hand-made tie,

laughing friends to surround me and sweetly sigh,

and give all the true love that money can buy, Lucky Guy -

Oscar Brown, Jr.

Ronnie and Rosemary at their wedding reception, 1962 embracing a Coca-Cola bottle.

Rosemary spends lots of time at our house and helps me with my French and Algebra homework and teaches us,

Chicken in the barn yard scratchin' at the door

Granny will your dog bite" No, child no.

Little boy, little boy who made your britches?

My mama cut 'em out and my daddy sewed the stitches.

When the singer Wilson Pickett becomes popular Rosemary says, "Don't he look like he stink?"

Sissy at the reception, Dancing w/ "Shotgun" The Buccaneer

On a late spring afternoon in 1965 as I sit in the living room after school falling asleep in front of the TV, across the small room, in the chair opposite me, I see through my half-nodding eyes, an apparition that looks like an Italian man in a white, sleeveless undershirt. It's like I'm seeing "The Boogerman" from his fire escape on Vernon Ave. up close. He sits there with his arms folded across his chest and his black hair combed straight back, looking at me. My eyes are half open and I don't move. I get a good look and decide to slowly open my eyes as he slowly dissolves. I'm not scared but surprised and startled and I tell my parents and everybody in the family and all my friends, and I give him the name Sam.

One evening in November 1965 a kid named Kevin and I are upstairs in the kitchen shooting dice on the floor when all of a sudden the lights dim. They come back on full then dim again, and finally go out completely. "C'mon." I tell Kevin. "Let's go outside." We pick up the dice and start heading for the door and I say, "Imagine if when we get outside, all the lights in the whole city are off." Kevin says, "Yeah man, that'll be a goof." When we get downstairs and open the hall door the streets are black, traffic lights are out and horns are blowing and the only lights are from cars, trucks and buses on the street. It's the big blackout of 1965, and I think about the comet I saw back on Willoughby.

The liquor store is right across the street, and almost anybody going in or out will buy you a bottle for an extra quarter. Gypsy Rose wine is 50 cents a pint and it, along with Tiger Rose, Twister and Swiss Up, are selling rapidly, beginning at 8am. A popular cocktail is pouring a pack of Kool Aid into a

pint of Swiss Up making a drink called a "Shake 'em up". By
the winter of 1965 the movie Goldfinger is out along with the
'65 Mustang and Mustang Sally, and one of the school-band
members, a Puerto Rican kid named Waldo, plays trumpet and
plays the theme from Goldfinger at the school talent show,
but not before turning up a bottle of Gypsy Rose in the
hallway of the building next to the school at 8:30 in the
morning. As he plays Goldfinger beautifully with piano
accompaniment and his faced flushed red with wine, he
finishes to a standing ovation. We're 15 and in the 8th grade.

Artis has a friend of his family that we all call "Grandpa", who's
about 60 and drives a white 1960 Imperial like Al had, and
Artis says he used to be an NYPD detective, and he comes
around and hangs out with us, and buys liquor along with
paper cups, and he parks his car on Park Place and we boys
and girls crowd in and he pours us drinks and we drink, talk
and smoke cigarettes with him, and he tells us dirty jokes.

I learn to drive by telling Ma that I want to wipe off the car for
her and that I need the keys so I can clean the inside of the car
as well. I always tell her this when the car is parked around
the corner on Sterling Place where she can't see it, so when
she gives me the keys I get in the car and practice putting it in
drive and in reverse to get the feel of the brake and the gas
pedal, and see how it feels to operate a vehicle, moving it up
and down in the parking space. One day Mike King is in the
car with me and I finally pull it out of the parking space and
aim it towards Buffalo Avenue and Mike says, "Ed, what are
you doing?" Mike is the first friend of mine to call me Ed. I
drive the car all the way around the corner and bring it back to

Sterling Place in time to get it back in its original parking space.

Pretty soon I think I'm comfortable enough with the car to move it up and down in its space right on Ralph Avenue in front of the house, and it's a 1959 Ninety-Eight Olds with the long tail fins on the back, and I pull it out of its parking space and drive it around the corner and when I get back to Ralph Avenue to park it in the same space, I bump into Mr. Rockford's car while backing it up and break his headlight. Mr. Rockford owns Rockford Moving and Storage on the corner of Ralph and Park Place. He has three moving trucks and is always drunk. He has blonde and brown hair and blue eyes and sits on a wooden milk crate in front of his moving and storage all day, smoking and taking nips out of a liquor bottle that he keeps in the back of the wooden ,milk crate. The three moving trucks that he owns are the really old ones from the 1950s where the steering wheel is located almost in the center of the cab so that there is a space next to the window for one of the helpers where the steering wheel should be. When these old moving vans come down the street the man sitting where the driver's seat should be is often fully asleep, with his head resting on his sweaty arm that hangs halfway out the window, so that the truck looks it's being driven by a man who is fully asleep. All of the men who work for Mr. Rockford are black, and they look drunk all the time. It seems that all moving men are always drunk.

When I backed Ma's car into its space and broke Mr. Rockford's headlight he said with his drunk face and his wet lips, "Eddie what are you doing? Look what you did to my car !

You broke my headlight ! I'm gonna tell your father right
now!" I begged Mr. Rockford not to tell Dad and that I would
pay for his headlight myself. I was working at Normie's and
making money. So when I got paid I took about $35 and went
down to Strauss Auto Store on Pitkin Avenue and Howard and
told them I needed a headlight for a 1963 Chevy Impala and
when they rang up the bill it only came to about $3.00. I had
no idea. I don't know anything about auto parts and what they
cost. I went home and got a screw driver and changed Mr.
Rockford's headlight myself, and still had over $30 in my
pocket. I was glad and felt wiser.

I'm enchanted by big sounds in music and especially in love
with the arrangements of Oliver Nelson, Claus Ogerman and
John Barry, serenaded and connected to the grand
orchestrations and the urban flavor of Oscar Brown, Jr., and
the 1960s big band of Maynard Ferguson, who Ronnie
introduces me to. Bossa Nova enters the jazz and pop media,
and we watch the pretty girls walk down Ralph Ave. to Stan
Getz and Astrud Gilberto singing The Girl From Ipanema, and
Lou Rawls singing The Girl from Ipanema from his album, Lou
Rawls Live. We're hearing all the pop singers of the day on
WNEW 1130AM and WHN 1050AM, which are always on in
Ma and Dad's bedroom, and they're playing Jack Jones,
Robert Goulet, Rosemary Clooney, Shirley Bassey and Frank
Sinatra on WNEW's Milkman's Matinee and The Make-Believe
Ballroom. We all know how to dance the latest dances, and
we do the Brooklyn Hustle, the Twine and the Prep Skip, we
know how to Cha-Cha and Mambo to the music of Joe Cuba
and make romance to the dreamy ballads of Jimmy Sabater,

Johnny Colon, Joe Bataan, Tito Puente, Ricardo Ray, and we're hearing the latest New York Latin music on the popular stations like WMCA and WABC. This is before the word Salsa was even thought of musically. Spanish music was called Latin and dancing Spanish was called Latin. Latin-Soul Music enters into its' own, a genre specific to New York. Blacks and Puerto Ricans, Cubans and Panamanians are dancing together and dating each other because unlike the Mexicans, all the Spanish Islands of the Caribbean have blacks who'd been there since slavery, just like the blacks on the east coast of America. Herein lies one of the vast differences in the cultures of East and West Coastal America. Blacks and Hispanics on the west coast are almost like enemies because there are no blacks in Mexico for the most part, and the Spanish people in California know that they were there first, before blacks, but in New York, blacks were here before Spanish people.

WLIB 1190AM is playing Gospel and Jazz music with pianist Billy Taylor hosting an afternoon jazz program. WWRL 1600AM is playing all the latest soul sounds, and Disc Jockeys Eddie O'Jay and Frankie Crocker are superstars. Jazz is heard everywhere because we're in New York - in the barbershop, the bars, the pool rooms, in people's cars, and hipsters are walking around carrying jazz albums, on their way to or from someone's house, jamming.

One day a young man rents a small apartment on the ground floor a couple of doors down and leaves his personal belongings in view through a window with no curtain and there are jazz albums among the items. I peep in the window and can see the album on top, which says "Miles Davis, Quiet

Nights". My friend Mike says "Let's get 'em!" We go in the hall and force the door open and scoop up the albums and we're gone. Also included in the stack of records is the album "Lou Rawls Live", and I learn the lyrics to St. James Infirmary, The Shadow of Your Smile, and a song called I'd rather drink muddy water, which I play over and over until Grandma, visiting from Newark says, "Boy? Aintchoo done drunk about enough of that muddy water now?"

Granddad's been dead two years now and when Grandma comes and stays with us, she cans fruits and vegetables and makes apple butter and lye soap and she cooks chicken feet and she makes my sisters wash bed sheets by "walking" them clean in the bath tub, and ridicules them more and more as they become teenagers about where they're going, how they talk, walk and dress. Although Grandma is a Born-Again-Christian woman, she is keenly aware and sometimes surprises you with her observations and comments. When the early 1970s brings "Hot Pants" on the scene, Grandma catches my cousin Donna-Jean on her way out the door one Friday night, and Donna, who is tall, slim and dark, has on electric-blue Hot Pants and Grandma hollers at her: " WHAS *WRONG* WID YA? WHERE YOU SUPPOSED TO BE GOIN LOOKIN LIKE THAT? LOOKATCHA !.......... SHOWIN' ALL YA **COCK** !" We all fall on the floor laughing as Donna-Jean stands there with her mouth hung open, then she rolls her eyes, sucks her teeth and walks out the door. When she rolls her eyes Grandma says, "You can roll 'em but you can't shoot 'em." One day Grandma's got her coat on and her pocketbook on her arm, waiting for Ma to take her somewhere, and she looks at the clock and says, "C'mon Ollie, it's time for us to *book. "*

Grandma

Living on Ralph Avenue exposes us to violence and bloodshed. We're growing up with kids who carry knives, 22s , brass knuckles and blackjacks, and we learn how to make zip-guns using a wooden coat hanger and a 6" length of a car antenna, some rubber bands and tape, and a 20 penny nail. The nail triples as the hammer, trigger and firing pin, and a .22 cal. round seems custom made to fit into the car antenna, the barrel. Car antennas are regularly snatched off to quickly use as a weapon in a fight.

Sissy's boyfriend Artis shows me how to make zip guns. Artis is real funny and loves to watch Road Runner cartoons and laugh and eat peanut butter sandwiches with no jelly. Artis goes to 210, filled with Chaplains. He's the first person I ever hear say "Un-Ass", meaning to give up or give back something. If you owe him some money he says "Yo man, when you gon' un-ass my swag?" He also uses "a case of the ass", describing somebody who's angry. "I can't go home right now 'cause my mother got a case of the ass." Artis is also the first one I hear describing his best friend as his "Ace Boon Coon". And if you say "Are you serious?", He'll say, "Is a pig's pussy pork?" Or if somebody doesn't believe something or is hard headed, he says, "Yeah cause he don't believe shit stink." He teaches us to sing,

Nuts, nuts, we want nuts,

Get em at your favorite store.

Looka dat man up on the wall,

he aint got no balls at all I say now,

Poontang, Poontang, I don't want it cause you

slept all night wid your hands upon it now

gimme some of dat yum yum

before I say goodnight.

Artis is jealous and possessive when it comes to Sissy and he has twin cousins named Clyde and Clement who come around and hang out with us. Sissy has keys to Ronnie's apartment on Willoughby Ave. and babysits for Ronnie and his wife Rosemary, and sometimes we play hooky and go up Ronnie's house. Artis carries a blackjack in his pocket and one day suspects Clyde of making a pass at Sissy, or looking at her butt. We're about to leave Ronnie's house and he says to me, "Ummo crack that mutha-fucka upside his head when we git outside, watch." I don't take him seriously. We're standing in the hallway waiting for the elevator when Arty, in a flash without warning, smacks Clyde twice in the forehead with the blackjack and Clyde falls down, grabbing his head with blood sprinkling through his fingers, onto the walls of the hallway. Arty is immediately regretful and panics and starts crying and apologizing and calling for us to get the ambulance. The police and ambulance arrive and Artis makes up the story that Clyde was attacked by someone else out of nowhere, who hit him and ran down the stairs. Poor Clyde goes along with the story. I'm horrified and full of remorse. Clyde gets killed about a year later by falling over backwards onto a concrete staircase from the banister of a stoop around the corner on Park Place. Years later, one of our friends Ronnie, from Putnam Avenue, who served in Vietnam, is killed the very same way, falling over backwards off his own stoop to the concrete staircase below. Artis dies in his 40s from a life of dope.

Artis

I know five guys named Michael around Ralph Avenue,
Mickey, whose real name is Miguel, which in English is
Michael, Michael Black, Michael Young, Michael King and
Michael Higgins. There's a hit song called Michael The Lover,
and Dionne Warwick has the song Message to Michael.
Michael King is my best friend and he and Michael Young,
Michael Higgins and I are in the same class. We give Michael
Higgins the nickname "Skiggy". He's the best dressed in the

class, and always wears starched, tab-collar shirts. He doesn't have brothers and sisters so he's always wearing new clothes. Michael Black's sister Christine is also in our class and Michael and I are friends. He has a part-time job working at the corner news stand on St. John's and Buffalo and puts together the Sunday Daily News when they come in off the newspaper truck. It's a candy store where they also have a soda fountain and make chocolate egg creams and sell cigarettes, cigars and candy and gum and chewing tobacco and pipe tobacco and pipes. That's when Mike and I started smoking pipes and buying Cherry Blend. He comes from a large family and his brother Harold, the oldest, is a bully and an expert boxer. He's good and notoriously fast with his hands, to the point where we're all dazzled by his ability to block and throw punches so rapidly. He's a couple of years older than we are and bigger than us. One night he and I get caught in Albany Chaplain territory, in front of Alexander Hamilton High School on Pacific and Albany near the Albany Projects , and get jumped by about 6 Chaplains. We fight our way away from them and run home down Dean Street back towards the Kingsborough , in Corsair-Lord territory where we live.

The Albany Projects, Bergen Street view

Harold is abusive. One cold, winter Saturday a guy named
Charlie from Amityville is hanging out with us, and we're
drinking and goofing around in the hallway around the corner
on Park Place. By the time it gets dark I go out into the street
and look for Diane and take her down into the basement.
After that I walked her home and when I came back to our
hallway I heard voices from upstairs on our floor . When I got
to the top of the landing and turned to my right Harold was
standing over Charlie, who was drunk and sitting on the steps.
Harold was pushing him around and trying to provoke him.
When I asked Harold what he was doing he looked at me like
King Kong and said "Shut the fuck up and mind your business!"
He didn't yell. Then he started beating Charlie, quietly and
methodically. He punched him in his head repeatedly. At first
I thought he would stop after about two blows. But he didn't. I

pleaded with him to stop but was afraid to intervene physically because I knew what he'd do to me. This was happening right outside our apartment and Dad was inside but I didn't want to call him because I knew Harold was Crazy and huge and he'd hurt Dad too. He must have hit Charlie 25 times. He finally stopped, pushed past me and left. Charlie is sitting on the steps and there's blood all around him. His lips, eyes and nose are torn apart and are swollen, and he's drunk with blood soaking his coat. Charlie had been afraid to fight back, and I had been afraid with him and now I feel ashamed. It was something I did once but I never did it again. He wasn't from Brooklyn, just visiting. I'd never seen anyone in person who'd been so viciously beaten. Every week it seems Harold is beating somebody up, and he goes around singing the record How Glad I Am, by Nancy Wilson.   He dies young, at age 27.

His brother Michael was familiar with the song, Red Roses For a Blue Lady by Robert Goulet because he'd hear it on WNEW while working at the soda fountain, and also coming from his parents' bedroom late at night as he lay in his bed falling asleep.

Michael King is my best friend and a creative genius with words and voices and imitations, good at science, electricity, math, logic and outrageous hilarity. Mike's nickname is Skipper and his father owns their house on Sterling Place between Ralph and Howard, a block that's crowded, noisy and dirty, and home to two local gangs, The John Quells, and the Puerto Rican gang, The Dragons. They live on the top floor and he always has to be upstairs at 6pm to sit down at Dinner with his family. His dad is a high-strung, hard-working, tough,

northern man who's lived in Chicago, Detroit and New York
and disciplines his 4 children, takes pride in being smart, and
was a Sgt. in the Army. He wakes his kids in the morning by
singing,

Layin in the bed and callin' it a bunk ,

eatin good beans and callin it junk,

layin around wid your eyes all red,

butchoo gon' get up now unless you dead.

Mike's Dad doesn't keep friends and often brags, saying,
"Hey, I went to school with Con Edison!"

One day as Mike and I approach the top of the stairs in the hall
his dad meets us outside the apartment door, walks straight
up to Mike and says "I thought I told you to put some water in
the boiler." Mike stumbles for an answer but gets slapped
across the face quicker, harder and louder than I'd ever heard.
It makes me jump and it echoes with a splattering off the
yellow-painted walls and up to the skylight and back down the
stairs. Mike grabs his head and cries. A couple of months
later he comes over my house with tears in his eyes telling me
that his father had a heart attack and died.

Mike had a dog named Yankee who accidentally jumped off
the roof to his death while he and Mike were playing "jump
the roofs". The houses on his side of the street are all
connected but some of them have driveways. Mike and

Yankee would go on the roof and run down the block across the rooftops jumping over each ledge that separates the houses, then turn around and go back, but one day instead of turning back with Mike, Yankee jumped over the last ledge and fell to his death, landing on top of a car parked in the driveway.

One early spring evening me and five of my friends are sitting in Dad's car parked right in front of our house and I'm sitting behind the wheel. The windows are down and the motor is off and we're just sitting in the car hanging out and a cop car pulls up beside us and the officer asks for my license and registration. I don't have a license and I'm not driving and the car is off and I don't plan to drive because I know Dad's upstairs. I tell the cop it's my father's car and we're just sitting in it and the officer tells me to go upstairs and get my father. I tell Sissy to go upstairs and get Dad and when Dad comes down and sees the police and listens to what the cop says he suddenly slaps me completely across my entire head and face before I could say a word, harder than I'd ever been slapped before, shocking me into a stun and I hear a whistling sound. He's furious just because of the mere fact that I'd brought the attention of the police to the house. He slapped me the way Mike's dad slapped him.

Mike and his family move to Detroit right after Junior High School, and Mickey and I start High School together at Thomas Jefferson.

Sissy and Linda end up going to Franklin K. Lane High School, famous for being surrounded on 3 sides by Cypress Hills

Cemetery, and tough white boys who fight with blacks and Puerto Ricans each day after school, chasing them up to the train station.

Franklin K. Lane High School

Mickey lives right around the corner on Sterling Place with his two brothers and his mother. They're from Panama and speak Spanish and have been in Brooklyn about five years. Thomas Jefferson High School on Pennsylvania Ave. in East New York has an equal representation of Blacks, Whites, Spanish and Caribbean students and I play in the school orchestra where we play Wagner's March of the Meistersingers, the concert band where we play Modest Mussgorsky's Great Gate of Kiev and Mitch Leigh's Man of La Mancha. By this time the next James Bond movie Thunderball is out, and Yvette Davis and I confess to each other that we saw it three times just for the music. Yvette has a younger brother who likes the record, *Brown Skin Girl* .

The concert band at Jefferson is under the direction of our teacher Jack Levine, and the orchestra is under the direction of Mr. Iijima, who is Japanese. We're also in the marching band, also led by Jack Levine, and play for all the football games of "Jeff's" notorious Orange Wave, regular city champions with legendary coaches, the brothers Eddie and Moe Finklestein. Moe Finklestein, the head coach, openly slaps players in the face on the field during Saturday games, in front of their parents and all. One of the team's stars is a halfback named Jesse Claire, # 44, along with John Brockington who goes on to Syracuse and then to the Green Bay Packers. Our biggest Brooklyn rival is the big, tough team of boys from Boys High. Our school cop is "Harry The Cop".

Thomas Jefferson H.S., Pennsylvania Ave.

Main entrance to TJHS

Boys High School, Marcy Avenue

It's early summer of 1966 and I'm playing Chinese in front of the house when Diane's mother gets off the bus carrying Diane's green maternity smock and we look at each other and she acknowledges with a weak smile that Diane had a boy and says she named him Darren. When they come home from the hospital Darren goes to live with Diane and her family, and we split up. A month later my family moves out of the neighborhood.

I've formed a tight circle of friends at "Jeff" and I'm popular in school. Eddie, Craig, Montclair, Ervin, Mickey and I call ourselves "The Cowboys". We're all musicians except Mickey. Montclair Wilson has a real deep voice and plays tuba in all 3 bands, and he's also 1st Chair, 1st Tuba in the prestigious All-City Orchestra.

We hang out at Metrick's luncheonette on Pennsylvania and Livonia, and Jack Metrick makes burgers behind the counter and malteds, and has a juke box with all the hit songs. We go to school with lots of kids who grew up in East New York, and went to George Gershwin Junior High School.

Gershwin JHS on Van Sicelen Avenue

James Brown is singing Cold Sweat, the Supremes are singing Love is Here and Now You're Gone, and Mitch Ryder and the Detroit Wheels are singing Devil with the Blue Dress On. We hang out with our gang of friends. Steven Lang, Jack Amariglio, Bobbie Becker, Maritza Meyers, Lynn Morton, Norman and Toni Richardson, James Talbot, Miram Parker, James Cummings, Skippy, who soon tragically drowns at Rockaway Beach, and Yussic, and Jeep, who wears thick, black eye-glasses and looks like a jeep. The word "Skank" comes into play, describing ugly girls, then there's Schenck Avenue, which is pronounced Skank. Don't be a girl who's not pretty, and live on Schenck Avenue. You never live it down.

I meet Yolanda, my high-school sweetheart, on the bus one Saturday after a victorious football game and I'm in my band uniform and she's in her booster uniform and there's a party on later, downtown on St. John's Place, and we agree to meet there. The drummer Max Roach's daughter comes to the party and I ask her to dance slow with me and she does, to Brenda and the Tabulations singing "Dry Your Eyes". I didn't know she was Max Roach's daughter until the record was over when my friend Eddie Beasley, who also plays drums in the school band, told me. "Yo man, you know who that girl is? She's Max Roach's daughter." "What? Git the fuck outta here I say."

Yolanda is Spanish, of the Spanish Honduras, but I don't find out until I go over her house for the first time, and her mother speaks to her in Spanish. The first time I go over Yolie's house the radio is on and Lee Dorsey is singing Holy Cow.

One day after school we're waiting for the girls to come out into the school yard when Mickey sees a girl that he likes and plans to "rap" to her. As she walks by I notice she has a booger on her face but Mickey doesn't know it's a booger and he makes a chivalrous gesture saying, "Excuse me sweetheart but you got something on your cheek", and he wipes it off with his finger but it sticks, and he's standing there trying to fling it off and we laugh and laugh and the girl rolls her eyes and walks away and we call Mickey the "Boogerman" and say we won't shake his hand anymore. He's the only one of us who doesn't know music, and can't harmonize and is always fascinated when we start crooning in five-part harmony, imitating the Miracles and the Temptations. We're doing like dad and his friends used to do on Willoughby Avenue.

Mickey and I are buddies and he spends lots of time at our house and gets to know my family, including cousins, aunts and uncles. His parents are separated and his father is back in Panama and has never been to the States. He's alienated from his mother, who has a bizarre obsession with ordering household items and appliances from TV, and her bedroom and bed are cluttered halfway up to the ceiling with unopened and unpacked goods she's received, and she sleeps on an isolated portion of the mattress among boxes and boxes of unopened mixers and blenders and toaster ovens and coffee makers and vacuum cleaners and household gadgets. It's as if she's opening a business or planning to ship all this new stuff to Panama but never does. It just piles up year after year. Mickey says sometimes in the middle of the night he hears boxes tumbling in his mother's bedroom, as she tries to sleep among the growing heap of tempting, American commercialism. The thing he cherishes most about his mother is the way she makes rice, mixed with cocoanut.

I'd taught myself to drive when I was 15 and I sneak the keys to my Ma's car and drive around the neighborhood with my friends and every time Mickey is with me in the car he tries to get me to run over people. "Buck, run that motha fucka over man, c'mon.............aw man,............ you coulda ran that motha fucka over....Look there's another one!.......... Looka dat nappy-head bitch, Buck, hurry up. Run that bitch over Buck!" We're laughing our asses off but all the while he's dead serious about it. Mickey makes me think back to Mr. Blunt when he slapped that guy in the face while Dad was turning onto Hart Street. The most fun we have in the car is when a bunch of us pile in and head towards East New York and going up Highland Boulevard, looking forward to the six of us in the car, laughing and roaring down the famous Miller Avenue hill.

The Miller Avenue Hill looking south over East New York

During the summers when school is out I go over to Cohen's back on Vernon Avenue and work for spending money.

Normie Cohen is very generous. In the summer of 1964 I'm making $100 a week, $20 a day paid in cash at the end of each day. My mother wakes me up at 5 am so that I get to work on time, and I ride my bike over to Cohen's in the morning dark, and work from 6am to 5pm. A lot of the time I go out on the truck with a driver named Joe Cascio, who's Italian and lives on Central Avenue. We deliver to stores all over east Brooklyn, from Williamsburg to Canarsie. Joe teaches me this dirty song that starts, *"When I was young and in my teens I met a girl from New Orleans and she was young and darn nice too, and she had something called a ding dang roo "*.....

The trucks are refrigerated and Joe tells me about the time when he was making deliveries by himself one day in the winter and got locked inside the truck.

"So I was parked in front of the deli and it's fuckin 25 degrees outside, so it's already cold okay? I load the hand truck and wheel it inside the deli and I come back out to grab some Genoa and Mortadella. I open the door and hop up in the truck and the fuckin wind blows the door shut. It ain't got no handle inside to get outta there. I start bangin on the goddamn door, then I start bangin on the side of the fuckin truck and yelling and screamin for somebody to let me out. I bang, then I stop to listen if I can hear somebody walkin. I can't hear nothin. I start thinkin "Fuck, this is it !" My stomach starts turnin and I'm thinking about my wife and kids and me, dead-cold and stiff. Now I'm moanin and cryin and it's gettin colder and colder and I'm fuckin gettin desperate and I'm screamin and kickin and bangin and finally after about 5 minutes, this guy walkin by hears me and he opens the door, thank you Mary, mother of Jesus, and I jump down and I swear I fuckin grabbed him and kissed him. Then I had to go straight home and change cause I'd shit my pants."

VII
The Hotel

Houston St. looking west to Allen St. and the 2nd Ave. El. 1929, before it was widened.
The last building on left before the El. is 175 East Houston Street. The sign reads: The
Houston Furnished Rooms. Brian Merlis Coll.

Ben Guberman operates a small transient hotel on the
southeast corner of Houston and Allen Sts. on the Lower East
Side, just above a Kosher meat market called Ershowsky's
Provisions, and right next door to Russ & Daughters

delicacies. Ma started working there as a clerk and clean-up woman in 1963. She works there part-time and loves going back and forth , sometimes on the subway, sometimes on the B39 bus from Williamsburgh, sometimes driving, and on a gorgeous, early afternoon, she'll take the J train to Marcy Avenue, get off and walk across the Williamsburgh Bridge, enjoying the views of the East River and the Manhattan and Brooklyn Bridges and New York Harbor and the concrete canyons of Wall Street, the hypnotic hum of traffic underneath her, the smells of the Schaeffer Beer Brewery and the pepper from the spice importer warehouses, and walking and talking with the Jews back and forth. When she drives to work she routinely picks up the Hassidic men waiting at the hitch point on Havemeyer St. just across Broadway, and gives them a ride across the Bridge, and on the way home she picks them up on the south side of Delancey St., at the bus stop by the liquor store, and takes them across to Brooklyn.

The prostitutes who work the neighborhood of Delancey from Allen St. west to the Bowery use the hotel to bring their tricks, and drug addicts also rent rooms so they can "get off". Some of the prostitutes, after turning a trick, also often get off before going back out on the streets. The tricks are an assortment of the sidewalks of New York. All colors and ages, and people you wouldn't expect, like some of the Hassidic men who operate businesses all over the neighborhood, and lots of men from Chinatown. The hotel is open 24 hours a day and smells like the miniature soap bars that each patron receives upon renting one of its 14 rooms, and you can sleep overnight for $8.00 in 1962, but most of the money is made

from the "short stay", 1-2 hours, which is $4.00. My father
eventually starts working there part time also, in addition to
his fulltime job as a custodian at New York City Community
College on Jay Street. He's grateful to have a secure job,
working for the City. At the end of each day at the hotel, my
mother comes home smelling of its miniature soap bars. She
quickly becomes familiar with the immediate surroundings of
the east-side neighborhood and makes acquaintances with
other small business owners in the area.

175 East Houston Street today

The first time I ever went to the hotel was back on Ralph Avenue when one day Ma calls the house because she'd left her reading glasses home, and tells me how to take the subway there, so I walked down to Ralph and Fulton and took the "A" train to West 4th, changed to the "F" towards Brooklyn and got on the front of the train to 2nd Avenue. As soon as I came out of the subway I looked across Allen Street and Ma was up in a side window of the building waving at me and smiling, reminding me of the Jewish woman across the street on Willoughby, waving me upstairs to do a chore.

While Linda was on an 8th-grade class trip one day, the school bus unexpectedly passed right by the hotel, and she caught a glimpse of Ma sitting in her side window on Allen Street. Linda secretly cried, because here was our own Ma, looking out at the traffic passing by, not even remotely knowing that her daughter is right beneath her, amongst the thousands of people passing by. While Linda was excitedly happy amongst her classmates dressed neatly and being educated, Ma was also grateful and happy for herself too, doing her domestic job, all she knows how to do.

Allen St. view of 175 E. Houston from "F" train exit.

When I got upstairs to the hotel with her glasses she said, "You hungry?" She handed me $3.00 and said, "Go down to Katz's Deli on Houston and Ludlow and get yourself a brisket-of-beef sandwich with mayonnaise. Put some salt and pepper on it. Tell 'em to slice it thin. And get a black-cherry soda." It was the best sandwich I ever ate. The "Dr. Brown's" black-cherry soda became my soda-of-choice at Katz's, where they also sell celery sodas, called Cel-Ray.

Ma buys dress pants and suits for Dad on Orchard Street where she can drive bargains with the Jewish merchants, and if they need alterations she takes them over to an Italian woman named Marie who has a tailor shop on First Street.

Katz's Deli on Houston and Ludlow Sts.

The hotel has no solid security against bandits and has been robbed in the past, late at night, by men who point guns and demand cash from the drawer. One night the stick-up men come while Ben Guberman is working alone and force their way into the little office, tie him up, steal the cash and run down the stairs leaving Ben on the floor, gagged and bound, where he dies of a heart attack. After settling his affairs his wife tells Ma and Dad she no longer wants anything to do with the business, and offers it to them to run, if they want it. They won't own the building, just run the hotel. The building is owned by Harry Ershowsky, the red-haired Kosher butcher downstairs.

VIII
Putnam Avenue

With Dad having a steady, full-time job with the city, and now running and earning from the hotel, we soon move into our own home in the summer of 1966, to a 2 family house at 1124 Putnam Avenue between Broadway and Bushwick. We're elated. It has 6 bedrooms, 2 1/2 baths, finished basement, backyard, front yard and stoop, and it cost $17,500. Our new phone number is Hickory 3-0171. Ma even finds a store on Broadway that has one of those old washing machines for sale and she sets it up in the backyard. I hang a clothes line upstairs that's attached to the frame of Ma and Dad's bedroom window and runs out to the telephone pole in the backyard. There's a Scuppernong grape vine that runs along the back fence, planted by Italians who lived here a generation ago. The backyard next to ours has a pear tree in it, and the house is owned by a Jamaican man named Mr. Roberts.

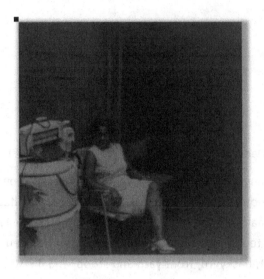

Ma and the washing machine in the backyard on Putnam.

We have that good home feeling like we had when we moved to Halsey Street, except that this is our house. Our family occupies the ground floor and the parlor floor, and we rent the top floor to a Puerto Rican woman named Ruth and her children. Ruth sends her son Wilfredo to run errands and take messages up and down the stairs to Ma and Dad. She says to him, "Tell Mr. German to come upstairs." Wilfredo knocks on the door and when we open it, he says, "to come upstairs". Back in the 2nd and 3rd grade in P.S. 25 one of my classmates, Jose Garcia used to say "Teesher - I broke my paper!" Or if he tore his pants he'd say I "broke" my pants, and when we're outside in the schoolyard or on the sidewalk, he calls the ground, "the floor".

Out of all Ma and Dad's family, we're the only ones in Brooklyn with a private house and a backyard, so we start having lots of parties and Bar-b-Cues with Ma's family coming from Newark and Dad's family from Brooklyn and Queens and Long Island, eating and getting drunk in the backyard.

One day I'm standing in the front yard when Daddy's cousin Rose, a notoriously bad driver, pulls up in his 1974 light-blue Coupe De Ville already drunk, with his thick eyeglasses and his spit-soaked cigar between his wet lips, double parks and says to me, slurring his speech, "Hey Bucky, do you know how to park a *CCCCadillac* ?" Rose always drives a Cadillac, but he's always lived in the projects.

Rose, Lizzie and Dad

Dad's cousin Lizzie Hendrix, Rose's sister, arrives at the house smiling and in a good mood, but once she gets drunk, she gets mad. She went to a party once at Dad's cousin Shorty's house, and got real drunk and went to use the bathroom and when she got in the bathroom she lost her balance and leaned against what she thought was the wall, but it was the shower curtain, and she fell into the bath tub and broke her rib on the side of the tub. She was 75 when this happened.

Dad and his Hendrix cousins. Top, Lottie, Gussie, Frankie, Helen. Bottom, Dad, Lizzie, Shorty.

The first kid I see upon arriving on Putnam Avenue is Bobby, who lives two doors down from us and is my age. He gives me a dirty look when I hop onto the moving truck we rented to begin unloading our belongings. It's the summer of 66, Carla Thomas is singing B-a-b-y, The Supremes are singing You can't Hurry Love and Joe Cuba is singing Bang, Bang. Bobby later catches the nickname Bobby Wayne, after John Wayne, because he starts wearing cowboy hats and winds up becoming a wino and being dead by 1973.

There is still 1 white family living on the block, directly across the street from us, and on the corner is the real estate office that sold Dad the house, which is run by white people. There are still lots of white people living and owning businesses in the neighborhood, and the same bleach man, way back from Willoughby Avenue, drives through yelling "BLEACH"!

Sam The Ghost has followed us to Putnam Avenue and many people, family and friends claim to see him in the basement, and describe him just as I saw him on Ralph Avenue. Every time new friends or cousins come to visit, we tell them about Sam The Ghost. I take my young cousins in the basement where we have a record player set up, then I make the room real dark and tell them that I'm going to explain how I met Sam The Ghost. As I'm telling them about Sam, Miles Davis' album Quiet Nights is playing in the background, and I play "Song No. 1" that starts with an orchestral bang and becomes real spooky. All this time I'm describing Sam as an Italian man in a white, sleeveless undershirt with black hair combed straight back. Then the song "Summer Night" comes on and at the end of the song I say "listen, I think I hear him", and Miles

Davis' spooky, raspy voice surprisingly says, "Tell em to play another one", and all the kids start screaming and running upstairs.

It's a summer weekend and Ma's getting ready to fry some pork chops and relatives are in the backyard sitting around drinking and playing cards. The grease is heating up in the frying pan and the pork chops are seasoned and floured and ready to go in the pan. When the grease gets hot Ma puts 5 pork chops in the pan and steps out to the backyard for a couple of minutes then comes back in the kitchen to turn the chops over and when she steps in the hallway there's a half-cooked pork chop on the floor in the hall with a bite taken out of it and grease all around it. There are 4 pork chops left in the pan and grease has been dripped on the floor leading out to the hall. Nobody sticks their hand in a hot pan of grease for a half-cooked pork chop, takes a bite and throws it on the hall floor.

There are teenagers all over the block and my sisters and my brother Don make friends quickly, but I never become close to anyone on Putnam Avenue, except Diane Cooper across the street whom I soon start kissing, and she asks me one day, "Do you know the definition of a kiss?" When I answer no she says, "An upper persuasion for a lower invasion".

I already have my crew who are the kids I go to school with at Jefferson, and most of them live in East New York.

One night me, Eddie, Mickey, McGee and Montclair are walking down Atlantic Avenue and when we turn the corner on Jerome Street we see a tall, heavy-set Spanish girl wearing flip flops and a soiled white dress with flowers on it and she says "Whas goin on, whatchall up to?" We look at each other and walk past her laughing and when we turn around and look back at her she's scratching her crotch and saying, "Y'all wanna do somethin? Whatchall wanna do?" We stop in our tracks, laughing, while she stands there still scratching and mumbling.

One day we're walking down Fulton Street in East New York across Pennsylvania Avenue, and it's me, Mickey, Montclair, Eddie and Craig Beasley and McGee, and we see a man ahead of us standing still in the middle of the sidewalk, nodding. As we pass him, deeply into his nod and leaning to the right, I notice he has a stack of jazz albums in his left hand. This time it's my idea.

"Yo, he got jazz albums in his hand. I'm gonna double back and snatch 'em and run!"

"Naw man, don't do that", Eddie says . But I say. "C'mon man, that's what he gets for messing with dope, and once I snatch 'em he'll never catch me cause he's high. All we gotta do is run a couple of blocks and lose him."

So I double back past him as my boys cross to the other side of the street. I give myself room to pick up some speed, turn around, run up behind him and snatch the stack from him and run. He immediately comes out of his nod and is fully awake, right on my tail yelling *"C'mere you mutha fuckal!"* When I turn around and see him right on my heels I say out loud, "Oh

Shit", then I really start booking with all my strength and when I look back he's still right there. "DAMN". I think. After three blocks I can see the entrance to the train station ahead and when I look back he's leaning against a car panting, a block behind. I run another block for extra measure, past the front entrance and go up the rear entrance, flying up the stairs and fishing for my train pass, flash it to the booth attendant, run through the gate, shoot up the steps and see the lights of the "JJ" train two stations away. I lean against the wall of the platform heaving to catch my breath, but with a handful of jazz albums. My boys all split up and ran different ways once I snatched the records, to their own houses right in the neighborhood, but I'm on my way home to Bushwick. When I finally get on the train and the doors close I lean against them and look at the records and I have albums by Wes Montgomery, Duke Pearson, and Willie Bobo. I look out the door window with the albums in my hand, and as the train's iron wheels screech around the corner from Fulton Street crossing East New York Avenue at Broadway Junction, I see the tall, light-skinned woman in light blue pants and light blue top rounding the corner past the bus depot heading north up Broadway, with the 16 oz. Pepsi Cola on top of her head.

There's a large family down the block across the street, The Simmons, who are in the demolition business, also known as "nigger construction", and they tear down abandoned houses all over Brooklyn and three of the 7 kids, Duke, Connie and Terry all die very young from working, drinking and drugs.

I'm also hanging out with my cousins in Amityville. My cousin Cedric joins the Navy in 1965 and his brother Larry joins the

Marines in 1966. Their older brother Maurice, dies in a
Connecticut prison years later. I relate more to my friends in
High School than the kids on the block because of music. I like
going to Amityville because Larry and Cedric are the coolest
cats I know, dressing nice and driving cars, and they're real,
New York suburban kids who go to Drive-In movies and have a
pool table in their basement and are popular with the girls,
and I secretly have a crush on my cousin Michelle, who is light
skinned with freckles, green eyes and looks like a combination
of Barbara Streisand and Cher Bono. Their father, my Uncle
Dowdy, likes jazz and has albums by Chico Hamilton and Cal
Tjader and an album that we play a lot by Sonny Stitt called
Primitivo Soul. I like Uncle Dowdy a lot. He smokes cigarettes,
cigars *and* pipes and is generally good natured and friendly.
We play Chico Hamilton's Forest Flowers until we wear the
record out. Larry and Michelle have worked out a routine
that they act out when we play "Big Boy Pete" by the
Olympics. Larry plays Big Boy Pete and Michelle plays
"Brown", who "cut that black cigar right outta Pete's mouth".

One day Larry says to me, "There's a place in Massapequa with
a sign that says Parking for Whites Only!" I don't believe him.
This is New York and it's 1965. "I swear", he says. "I'm gon'
show it to you right now." We get in the car and he drives
over to Massapequa to a department store named White's of
Massapequa and right in the parking lot there are several signs
along the fence that read: PARKING FOR WHITE'S ONLY.

Cedric's mother, my Aunt Lil, is my favorite aunt on my
Father's side, and she makes us clean house. Aunt Lil is very
attractive, very light skinned with green eyes also, like her

daughter Michelle. She makes us clean house all the time and keeps us busy running errands and scrubbing floors and says 'All right now, make sure you clean those floors thoroughly, I don't want any "slut cleaning". Whenever I arrive from Brooklyn she says, "Come here Bucky and sit down and tell me all the news and business." If she finds people irritating, she says they give her asthma. "Oooh Bucky, I can't stand those ignorant people. Ignorant niggers give me asthma!"

Cedric's father Dowdy is also very light skinned to the point that he looks Spanish. Their grandmother's name is Emma, the same as my grandmother, and is my Father's aunt. She was also my Father's school teacher back in Georgia. One time I heard her say, "You can run rabbits like a dog and eat shit with a knitting needle." And if she sees you walking too slow she'll say, "You walk like you got cotton in Birmingham and niggers in Augusta."

Getting on the Long Island Railroad and escaping to Amityville is exotic and it expands my eastern horizon of New York, as The Hotel is expanding my western horizon. Larry and Cedric are notorious in North Amityville, and known by everyone. When I take Mickey to Amityville, Cedric likes to show how tough he is by throwing up his dukes against us and saying, "C'mon you punk motha-fuckas, I'll take both you niggers on right now. Come on!"

Mickey and I hang out in a pool room on Madison Street owned by an Italian guy named Vic and the name of the pool room is Vic's Dive. Vic has 6 regulation-sized pool tables and a soda fountain with stools and photos of celebrities and movie stars behind the counter and a jukebox that has music in it by Joe Cuba and Jimmy Sabater. When we're not shooting pool in Vic's we're shooting pool in the upstairs poolroom on Broadway and Halsey, or in my Uncle Pete's club in Newark.

The G & G Rod & Gun Club on Wickliffe Avenue in Newark is my Uncle Jewel's (who nicknamed himself The Peter) private, members-only after-hours club. It's walking distance from downtown Newark and Pete gives me a set of keys to the club and Mickey and I take the 118 bus from Port Authority and go to the club on Sunday afternoons to clean up and hang out. There's a pool table, a liquor cabinet, and a juke box that has Wes Montgomery's A Day in The Life in it, Lee Dorsey's Get Out My Life Woman and Bobbie Gentry's Ode to Billy Joe, which is one of Mickey's favorites. Uncle Pete is a member of the Masons and has the Masonic decal with the compass as part of the club's logo outside on the window. Sometimes when he goes to meetings at the Masonic Lodge, all the men have on black suits and white shirts with red ties and they're wearing red socks. There's a gambling room at the rear of the club, up a flight of stairs, where a card table and a craps table are set up.

Jewel (The Peter) Harris

One Sunday Mickey and I arrive at the club, open the gambling-room door and gasp. There are $20 bills all over the floor and all over the crap table and the card table, where a paper cutter has been left. Some of the bills are light green and some are dark green and some are cut crooked and some look very good. My heart is beating. How could they leave this like this? I tell Mickey, "Don't mess with any of it, leave it alone". But the following Saturday, he passes one at the Thomas Jefferson Saturday football game. Having keys to the club at age 17 is like having our own bar, sufficient with all the trappings to lure girls passing by, and they take a look inside, hear the jukebox playing and see the liquor cabinet, and in a little while we're all partying. Uncle Pete doesn't show up until sometime after dark. One day my Uncle Buck walks in and I'm at the pool table and Mickey has a girl in the back room and as he opens the door they jump up from the little couch and Uncle Buck watches the girl rush out the front, looks at Mickey who's fixing his pants and warns him saying, "Go wash your dick!"

Partying in Pete's Club 1966. Top, Uncle Norman, bottom, Maggie, Uncle Norman's wife, Uncle Buck, Aunt Sarah, Ma, Dad, Rhoda, Pete's Girlfriend and Thelma, Ma's friend from Willoughby Avenue

My mother's brothers make money any way they can in the 50s and 60s, from working in the fields around Bridgeton, driving Mr. Softee trucks in Newark, running used furniture stores and fruit and vegetable stands, and once Uncle Norman opened a seafood take-out restaurant called The Clam Box in Newark, on Avon Avenue. Everything they do involves gambling, and when they have regular jobs they still play cards for money on the weekends. My Uncle Bill keeps a brown paper bag in his car that's full of dice, the way a kid keeps marbles.

We still go to Bridgeton on weekends, driving down with Ma or sometimes even taking the bus. It's a getaway from the city, and adventure in the country, and a bunch of cousins and friends to hang out with. Uncle Bill's sons Charles, Stanley and Gary are still bad, and are always in and out of jail. Charles is oddly mysterious and spooky. One night he takes a carload of friends and cousins to Harlem to buy dope and when they get back to Bridgeton they're pulled over and searched by the police who find the dope in the car. All the occupants of the vehicle are lined up against a wall and about to be locked up when Charles asks to speak to the arresting officer. He whispers something to the officer that he never reveals to us, and the police let everybody go free and allow them to keep the dope. My cousin Tony says that one night Charles drove from 145th Street in Harlem to Bridgeton in 90 minutes.

It's a summer weekend in 1966 in Bridgeton, and a bunch of us pile into a car with Charles driving and I'm sitting in the back seat directly behind him. We're going down a two-way country road through a no-passing zone where the double-yellow line divides the road, doing about 55 mph and coming up quickly on a car ahead of us, almost at the crest of a hill. Charles does the unthinkable. He crosses the double-yellow line and passes the car going blindly over the hill as I sit behind him too dumfounded to even scream. I think we're going to die. There could be another car coming up the hill or worse, a truck. He makes the mover quicker than anyone can object.

It's over in a flash and I realize that he's crazy. It's the last time I see him. He comes over to the house once on Putnam but I'm not there, and shows up with his hair in pin-curls and rollers like a woman, and Ma makes him leave.

Uncle Bill has 11 children. The first 7 are boys. Charles is the third born. Of Uncle Bill's 7 boys there are 3 living. Aunt Sarah has 7 children, 3 girls and 4 boys. Of the 4 boys, 1 is living. All of the ones who do bad things to others die young or have miserable, long lives. Charles dies in his 20s on Riker's Island from Gangrene and is buried in Potter's field with his brother Gary who gets stabbed to death on Riker's Island and is also buried in Potter's field.

Uncle Bill (top), Uncle Preacher and a neighbor 30 Birch Street Bridgeton, New Jersey

One weekend in August of 1967 we're in Bridgeton, New Jersey visiting Ma's family and a bunch of us pile into the car and head for the grocery store and Ma is driving. Ronnie, my cousin Stanley and my Uncle Buddy and a friend of my cousin's named Willie all squeeze in together laughing, riding and talking. The warm, country air is sweet with the smell of the Hunt's Tomatoes plant cooking tomatoes, and Uncle Buddy wants to stop by Mottas' Bar to pick up a package. Many local people work picking tomatoes in the fields, where a 5/8 bushel basket pays 14 cents, the same as it paid in 1947.

As we approach the little country bar, situated on the end of a street , Ma aims the car for the dusty, dirt driveway leading to the parking lot. Motta's bar is the ground floor of a large rooming house and the local borders are all sitting around outdoors in the shade by the side of the house, cooling off from the day's heat, talking, drinking and watching us as we approach the driveway, taking notice of our New York license plate. There's a car blocking the driveway with the driver talking to a man leaning on his door , who is visibly drunk. We sit patiently waiting for about 30 seconds unconcerned because we know they've seen us and will move soon. They know they're blocking the entrance. But they don't move. Ma toots the horn lightly. Nothing. She toots it a second time. They ignore us. Finally Ma says "Would you please move out of the driveway so I can park?" And the drunk man says, "You wait a damn minute, shit". Then he leans even harder on his friend's door resuming his chat, and Ronnie says, "Yo man, move the car!" The people on the side of the building take notice. The drunk man shouts back, "I said wait a Goddamn minute!" His bottom lip hangs down, pink and vibrating. Ma says, "Oh, the hell with it, let's just go!" By this time we boys in the back start "selling wolf tickets" and the crowd thickens and closes in around us and a coke bottle comes flying and hits the side of the car and that's when we burst out, each one of us aimed at somebody in the crowd. We know this will be a rumble and so do they. We grab each other throwing punches to the head, back, stomach, anywhere, tussling in the dusty parking lot. There must have been eight of us involved in this brawl, while Ma sits behind the wheel screaming for us to stop. I land in the bushes, tangled up with some roughneck when I see Willie pick up a piece of 2 by 4 that has large, rusty nails on one end of it. He swings it at a man and hits him three times in the head. Somebody grabs me, separating my fight and we all jump back in the car bruised and scratched, breathing hard and nervous and head back to Aunt Evelyn's house on Birch Street, where Aunt Evelyn, Uncle Bill, Aunt Sarah and Uncle Preacher are playing cards.

The police arrive in about 20 minutes along with a witness from the parking lot who begins pointing fingers and they arrest all of us, including Ma. There's been a serious injury during the fight, but where is Willie? None of us know. We spend three days in the county jail and it was painful to see Ma taken into a jail cell, but we're all released and we go back home to New York except Ronnie, who remains in Bridgeton and gets a job there but he's arrested days later when the injured man dies. He was singled out for some reason by the crowd, probably because he's from New York, and he is being held on homicide charges for beating a man to death with a rusty-nailed 2x4.

In September, 1967 I try out for Jefferson's football team and get accepted after passing a running trial. I haven't even made my first team practice when "Harry The Cop" catches me cutting algebra class. When I naively tell him I'm on the football team, his eyes get big and he takes me down to Moe Finkelstein's office, the football coach. Moe looks at me and says, "You'll be here for practice at 4:30." When I show up for practice Moe gathers the team around in the locker room and points me out and says, "Alright, we take our team commitments very seriously and we also take our academic commitments very seriously but one of our new team members was caught cutting class today. So what does he get now?" The team responds, "The 21-gun salute!". I don't know what they're talking about or what to expect and I'm smiling, then Moe says, "Okay, hop up here, on your stomach." He puts me on top of a table face down and 21 team members whack me on the behind with a paddle, as hard as they can, and I almost black out. I never felt that kind of pain, and on the way home, I can't sit down on the bus. I never go back to the team, and never see Moe Finkelstein again.

IX
Vietnam

My cousin Cedric, 1965 - The photo that made me and Mickey join the military.

I become restless and bored with school, cutting most classes except music and English. My cousin Cedric is in the Navy and writing letters from cruises in the Mediterranean, and saying things like "Yeah man, we just sailed through the Straits of Gibraltar!" His brother Larry is a U.S. Marine and stationed in California, and Sissy's boyfriend Artis is in the Army, stationed in Germany. My cousin Sonny is in the Army and stationed in Saigon. The war is going on but not everyone is going to Vietnam. Mickey and I want travel and adventure in *our* lives so we go to the recruiting station on Flatbush and DeKalb and ask about going in the Navy. I think I'm finally getting a chance to wear the Sea Cadet uniform for real now, but the recruiter says we're too young and have to be 18. But we're 17 and want to go now.

"The Marine Corps will take you at 17, assign you to Sea Duty, and you'll be stationed on ships with the U.S. Navy, and sail all over the world," said the Marine Corps recruiter right next door.

We'll show Moe Finkelstein *and* the football team what tough really is and what it's like to be real men.

We could have joined the Army but we wanted to be special and do something bold. Our parents have to sign us out of school, and on November 10th, 1967 we take our oaths of service and are sworn in. We don't know it but it's Marine Corps Birthday. We have a going-away party at my house and we're in the basement dancing to the song, Expressway to your Heart. A few days before we have to report for to report, I see Al, the owner of the pocketbook factory when I was a kid back on Willoughby, standing on the corner of Monroe Street and Howard Avenue in front of a warehouse building near Broadway where he's just moved his factory.

"Hey Al, how you doin? You remember me ? Eddie, from the pocketbook factory you had down on South Elliot Street."

"Yeahhhh.....Eddie......You were a little boy back then!"

"I know. I just joined the marines. I'm leaving for boot camp day-after tomorrow."

"Is that right ! Well good luck to ya'. You go on over there and I'll hold down the fort over here." He was still looking sharp. Still wearing a process with a paisley doo-rag with his green eyes, standing next to his white Cadillac.

We assemble at Ft. Hamilton Brooklyn and get divided into groups and another recruit named Lutz is in charge of ours . We arrive at the Marine Corps Recruit Depot about 2am, half drunk from the pyramids of beer that we'd consumed at the Charleston Airport while waiting for the buses to take us to Parris Island. The smell of the Union Bag Paper Mill across the Savannah River meets us as we get off the buses. Everything changes. I realize for the first time that I've done something serious and for the first time, Ma and Dad can't help me. I can't quit like I did when I quit the football team. We want to be heroes.

Our talk changes to nautical language. The floor becomes the deck, doors become hatches, walls are called bulkheads, left becomes port and right becomes starboard, upstairs is topside and downstairs is below. A bed is called a rack and drawers are called skivvies and a whorehouse is called a skivvy house. I'm called nigger by a white man for the first time on our first day there, because I thought I *could* quit. When we arrive at Parris Island half drunk, a big, black Drill Instructor gets on the bus and says: "ALRIGHT, SHUT UP AND LISTEN UP ! IF YOU SMOKIN CIGARETTES PUT EM OUT. IF YOU CHEWING GUM, SWALLOW IT. THERE'S YELLOW FOOTSTEPS PAINTED ON THE DECK OUTSIDE THIS BUS. YOU GOT TEN SECONDS TO GIT OFF THIS BUS AND FIVE OF 'EM ARE GONE. NOW I DON'T WANNA SEE NOTHIN BUT ASSHOLES AND ELBOWS! MOVE !!"

There is Right Guard Deodorant, Dial Soap, Colgate Toothpaste, Scope Mouthwash, Marlboro Cigarettes, M-14 rifle, cleaning rod, linseed oil, pain and torture, regimentation, humiliation, laughter, patriotic indoctrination, intro to C-rations and synchronized perfection. We have 3 drill instructors. Staff Sgt. Ramsey the senior, Cpl, Fredendahl the junior, and Sgt Reese the meanest and funniest ,in the middle. Reese tortures and taunts us the most. He walks up to recruits and puts his face in theirs and says, "Well listen sweetheart, you better forget about your girl back home, what's her name? Suzie Rottencrotch? She belongs to Jodi now." And he says "A lotta you maggots'll never make it as real marines 'cause you're just a bunch of shit birds!" Sgt. Reese literally struts up and down the squad bay proudly, and I'm mesmerized by his duty uniform with the brass, belt buckle glistening in the sunshine coming in through the portholes, the emblematic eagle, globe and anchor on his duty cover. I'm enchanted the way I was back on Willoughby Avenue when I saw Raphael in his dress blues.

There's a complete feeling of indoctrination and regimentation that saturates my senses because we all live in the same room called a squad bay, and we do everything at the same time, so you have the smell of 82 freshly-showered and clean-shaven recruits smelling of Right Guard deodorant and Mennen after shave, all polishing our boots with Kiwi shoe polish at the same time, and we begin to feel like one, more and more each day. We march and chant together and we're fresh, young and strong.

I weigh 145 lbs. upon arrival in November and a lean-cut 186 lbs. in full-dress uniform at graduation, on January 15, 1968. During final inspection our Battalion Commander, Lt. Col. George T. Sergeant snatches my M-14 from me, looks down its glistening, immaculate barrel, hands it back to me and says "Good luck in your future, marine."

After graduation on January 15th we're allowed to go to the Enlisted Men's club for the first time. But this is not the regular EM Club, it's the base's Recruit EM Club, also known as the "Slop Shute" . It's called the slop shute because graduating recruits routinely use this place to drink the only alcoholic beverage available, the 3.2 beer, and most, after graduation, guzzle the beer in such quantities that they wind up throwing up so much that you can smell the vomit coming from the "head" all the way to the bar. When we walked into the slop shute in our dress uniforms after graduation that evening, all we could smell was beer, cigarettes and vomit.

Edwin S. German, Parris Island, December, 1967.

Miguel A. Goring, Parris Island, December, 1967

Me and Mickey, 4th row down, 6th from left

After infantry and M-60 machine-gun training at Camp Lejeune, North Carolina, we come home on our first leave. Mickey arrives before me because I get food poisoning at Camp Geiger and I'm set back two weeks in training.

Edwin S. German, Camp Lejeune, 1968

My girlfriend Yolanda gives me a surprise welcome-home party and the Marvelettes are singing My Baby must be a Magician. Yolanda is sweet, sexy, pretty and smart, and I want to be her hero. We don't watch much news and have been deprived of current events and have become marines. We walk like marines and are taught that marines don't use umbrellas, not in uniform.

On April 4th, 1968 I'm at Yolanda's house in my tropical, Gabardine uniform, sitting on the couch with my arm around her, when her father bursts in the room and screams that Martin Luther King has been shot. By this time Mickey, a couple of months older than me and already 18, is at Camp Pendleton California in staging battalion, on his way to Vietnam. We don't get Sea Duty like the recruiter said we would. Just before we graduate the 1968 Tet offensive is launched and the war escalates. By the time we get to Camp Lejeune we know we're going to Vietnam. I arrive at Camp Pendleton just before my 18th birthday and avoid staging battalion by being with the 5th Marine Division Band for a couple of months and I'm desperately lonely, isolated and disoriented. Yolanda gives me her portable, battery-operated record player and I spend evenings alone on the beach at Oceanside, watching the Pacific Ocean and listening to the dreamy arrangements on Wes Montgomery's albums California Dreaming, Tequila, Goin' Out of My Head and A Day in the Life. All the members of the marine band are Vietnam Veterans and consider me a "boot" and they have little to do with me. I do make friends with two band members, Joe from Louisiana, and Paul from Boston. It's 1968 and Paul has a '68

Pontiac Le Mans 4 speed, in which we almost lose our lives when he totals it on the freeway coming back from Tijuana one night. He falls asleep at the wheel after taking "downs", and crashes into the guard rail breaking it on impact, and a section of it smashes through the windshield splitting Paul's top lip all the way to his gums. Joe ends up with windshield glass all in his face and hair. I was laying across the back seat asleep when it happened and got knocked between the seats but not hurt.

The first time I ever smell a skunk is late one night as Paul, Joe and I are coming in from Tijuana. Paul is parking next to the barracks and Aretha Franklin is on the radio singing Ain't No Way, and we sit in the car until the song ends. When we get out of the car we see a skunk and chase it around for a few seconds until we smell his assault. Until then, I'd only seen skunks in cartoons and on TV, and never smelled one.

Mickey arrives in Vietnam in May, '68 and is assigned to Charlie Co. 1/9, "The Walking Dead". A few weeks later Robert Kennedy is assassinated and one evening when I'm checking in at the barracks the NCO in charge looks up at me briefly, then quickly again from his typewriter and he's listening to Wolfman Jack on the radio.

"Uh, German, I think you better take a look at the bulletin board."

Under its florescent light, the white bulletin board had me listed in black marker;

GERMAN, EDWIN S./ 2292518 / ON ORDERS:

WESTERN PACIFIC. 1 JULY.

I've received orders for staging battalion, then Vietnam. My heart beat in my mouth. And the song playing on the radio is,

I think it's so groovy now,

that people are finally gettin' together,

I think it's wonderful now,

that people are finally gettin together.

The very next week Wes Montgomery dies. He's one of my musical heroes, with his records going to Vietnam with me, packed away in my sea bag.

The three weeks at staging battalion pass quickly and we find ourselves, one sunny afternoon at the end of July, on a bus headed for El Toro Air Base, where we'll depart for the Western Pacific. In boot camp we trained on the M-14, in ITR we trained on the M-1, and in staging Battalion we trained on the M-16, the newest automatic weapon, which most of us will carry in Vietnam.

On our way to the airport on the Freeway, we pass a young, white couple riding in a 1963 Chevy convertible with the top down. They look like they're coming from the beach. The girl is hanging on her boyfriend's arm, wearing a mini-skirt which reveals slightly, her freshly-tanned behind, as she leans on her left hip with her legs crossed and her behind facing us. As we ride parallel to them we whoop and holler and poke our heads through the open windows to get last views of what we cherish and look forward to again. The couple look up at us, their hair blowing in the wind. We're gesturing for the girl to show us more , because we're going to Vietnam and deserve a last look. Her boyfriend says something to her, she looks up at us, smiles teasingly and pulls her skirt all the way up, giving us a last show. We scream. No panties at all, and the brunette hair between her legs also sails in the wind, like a flag.

At El Toro air base, a half hour before boarding, we're given a final flight orientation and briefing and our sea bags are inspected for items not permitted on the flight like flammables, aerosols or anything explosive. A Gunnery Sgt., after inspecting our gear and throwing away our spray deodorants and colognes, wishes us well and says in a thick, southern drawl, "Now I wantchall to go over there, kick some ass and take some names and come on back home, hear?"

The flight to Vietnam is intriguing and bizarre, because after the final briefing we board an American Airlines jet with civilian crew and female stewardesses who are attentive, attractive and compassionate. They serve us cocktails, food and coffee and chat briefly with each one of us above the clouds, over the waters of the Pacific Ocean. The last thing I expected was to go to Vietnam in an American Airlines jet. I thought we'd be in a droning, drab, olive-green, windowless, military aircraft. The flight is long, about 16 hours with a brief stopover in Hawaii where girls drape leis of flowers around our necks, then Okinawa, where we spend the night in the Marine Barracks. A couple of hours after we fly out of Okinawa, the cocktails stop and breakfast is served aboard the flight, and after that, the crew gets everything into place and the Captain addresses us in a confident voice.

"Uh, Good morning, this is the Captain speaking: On behalf of our entire crew, American Airlines and The United States of America, we salute you fine marines."

Cheers and battle grunts explode from our chests.

"We're now approaching Da Nang Airport. We hope you had a pleasant and fun flight and we know most of you did, with all the partying."

More cheers and OOh Rahs.

"And on behalf of all of us, we look forward to bringing you all back home when your tours are over."

A final cheer.

The plane's engines hum to a higher level, we feel a drop in altitude, a gentle bell sounds and "No Smoking" lights come on.

"We'll be landing in Da Nang in about 15 minutes now. The time is 11:45am the temperature at Da Nang airport is 92 degrees, it's slightly overcast on the ground and the humidity is 85%. Please place your seats in an upright position and fasten all seat belts, thank you."

The coastline of Vietnam finally comes into view on this hot, steamy day of August 1st. The tropical-colored houses are pastel pink, green and yellow and white, set within brilliant green grass and rice paddies. Jungle hills are pock-marked with bomb craters. As we make our approach the place seems too confusing and crowded.

Da Nang airport is busy with military aircraft, trucks and jeeps, piles of merchandise and military hardware stacked two stories high, and servicemen and Vietnamese employees. The U.S. servicemen are wearing light-weight tropical-green camouflage uniforms and we're getting off the plane in our thick, hot, stateside utilities and stateside boots, while their boots are tropical, salty and faded. We're totally green, pale and new, and I'm still feeling the warm goodbye hugs from the American stewardesses, and can still sense their cologne and some of us have lipstick on our cheeks as they kissed us bye. I'm on the other side of the world, in a place where young Americans are dying.

After getting off the plane we assemble at a temporary holding station under a canopy, waiting to board trucks on a convoy to our duty stations. Servicemen who've finished their tours or have been wounded pass by us, boarding the same plane that we got off. Some are walking, some are in stretchers, and some are being helped along by others, all on their way home.

"Hey boots..........Good Luck.......You got a lonnnnng way to go Bro......Man, Ah feel sorry for y'all asses."

Some are laughing and grinning as they taunt us in our predicament, some simply stare at us with blank expressions that show relief, fatigue, impatience and anxiety, sorrow and melancholy pity and the joy of finally going home, that dream-like fantasy so far out of reach for us now.

They've done theirs..........we have ours to do.

But when the dead pass us they say nothing, and don't look at us. They'd died here and are wrapped in the appropriate manner for their final overseas voyage, back home to their loved ones to be mourned over and buried with flags. They're quiet in their forever youthful sleep, not able to respond to the wrenching anguish, sorrow and anger of their loved ones, not able to answer or explain what happened, not able to rejoice or weep in their return. A Sgt. standing nearby snaps to attention and we follow his example and salute comrades whom we can't see and never met, being carried devotedly, following the living back home after so much strife. I feel alarmed, sober and numb. I wonder where Mickey is. I know he's with 1/9 but where's 1/9?

"Alright listen up. When I call your name, pick up your gear and follow the detail out to the road to board the convoy. Davis, Dalton, German, Hernandez, Zurita.........."

We lift our sea bags and file behind a corporal who leads us to a long line of six-by diesel trucks. Each truck carries 18 men just arriving "in country", plus 2 seasoned marines on each side who carry automatic weapons for our security, and another marine who sits behind an M-60 machine gun mounted on a tripod, at the helm of each truck. We're going 15 miles south of Da Nang. Each truck also carries a block of ice in a box, under a green towel. The signal is given for the convoy to move out and as the line of ten trucks starts their engines, the smell of diesel fuel from their exhausts hits me, a smell that will become synonymous with the war. We leave the airport about 1330 hours and drive all through Da Nang towards the outskirts of the city, south. We're seeing sketches of life of the Vietnamese as we ride through villages. The smell of smoke from burning wood is everywhere, the smell of incense from houses, temples and churches. The smell of buffalo dong floats across the road coming from the rice paddies. People walk, run, drive, ride bikes and trot goods. Women have black teeth. Children run alongside our trucks with their hands out, begging for anything we care to toss at them. We're traveling down a two-lane, so-called highway of dusty, red dirt, which gradually but completely covers our faces, including our eyelashes until each one of us wears a mask of dust that creates bizarre, masquerade-like looks. We look like ghosts. As the kids run alongside our truck a boy catches my eye and says rapidly, "Hey Soul Brudda, Hey Soul Brudda you gimme chop chop..... some candy......how 'bout one cigarette?" I throw him a piece of gum which he catches and adds, "Soul Brudda numba one!" He holds up a small, clenched fist as he stumbles over rocks and avoids running in the ditch. We're moving 10-15 miles per hour, slow enough for the kids to keep up with us momentarily, long enough to shout greetings and beg with their out stretched, dirty, nimble little hands. By this time we're chipping off pieces of the ice and crunching it in our dusty, thirsty mouths. That's what it was put there for. We start throwing chunks of ice to the running kids, who catch them, drop them and pick them up, sucking on them like popsicles. Already, a simple thing like ice has become a rare treat.

Vietnam. I know nothing of these people, this land. Where am I going? What will it look like? I want to change out of this hot, thick, stateside uniform and get my tropical utilities and jungle boots and be more comfortable and blend in with the rest of the seasoned men. I look new. I am new. My boots still have black on them. Even when I get my jungle boots they'll look new too. It'll take a while before I can look "salty" like these guys.

About 3pm we pull into the base camp, a place called Twai Lai, or "Twilight". It's an operational area set in white, beach-like sand, in the midst of rice-farming lowlands of Quang Nam Province, where some are Viet Cong, "Farmer by day and fighter by night". I'm assigned to a marine rifle company, Bravo, 1st Bn, 27th marines. Back at Da Nang airport, I met a Puerto Rican marine from New York named Rob after we'd been assigned the same truck to make the convoy. We introduced ourselves.

"How you doin Bro, My name's Rob."

"Hey what's happenin, my name's Eddie. Where you from?"

"Um from New York."

"Yeah? Me too. What part?"

"Um from Man-hattin' - The Lower East Side."

"Um from Brooklyn!" But I know 'bout the Lower East Side."

"So we home boys."

"You know that".

"Yo man, there's another brother from New York here too. Yo Hernandez!"

A tall, heavy-set Puerto Rican shuffles down the isle of the six-by over to us with a wide grin on his face, flops down on the bench and we shake hands. Hernandez is from Harlem, 103rd and Lexington. Rob says "Yo man, pretty soon we gon' have us a whole gang of mutha fuckas from New York." Rob is Puerto Rican but sounds like he's black. He has a complexion like a Native American and a long nose like an Arab. He talks slow, with a drawl. He does everything slow. His last name is Zurita.

We check in at the command hooch, we're assigned rifles, pick up our 782 gear from supply and begin to settle in. We don't know it now, but we'll only be with the 27th Marines about five weeks because the unit is about to leave Vietnam, for Okinawa. We're assigned to a 12-man tent and after we stage our gear under our cots in the shade of the tent, it's chow time and we're hungry. We follow the men to a field mess, about 200 yards from the compound, where assorted marines are assembled for the evening meal, my first meal in a field mess hall, situated in what seems like a very small valley, surrounded by jungle green and set up on plywood boards upon which sit wooden benches and tables, all makeshift, with banana trees protruding from the enclosing walls of miniature jungle. The food-prep section is housed in another area and between these two sections is the chow line where all of us wait, for our ration of mashed potatoes, Salisbury steaks from a can, string beans, rolls and Kool Aid. There's also ice. As we eat, Rob me, and another Puerto Rican we meet from New York, Roberto Saldana, (Lil' Man) sit together with Hernandez. Lil' Man likes to sing all kinds of music, from the Temptations to Frank Sinatra and knows the words to lots of popular songs. He thinks he's Sammy Davis, Jr. I know we're gonna be friends. Lil' man and Rob are both from the Lower East Side. Rob from the projects on Avenue D, and Lil' Man from Eldridge Street, near the hotel. A Sgt. comes over to our table before dumping his tray and tells a Corporal that his squad will be going out on night patrol.

"Hell we just went out last night, shit!"

His complaint does no good. He knows he has to have his squad ready when it's time to go. Nobody likes night patrols.

We're all wearing our new jungle clothing but my boots feel a little tight, causing slight irritation to my left foot. By the time we dump our trays and head for the tent area dusk is approaching. As the sun begins to sink, the welcomed evening breeze from the east towards the sea begins to come in. It comes in around the same time each evening. This is when marines tend to their personal business of writing letters, cleaning weapons, laying back on the cot and listening to the radio, and playing bid whist. We meet more marines from New York and now there's about 10 of us. Our squad leader sticks his head in the hooch and drops two cases of beer on the floor, Falstaff. We all grab a beer and Lil' Rob makes a toast and starts singing "La Mer, Beyond The Sea", by Bobby Daren, as the wind from the ocean cools us off.

We leave the tent and I follow the crowd towards the edge of the compound where we gather under a 40 ft. guard tower atop of which there's a sentry standing duty. We're drinking beers and smoking cigarettes.

Then somebody takes out a plastic bag that's filled with pre-rolled joints of reefer and starts passing them around. It's the first time I'm smoking reefer. I don't know what to expect. The joints come 10 in a pack and a pack costs $1.00 They're passed around and we start to feel nice and begin laughing and goofing around and ranking on each other like kids, the New York crew ranking in broken Spanish calling each other names like Cabesa de mono (monkey head), carte de omnibus (bus face), and at this point I nickname Hernandez from 103rd and Lexington, "Chef Boy- Ar- Dee", because he looks just like the chef on the spaghetti can. Then we start talking about each other's mothers, like back in Junior High, laughing and laughing and walking back towards the tents. I just met these guys today and we're already comfortable enough to be talking about each other's Moms. We pop open more warm beers, squirting them all over each other as each can opens. It's my first day in country and now it's dark and I'm high, with a bunch of guys that I just met, in a new compound and I don't know my way around. I can only see the people directly near me and can't make out the surrounding facilities. There's a tape playing in the tent and Otis Redding is singing Ole Man Trouble. Back in California in Staging Battalion and in the 5th Marine Division Band, I was too young to have a drink. The drinking age was 21. Couldn't even go in a bar. But on the plane coming here we drank cocktails, anything we wanted. And back in the slop-shute at Parris Island, when I was still 17, they let us have 3.2 beer. What was the drinking age in South Carolina at the time? And now, they distribute beer to squad leaders in the combat zone for their men, and I'm only 18 !

"Yo man, don't they have any *cold* beer around here?" I ask, grinning.

"Sheeeit man!" Rob says, where the fuck you think you at? Coney Island?"

That comment becomes one big goof, and we laugh so much that the muscles of my face start hurting. We're standing in a semi circle just outside the tent....... BOOM !, KA BOOM....POW!! I hit the ground and look at faces for directions and they look back at me with big eyes and open mouths and holler INCOMING.....INCOMING!!

I'm looking back and forth and hugging the earth and BANG!! Someone yells "HIT THE BUNKER, HIT THE BUNKER, OVER THERE OVER THERE." I see sandbags stacked around a hole and I run and dive in and bump my head hard on a sandbag and land inside and I'm holding my head

between my knees........ then it's quiet...... and guys outside
are laughing. It wasn't "incoming", it was outgoing. The four-
deuce guns are just a few yards from our tent in a sunken gun
pit and they had a fire mission. I didn't even know they were
there. The joke's on me. My first day in country ends. My new
boots are too tight. Wrong size. Take em off, smoke a
cigarette, go to sleep, drunk.

The next morning we're ordered to saddle up and prepare to
move out on a company-sized operation. "Damn man, they
don't waste no time" I think. We pack up everything we own
except our cots and as I survey my gear I insert a magazine
into my M-16 and lock and load.

"Whatchoo doin, man? You betta git dat roun' outta dat
chamber. You ain't sposed to lock and load till you told to."

It's a brother from down south named Williams talking, who's
been here for a while now. Williams seems mad and doesn't
smile much. I want to be accepted by the marines we're
surrounded by and learn from them about this combat thing. I
eject the round from the chamber and reinsert it into the
magazine. My rifle's at sling arms and I'm saddled up. The
gear is heavy but I'm strong. We board trucks that take us ten
miles down the road, south. We get off the trucks and
proceed into the tree line which we penetrate and begin to
take high ground. By 12 noon we're climbing the hills, my first
time in the mountain-jungles. The smells are thick and
pungent because vegetation is being hacked away by men
carrying machetes and chopping a path through. Now I
remember Ramah of the Jungle and Tarzan, and watching

them with Ronnie. It's steamy and hot and the gear seems a burden. The heights of the hills seem endless and I feel like they're moving us too fast but I'm doing better than a lot of the other new guys who are having a hard time keeping up and are being coached along by their team and squad leaders. We're walking in a straight column, one behind the other, 160 men strong, 15 meters apart. My left foot is irritated bad and getting real sore. I feel the seam of the too-narrow boot cutting into the top of my foot with each step I take. I know damage is happening. We're climbing to the top of a hill to set up a night perimeter. We're seeking to make enemy contact by sending out patrols and setting up ambushes. It's hard-going, slippery and muddy with treacherous vines reaching out to trip you or choke you, and when you start sliding down the hill and grab onto one, it's full of thorns. I'm panting, straining, sweating and trying to exercise discipline by conserving my water. I've been placed in a squad but Big Rob and Lil Rob are in different platoons. I've never sweated so much. We take salt tablets each day to prevent heat exhaustion. We're "humping the hills".

About 1800 we're finally at a place where we'll make night camp. We begin to set up perimeter on a finger of land over a ravine where we clear fields of fire to put the enemy at a distance around us, set up trip wires, flares and claymore mines and we dig in. I'm thrilled to reach the top of this endless hill and throw off this heavy gear and rest. We've shed our back packs and cartridge belts but there's still hours of work to be done, digging the foxholes and setting up the hooches. The foxholes are 5 feet deep, 2 feet wide and 4 feet long, so they can hold 3 men in fighting position. Directly behind each foxhole we pitch our two-man tents. There are 3 men to each foxhole but one man is always on watch which begins at 2100 hours (9PM) and ends at 0600 hours. (6AM).

I'm here in the hooch finally laying down with my boots still on, thinking about today's march. There were times when we had to suddenly and routinely stop and be still so that we could listen and hear if we're being followed. At these moments we found opportunity to rest but to also feel the forbidding, outlawed jungle and its unfamiliar domain with its vast, threatening wildness. Earlier this afternoon during a pause in the march I felt feelings of nausea and dysentery from the new water I'm drinking, some of it coming from fresh-running streams. This long, hot trek with its stress and apprehension, and the pain of my blistering foot that I didn't take the time to complain about, is unshakable.

Halfway through digging the foxhole, I stopped, put my e-tool down and took off my left boot. I peeled off the sock where it stuck to the sore in the middle of my foot, a 1/4 inch circle rubbed down to the flesh, already showing pus and beginning to turn green around the edges.. I showed it to Hernandez, (Chef Boy Ar Dee) who said "Yo Bro, you better take care o' dat. Dat can turn to jungle rot real quick 'roun here." The land is so fertile with growth and moisture and heat that any wound, unattended, could become deadly. I put the boot and sock back on and finished digging the foxhole and afterwards removed them again to let the wound air out. Later on I was barely able to get the boot back on because my foot had swollen slightly.

It's almost dark now and some of the countless jungle insects are noisily retiring to their early-evening vigil, clicking, snapping and whirring. I'm not scared. We're 160 strong with automatic weapons, grenade launchers, 60mm mortars, disposable bazookas, hand grenades, radios to call in anything from hot beer to napalm. And we're bad-ass marines. We're told to light no fires and eat our chow before 8:30. I'm starving. I take out a c-ration unit can of beef slices and gravy and eat them cold along with a can of cheese of crackers, some cool water and a chocolate fudge bar. Chef Boy Ar Dee and I stand in the foxhole leaning on the dirt wall facing the perimeter, talking of how tired we are. Our shirts and trousers are still soaked and salty from sweat.

"Yo - I got last watch, bro. Whatchoo want?"

"I'll take first." I tell the Chef. "I'm not ready to go to sleep right now." I'll be on watch from 9-12 midnight, then I can sleep the rest of the night. By 6AM it's daylight and time for all to rise. The guy who stands last watch might lay down in the warm tent for a few minutes after his watch, and while we're making coffee he'll creep in the hooch and flop down with his rifle and get a few winks with his boots extending out, his head facing uphill, which is how we sleep on these jungle slopes. If it rains real hard and your hooch leaks you might find yourself waking up and starting to slide down the hill with the oily mud.

I'm exhausted as the other guys lie down and I begin my watch. I managed to force my boot back on and loosely lace it up but I can feel the sore, throbbing and itching. Now I'm seeing the total blackness of the jungle. When it first started getting dark I thought my eyes would adjust later as the night crept in. But now, it's totally black and the nearby insects and night birds have settled down to a quieter, rhythmic whir, like the sound of hundreds of tiny machines in a factory. I can't see my rifle nor can I see my hand held directly in front of my face. It's totally black. I remember the first outdoor blackness I saw when Ma showed us the dark on Route 77 coming from Bridgeton when we were kids. And "Raw-Head Bloody Bones". It's never this black in Brooklyn. There are foxholes to my left and right with men quietly sitting behind their weapons, looking out at blackness but keeping ears tuned in for any movement. Finally about 11:30 the moon moves higher and casts some of its beams through the jungle canopy overhead and offers us slight, night vision. Thank God for good eyes. The soft breeze coming in from beyond the perimeter brings the smell of burnt wood nearby. There's no wood burning on our perimeter. That means the smell of the enemy. It's 2400 hours and my watch is over. I see my way to the hooch and wake up my relief, a brother named Pope.

"Yo, it's your watch. C'mon, reveille. Git up man."

I'm falling into the routine. I lay down on top of the poncho liner, find a groove, let out a sigh and fall directly asleep.

Automatic rifle fire and M-70 grenade launchers rattle my repose. Rifles are popping and men are hollering. The whole line opens up. Grenades fly and red tracers from M-60s rip through the trees like tiny jet airplanes on fire. I throw on my helmet, take my weapon and jump in the foxhole and start firing into the tree line, which is lit up like daytime by a trip flare. Then I hear the words. CEASE FIRE ! CEASE FIRE !, as the Chef crashes into the foxhole landing on my sore foot. "Aw fuck man!" I yell out in pain. The line is quiet and we're listening. Nothing. Someone or something tripped a flare and one segment of the perimeter opened fire starting a chain reaction that caused the whole line to open up. Officers call platoon sergeants and squad leaders up and we remain on 100% alert for the rest of the night. My first operation is over in two days and I've had 1 hour sleep.

The next day we break camp and make a company-sized sweep of the area until we find ourselves coming out of the tree line where the convoy is there to take us back to base camp where there's hot chow, beer and the comfort of our tents, where I can take off this boot and get some medical attention. It's the smell of two-day sweat, caked dirt on our clothes and boots and the sounds of field marching packs, e-tools, cartridge belts, magazines, machine-gun ammo and weapons dropping to the floor and the commotion of chow call, mail call, beer call and getting our heads and asses wired back together, to shit, shower and shave and slow down.

As I air my feet I write Mickey a letter, my first to him since arriving in country. I tell him about my first operation, the near-enemy contact, my foot and the American Airlines flight over. Mickey is up north with the 3rd Mar. Div. Two weeks later I get a letter from him that starts:

DAMN BUCK,

"Whatchoo doin over here man? You shoulda stayed in the band niggah. Where you at, and who the hell is Bravo 1/27? Um wid Charlie 1/9. They call us the The Walkin Dead.".......... He signed off his letter as MAG 68, initials for his name, Miguel Alonzo Goring. And he wrote "Cowboys 67", forever.

It's dark evening and we're manning the bunkers of the perimeter, and on the northern horizon I see what looks like the long, red, electronic legs of a giant creature walking.

"Yo man, what's that down there?" I ask.

"What? You mean those lights? That's Puff The Magic Dragon, workin out." Says brother Pope.

Puff is a slow, low-flying, huge aircraft whose function is to spray the ground with bullets fired from its 4 mini guns, mounted on the starboard side of the craft. The mini guns spray bullets more rapidly than any automatic weapon and its lines of fire are marked by tracers that illuminate the night. Puff works only at night and is a spectacle to behold. The drone of its huge engines above and the sight of 16,000 bullets a minute being propelled to the ground with pin-point accuracy, each bullet hitting the ground one inch apart from the other, like rain drops. It literally rains machine gun fire and resembles a flying saucer as it "walks" on its legs of magnesium-burning tracer bullets.

Big Rob (Zurita) says, "Puff is out there fuckin up Charles!"

The enemy here down south is known as the V.C., for Viet Cong. In the military alphabet, "Victor" is for V, and "Charles" is for C. So the Viet Cong are known as Victor- Charlie, which is shortened down to "Charlie", and to some, "Charles."

The next day I make sick call for my foot and I'm told to wear flip flops for the next 3 days and I'm put on light duty, which doesn't go well with my platoon Sgt., while the rest of the platoon pulls duty at a small outpost called Tugboat and they're gone for 4 days. During my three days of light duty I perform routine tasks of filling sandbags and policing the general area for trash and cleaning my gear. When I'm not doing this I rest under the shade of our tent and mingle with the few marines who don't have patrol. The dry, beach-like climate of our compound helps my shoeless foot to heal quickly and I'm now able to wear a jungle boot again, this time the right size.

When the rest of the platoon returns from Tugboat they're just in time to clean up and get some hot chow, light some joints and pop open some hot beers, this time Coors. There are no patrols or operations the next day and after we perform our morning details word gets around that a few guys are going to head into Da Nang for some cold sodas and hamburgers at the snack bar at a place called Freedom Hill. Me, Rob, Lil Man, The Chef and brother Pope, led by an older guy named Johnson who knows the ropes go out past the main gate and hitch a ride on a six-by that takes us to the center of the city where we get off and make our way through the busy, crowded streets. I'm shocked by how skinny and frail the Vietnamese girls look. They're tiny. So many bicycles. They use bikes like cars. When we jump off the trucks we're directly surrounded by children who immediately thrust their hands into our pockets and start begging. I literally have 4 hands from 4 boys, 2 trying my front pockets and 2 trying to get into the back pockets. I gently begin removing their hands one-by-one but to no avail. It's like trying to shoo a fly away that just keeps landing back. We finally have to yell at the kids sharply,

"HEY, GITCHO' HANDS OUTTA MY POCKETS 'FO I KICK YOU IN YO' ASS!"

The six of us find our way through the crowded, main thoroughfare up to the snack bar where a juke box is playing and servicemen are lounging around eating burgers, hot dogs, and drinking cold sodas. We get sodas, burgers and potato chips in the hot, airy atmosphere and then James Brown comes on the jukebox singing, Say It Loud, I'm Black and I'm Proud. I can't believe it. It's my first time hearing the record and I'm hearing it in Vietnam. I get paranoid and start looking around, the way I did back in 1960 when I was 10 in Aiken's barbershop when I first heard A White Man's Heaven is a Black Man's Hell. I begin to relax more and I get up and put change in the jukebox and play it over 2 more times so I can remember it, because I can't believe it. When we come back to the snack bar two weeks later, the record is gone.

When our platoon gets duty to stand watch at the outpost Tugboat, we saddle up our gear, food, water, ammo and weapons and file out to the main highway, Route 9, and proceed to walk towards Tugboat. It's 10 AM as we find

ourselves on the hot, dusty highway, walking in two columns
on the port and starboard sides of the road, with rice paddies
on both sides, where farmers are using black water buffalo like
mules. Convoys of trucks and tanks and jeeps sweep by us. As
we sit on the shoulders of the road during a pause in the
march, a strange group of Vietnamese passes us, walking in
single file. Men, women and children with complexions as dark
as mine and some darker, carrying goods and dressed in
burlap sack cloth. They're a tribe of Montagnards and I'm
seeing them for the first time. The women are bare breasted
and some wear bells and chimes around their necks and
ankles, and they hold pipes between their teeth that emit the
burning smell that isn't pipe tobacco, nor cigarette, nor reefer,
but smelled sickening and alien. They have pitch-black,
squinted eyes and as the women pass me they throw wide-
eyed, teasing glances which seem to penetrate me, as if
they're surprised at my appearance because I'm as black as
they are and I'm staring at them. Their hair is straight and
black and matted in places and they smile showing gold and
black teeth. Their smiles are like grimaces and they make me
wince. They look like they can cast spells or something. I
didn't know that such dark people were part of Vietnam.
There are about 40 of them. To me, they're like black people.
They don't live in the villages with the other Vietnamese, but
live in the remote hills and keep to themselves. They're alien
and mysterious and show the ancient tribal appearances and
secrets . Who are they? They're not concerned about their
bare breasts with the bells and chimes that tinkle around their
ankles as they walk. They say nothing. I finally and naively say
hello to one of the women as she passes who shoots her eyes

through me, with smoke from her pipe curling around her dark cheeks. I wonder how they'd treat me if they ever got me alone, then I quickly dismiss the notion.

We're 1st and 2nd platoons assigned to this oval-shaped mound where 81mm mortars and four deuces are mounted permanently. We're relieving 3rd and 4th platoons and will be here about 4 days. I wonder why it's called Tugboat. I think it's because of its oval shape. As we approach the turnoff for the outpost a Vietnamese man comes along with cans of Coco-Cola, ice cold, $5.00 each. All of us in the immediate vicinity buy one. We don't care. If it cost $10.00 we'd buy one. The money we carry in our pockets is MPC, Military Payment Certificates, and to us it looks like monopoly money - but it's real money, issued by the military to be used in the combat zone. Money is bizarrely uncharacteristic here among us. It's not important to us here. It's almost irrelevant because we use it mostly to buy black-market stuff. Everything else is issued to us, including cigarettes and beer. A marine you don't even know will lend you $20.

We arrive at Tugboat and relieve 3rd and 4th platoons and begin making preparations for our stay. A patrol goes out from 1st platoon and after about 30 minutes a loud explosion comes from their direction and platoon Sgts. and Lieutenants grab PRC radios for news. A booby trap. The point man of the patrol walked into a trip wire that detonated an 82mm mortar round that immediately blew his legs off and showered others with shrapnel. Medevac choppers soon hover over the patrol. We hear later that the point man will live. I didn't know him or any of the other wounded. "Damn, soon as we get here".

As 3rd and 4th platoons left Tugboat they left a squad of Vietnamese Army men with us. They're called ARVNS, who've gained a reputation for not being worthwhile. They sit on their haunches like children, talking rapidly and laughing and scrambling some kind of meat with what looks like green scallions in a blackened, improvised wok over a wood-dirt fire in the middle of the compound. They say the ARVNS are incompetent, cowardly and deceitful. They casually acknowledge us as they stir fry their early-evening meal, smiling, nodding and smoking cigarettes.

I share a foxhole with a brother named Williams and a white boy named Harper. Williams is from Alabama and Harper is from Georgia. Harper came in country the same time I did, on the same flight, and the same convoy from Da Nang. Williams has been here 5 months now and is salty, rebellious about whites and the war. He seems mad. It shows on his face and how he speaks and moves. We work all day in the hot sun, fortifying the bunkers and foxholes, policing the general area and cleaning weapons. It's 2130 hours and I'm on first watch, sitting in the foxhole looking out at the blackness while my eyes adjust. I'm tired and all is quiet. At 2230 the Sgt. of The Guard comes by making his rounds, asking if everything is secure. "Yes". He disappears to the left side of the perimeter and I stare into the bush area in front of me. Another 90 minutes to go. How is Mickey? What's he doing now? Sleeping? Standing watch like me? On an ambush? In a fire fight? Where's Yolanda, and McGee and Montclair and Eddie

and Craig ? At Rockaway Beach? On 42nd Street? And Paul
and Joe and Ma and.................*WHACK !!*

I'm slapped hard on the right side of the face by the platoon
Sgt. Oh shit! I nodded out for a minute. Was so tired. Had
sweated so much. He hit me in my face! "Yo man, what the
fuck you doin?" I snap.

"Dontchoo ever Garddamn fall asleep on my watch you hear?"

"I wasn't sleep!"

But I guess I was for a minute. It only takes a second to die.
It's only my 2nd watch. How could I ?

The next day around noon Williams and I are in the foxhole
and the Sgt. comes by. "I want you two to clean the trash out
of that bomb crater and burn it." He walks away. Williams
says "Fuck him, I ain't doin shit!" I start cleaning out the bomb
crater that had been used as a dump and I'm shoveling trash
into a barrel. "Where's Williams?" Asks the Sgt. "He's in the
Bunker." "Tell him to git out here and help you." I stick my
head in the bunker and tell Williams what the Sgt. said and he
looks at me, sucks his teeth and turns his head away. He lay
there on his back with his feet crossed at the ankles, with a
scarce crack of daylight seeping through the sandbags,
outlining his dark features. "C'Mon Williams", I tell him.

"I said I ain't doin it!" He Blurts.

I return to the crater and the Sarge says, "Aintchall done yet?
Where's Williams?" "He's still in the bunker." "I thought I

told you to tell him to git out here and help you." "I did but he said he ain't doin nothin." The Sarge pokes his head inside the bunker and shouts. "Williams, gitcho ass out here before I write choo up right now!" Williams' lips emerge from the bunker squinting their eyes in the bright sunlight with hands on hips, looking first at me then facing the Sarge. "You'll have this Garddamn crater emptied in 20 minutes and I mean that shit. Now I don't wanna hear nunna yo' bullshit, understand?" Williams says nothing but snatches up his e-tool and starts furiously hurling trash with his black lips poking out even further. When the Sarge gets out of range he says "Why you do that shit man, why you tell on me? You a Unca Tom, das whatchoo you is, a Unca Tom." You let dat white man hit choo in yo' face!"

"Yo, I ain't did nothin to you man."

"Yes you did. You a Tom!"

Well I'll be damn. Here I am, less than a week in country, trying to do my job, following orders, trying to stay alive, and this nigga from down south calling ME an Uncle Tom. I've never been called that. I grew up with all kinds of people, had all kinds of friends. Who does this country-ass niggah think he is?" But I'm disappointed because he's a brother and he's salty and I'm a boot. I just got here. What was I supposed to do when the Sarge found me sleeping and slapped me? Shoot him, get arrested and put in the brig?

"You a country-ass, Uncle Tom, dumb niggah". I told him, holding my e-tool in my right hand, daring him to jump at me. He didn't talk to me for the next 2 days.

Later that afternoon we're on a local patrol about 1,000 meters from Tugboat walking along rice-paddy dikes that stink with still, muddy water and buffalo dong and we're up to our thighs in it, and it fills our socks and boots. Water buffalo are scattered here and there, fat, quiet and ugly, gazing at us with open nostrils, and we tease them and call after them and they turn their fat asses and try to run. They're tended mostly by children who carry little switches. Sometimes they ride them. I think back to boot camp to a recruit named Pvt. Daigle whom we nicknamed "Water Buffalo" because he had a wide ass that switched back and forth when he marched and his trousers hung in the back the way the sagging skin hangs on an elephant. We even made fun of his name, Daigle, because it sounded so much like bagel. It's eerie, out of the entire crew of 82 of us from boot camp whom we trained with, learned with, sweated with and lived with and became marines with, I'm here alone. Where are they all now? All split up, never to find each other again. Not even one of them is stationed with me now. Not even Mickey. All scattered around the world, never to meet again.

The patrol is over and when we get back Williams unloads his M-60 machine gun off his shoulder and mounts it on top of the foxhole. I unstrap my cartridge belt letting it fall off my waist, take off my helmet and jump into the foxhole and open cans of peaches and pound cake from my C-ration unit. Williams comes over to me.

"Yo man, I'm sorry about the other day, alright?"

"O.K." I said. "It aint nothin to it, bro". He smiled for the first time and later he got to talking.

"Man, these white folk ain't nothin but beasts. All dey wanna do is git us kilt, das all. You gotta watch yo back and we gotta look out for each other. We black, man. We ain't even sposed to be here." He has big, wide feet and his boots are salty from the wear of the sand, the jungle, the mud and the rice paddies. After a while we're talking and laughing."

"ALRIGHT, FIRST AND SECOND PLATOONS, SADDLE UP WE'RE MOVIN OUT! "

"What? We just got back from patrol. I'm tired." But it's good news. We're going back to Twilight with the rest of the crew. We pack our gear, saddle up and move out. The ARVNS are again squatting over the treacherous, little fire with the blackened woks, tossing around some rice and meat. Some say they're eating dogs. They ask for our leftover c-rations which we give up and they smile their tricky faces showing gold, white, and black teeth. "Soul brudda numba one!....so long soul......Peace." They hold up two fingers for the peace sign and a clenched fist for black power. We're glad to be heading back for some rest.

When we near the main gate of the compound there's activity and noise all around and even some vehicles blowing horns. Voices are hollering and calling and there's lots of yippies and yahoos. Marines are running and literally yelling and screaming and laughing. As we walk in a column, one behind the other the news quickly passes down to us. "*WE'RE GOING HOME.WE'RE GOING HOME.......WE'RE GOING HOME !!*"

The 27th Marines are leaving Vietnam in 3 days and going to playful Okinawa. From there, leave will be granted and men can actually go home. By the time we reach the tent area it's chow time but very few are hungry because of the excitement. Men start writing letters home and popping beers and playing loud rock n' roll music and singing the song, We Gotta Get Out of This Place. By 7pm half the compound is drunk, but me, Rob, Lil Man, Hernandez and Harper aren't happy like the others because we're not leaving Vietnam with the 27th Marines. We just got here.

They did theirs. We got ours to do.

We're all transferred to the 4th Marines, up north in Quang Tri Province. On the day the 27th Marines left Vietnam, my crew boards a C-130 and left Da Nang. After landing we board a convoy which takes us further north to a large firebase called Vandergrift, also known as LZ Studd. I'm assigned to Bravo 1/4 and both Robs are assigned to Delta 1/4. As soon as I report to Bravo I learn that Mickey's unit, the 9th Marines, are right across the road from ours. I shoulder my M-16, go across the road and ask for Charlie company. I walk over to Charlie Co. and ask for 3rd platoon. They tell me that 3rd platoon is over at Camp Carroll. I find out where Camp Carroll is, go down to the main gate, hitch a ride on a jeep, go A.W.O.L. overnight and find Mickey. I haven't seen him in 5 months and I surprise him when I locate his outpost. We grab and hug each other and laugh and he calls me by my nickname, Buck. He begins to tell me about the horrendous firefights they met in the Ashau Valley, and we eat C-rations and smoke reefer until midnight, and I stand watch with him in his foxhole. I report back to Bravo the next day and almost get written up for going away without permission, and the platoon Sgt. thinks I lost my mind, being new and traveling alone in hostile, unfamiliar territory. I'm becoming comfortable roaming in Vietnam and will travel alone and unauthorized many times.

My first squad leader is a Jewish kid from Brooklyn named Marty D'Giff, and I nickname him D'Giff-D'Jew. We become buddies instantly. One day a marine from down south calls him a Jew bastard and Marty beats him with a shovel so bad that he has to be hospitalized. He's already been in several battles and recently lost his best friend, Alejandro Diaz from Brooklyn, when they were ambushed. Marty told Alejandro to keep down but he didn't listen, and was killed by a sniper. Marty didn't just lose Alejandro on that horrific day, but Bravo Company, 1st Battalion, 4th Marines lost 25 men, Officers, NCOs, and Enlisted.

Marty D'Giff from Sheepshead Bay Brooklyn at Yankee Station, after the
death of Alejandro Diaz from Brooklyn, and 24 men from Bravo, 1/4.
Vietnam. May 24th, 1968

Williams is also transferred up north with the 4th Marines,
and goes to Charlie Company. I run into Williams at LZ Studd a
few weeks after we arrive and he tells me that brother Pope,
who sang in the foxholes with us in Bravo 1/27 and imitated

Otis Redding when he sang Amen, was killed on his last day in Vietnam, on a chopper that got shot down while transporting him to the rear, on his way home.

I learn to play Bid Whist in Vietnam from a brother named Allen Bonds from Chicago who calls himself "A-B from Chi", and he has a bunker on Vandergrift Combat Base (aka VCB, aka LZ Studd) with a reel-to-reel tape in it with Nancy Wilson singing Let's Go Where The Grass is Greener and West Coast Blues. We play cards with brother Howell and brother Lemon in the tents at Vandergrift and I become friends with Johnny Long from Jersey City who names me G-Man, Fee from Jersey City, T. Lee from Jersey City, Robinson from D.C., Holland from Delaware, Spivey from Houston, Slim from Brooklyn, Murphy from Alabama and Elwardo Roach who sings, "Who's makin' love to your old lady while you out fightin the war", from Georgia.

There's always a singing group wherever I am, going back to Dad and his friends on Willoughby, back to my boys in high school, and now here in Vietnam. We sing all the popular soul tunes of the day in 4 and 5-part harmony, taking turns singing the lead. Guys come and go. Either their tour is over or they get killed or wounded or arrested.

We patrol the mountainous areas in northern I Corps near the DMZ's western region bordering Laos, and we live in triple-canopy tropical jungles through the Monsoons, and sometimes go hungry and thirsty for days. I share a tent with Brother Robinson who is badly wounded one morning as we're abandoning our positions, and a hand grenade falls into the foxhole where he's burning trash and explodes in his face. The explosion rocks the area and I grab my rifle and jump in a foxhole, then I hear painful screaming and voices of marines scrambling over to the area of the explosion, then they start calling my name.

"G-Man, G-Man, it's Robinson, c'mon."

As I get close to where I left Rob I see him flat on his back, his face covered with blood and tears. The corpsman is wiping blood and calmly trying to calm Rob's contortions, begging for him to keep still. Rob and I were drinking coffee and watching the trash burn in the foxhole that we shared and I had just walked away from it. Now, Rob's face, shoulders and chest are imbedded with hot pieces of metal and he's delirious.

"G-Man, I can't move. It hurts. I'm burnin up G-Man!"

The Doc tells me, "G-Man try to keep him calm. The chopper's coming." Rob's face is torn up and his nostrils are split open. I keep my composure and assure him, "Rob listen, you gon be alright. You ain't gon die. You goin' home. You goin' back to the world. Take it easy Bro, the chopper's coming. I'm right here." I can only see the pain on his face. He's crying hard. I talk to Rob softly, holding back my emotion. I'm hurt by his pain too.

"It hurts G-Man, why they wanna do this to me? What's takin 'em so long? Tell 'em to hurry up, G-Man! Why this happen to me?"

The chopper sits down about 30 yards from us and a corpsman runs out with a stretcher. As we lift Rob onto it he yells out in pain and I hold both his hands as they lift the stretcher and run it towards the bird. The last words he says to me are, "I love you G-Man, call me when you git home. Hurry up and git me on this goddamn chopper. What took y'all so fuckin long Goddammit?" It hadn't taken them long. They were here in minutes. Rob's going home.

The next morning we're lifted back to L.Z. Studd. Once we settle in, clean up and chow down, word gets around that some sure nuff partying is gonna happen in the "alley". Johnny Long, T. Lee and I had made a run to Cam Lo Ville where we talked with the kids and I talked with a girl named Lana, and flirted with her and held her hands. We bought reefer from the kids and played a few hands of black jack with them, and I sang Love Potion # 9 for them. We get back to Studd just before dark.

"Yo brother G-Man, what's goin on?" It's Holland from Wilmington, Delaware, a dark, tall, good looking brother with a low-profile character and an alto voice. Holland melted into the group one day back in the bush when he heard us singing, and added his welcomed, versatile range to our harmony.

"Yo Holland, where's the party tonight?"

"It's over in the alley."

"The alley?" I laughed. "What damn alley"? I looked quickly around. "Ain't no fuckin alleys over here man"! Holland laughed. "It's a clearing back behind those bushes over there, G. Everybody's gon meet over there."

Back at the tent area we're planning our rendezvous under A.B.'s direction.

"So look. Dontchall be bunchin up, comin in the alley in no big crowd. Be cool. Come over 2 or 3 at a time. And don't be lettin everybody see you comin in there either. This is for the brothers. It's OUR motha fuckin hideout. We don't want nobody else stickin they head in there. You never know who the *MAN* is!"

The alley is truly unique. After we disappear through some tall bush we follow a narrow, winding path with tall 7 ft. grass on both sides of it. After about 25 yards it opens up to a round clearing. Once there, cases of beer are piled up and peppermint joints are being lit. There's a mint oil that we put on the reefer and it turns the joints into menthol and makes them smell like peppermint. We buy it from the kids who sell reefer. "Wow man, who found this place?"

"Don't worry 'bout it. Let's just hit some harmony. Pass me one o'them beers." Bonds is the boss of all the brothers now, cause he's going home in about 35 days. He feels and acts like a grandfather as he leads us and chooses what we should do. He's bossing everybody around, but we all love him. We truly feel like we have a special place in this alley, where we sit on mounds of dirt while the tall grass and winding path conceals and distances us from outside observers. This is a real pow pow, and is giving me a chance to survey everyone around me, a whole crowd of brothers from Bravo 1/4. As I look around, I know all by name. A.B., Johnny Long, T. Lee, Fee, Holland, Slim , Boyd, Murphy, Jackson, Lee, Roach, Larry Jones, Milton Brown, Darnell, Spates, Rogers, Swilly, and another brother we just call Rock Ape, to his disliking.

Rock Ape, Lt. Ludlum, Sgt. Hill - L.Z. Studd, Vietnam April, 1969

Bonds looks around and signals for the group, as he leads us into My baby Loves Me, by Martha and the Vandellas.

We stay in the alley until after dark when a single gunshot is heard. It's not unusual to hear the big artillery guns, the mortars or the ontos tanks on the lines doing their fire missions, but a single gunshot automatically attracts attention.

"YO, YO, HOLD IT, WHAT WAS THAT?"

There's a white guy in 4th platoon from Texas who's an M-60 machine gunner like me and goes by the name of Shorty. He stands about 5 ft. He has eyes that look a little Mongoloid and if he were Puerto Rican he'd be called Chino. But he's a good 'ol boy from out west and we always acknowledge each other when we pass, and sometimes talk because we're both gunners. The shot we heard in the alley had come from Shorty's bunker. They said he got drunk and was playing Russian Roulette. He'd shot himself in the head with his .45 pistol. All machine gunners carry .45s, but how can you play Russian Roulette with a .45? We never find out. But sadly, if one wants to play the game one will find a way. Shorty is dead now and didn't mean it. He probably thought the round was all the way down in the magazine, not close enough to the chamber at all. I know that for a split-fraction of a second when the gun went off he was immediately sorry but also quickly slipped into oblivion. If there's consciousness after death I know he's crying about the silly accident. He didn't mean it. He always smiled and seemed like he had lots to look forward to. His face is etched in my mind.

I lay back on my cot and dream of home. We'd been out in the bush for 25 days and uncovered 51 tons of enemy rice, 355 lbs. of salt, 15,000 rounds of small-arms ammo, 2500 mortar rounds, recoilless rifles and rocket ammo, 48 anti-personnel mines, destroyed 340 bunkers and killed 25 NVA. I'm a bonafide M-60 man now, and carry the huge machine gun over my right shoulder with belts of 7.62 ammo strapped criss-cross over my body and a .45 automatic pistol in a shoulder holster. The very next day we're lifted by chopper back to LZ Cates.

Cpls. Hazelton and Dyson LZ Cates, November 1968

Courtesy Lt. Victor Ludlum

"CATES ? WHO ? NOT ME! I AIN'T GOIN! UM SHORT! I AIN'T GOT BUT 11 DAYS. UM GON TO TALK TO THE SKIPPER."!

It's A.B.

Bonds is hopping mad early in the morning as he heads over to Captain Pierrepont, whom we call Captain "Peterpan". The skipper steps outside, peers at Bonds and listens, shifting his weight from one foot to the other, hands on his hips, glancing alternately down at the ground. We watch the scene from our tent as we pack our gear. Bonds faces Peterpan, gesturing with his hands and pointing his finger to his own chest, indicating himself. He's making a desperate plea to remain here at Studd for his last 11 days and not have to expose himself to the enemy in the bush. He wants to stay here and plan his re-entry into the world, bullshit with the brothers in the rear, play his tape recorder, some bid whist, get his hair trimmed real nice, buy some souvenirs and reflect on his survival of this past 12months of jungle combat. Bonds has been through the Tet Offensive of 68. Now he's walking towards us from his meeting with the Skipper, who denied his request. He has tears welling up in his eyes and his fists are balls of power.

"I could kill dat motha fucka, I swear. What the fuck is wrong wid him? Just cause Um a black man! They don't need me out in no field. Um Short! They gotta whole fuckin' company here. He just FUCKIN' wid me das all. MOVE! Y'ALL GIT OUTTA MY WAY. GODDAMMIT, UM SICK O' DIS SHIT!"

No sooner than we land at LZ Cates and settle in, the rain begins to pour. It rains all day, all night, all the next day, all the next night and into the next day. Thanksgiving is approaching and near the end of this 4-day rain on Thanksgiving morning the banging of white Murphy's M-60 wakes me out of my sleep and I jump into the foxhole. An NVA, apparently on a suicide mission had crossed the wire and was heading toward his foxhole and he opened fire and killed him. For the rest of that day Murphy lay in his bunker holding his stomach. Bonds is more irritable and nervous than ever. Rain that began falling on November 22nd finally ends late on the evening of November 25th. It brings cold, bone-penetrating air that makes us stay close to the bunkers, carefully guarding our gear from the wetness. When the rain does stop that night the jungle around Cates comes alive with the chatter of insects. A thousand, minute voices screech simultaneously.

Lt Ludlum shaving at LZ Cates, November '68

Bonds has sunken into a sullen, withdrawn, resentful state. I'm now living with Holland, Spivey, and Slim. Spivey's from Houston and is dark and overweight and loves singing songs by the Temptations and is proud of Archie Bell and the Drells from Houston. He's jumpy and afraid of all kinds of bugs, and will run like a child from a spider or a beetle. Bumble bees and centipedes terrify him, so this jungle experience is totally stupid as far as he is concerned. Spivey doesn't mind letting it be known that he's fearful of everything. He's a big, black scare-dy cat. In the hooch we sleep 3 across when conditions permit, with Spivey and me on the ends and Holland in the middle. Holland is skinny with long, lanky legs and particularly bony knees and joints that jut out at hard angles.

"Holland! Holland! Man, wake up and gitcho bony-ass elbows outta my side man. Damn. I can't even sleep G-Man. You ever lay next to this skinny niggah?"

"Yo man, dontcho be callin me no nigger."

"But G-Man. Every time I try to fall asleep Holland got his elbows in my side." Spivey, whose nickname is Tick, looks at Holland with a crazy, incredulous expression.

"Don't be looking at me wid that screwed up face Spivey, just move yo' big ass over das all."

"And you keep dem goddamn razor-blade-ass elbows out my side. G-Man, dis motha fucka got elbows like razor blades. Dat motha fucka can kill somebody wid dem shits!"

I look at both of them and laugh. "Yo, y'all remind me of Laurel and Hardy."

Tick, Holland and I split a nine-hour watch, sitting in the muddy foxhole 3 hours each, watching the 9 foot-high fog. The moon overhead is brilliant against the black sky and you can almost hear the stars move. "Damn, what a sight."

I sleep late the following morning and get awakened by Bond's calling. I open my eyes and Bond's head is looking in the bunker hatchway, with the blue sky and the whip-cream clouds hanging over Khe Sahn behind him. He's nervous, stuttering and jumpy, and holding himself like he has to pee.

"What's wrong Bonds?" I ask.

"G-Man - Holland - G-Man. UM GOIN HOME! UM GOIN' HOME! LAWDY, LAWDY, UM GOIN HOME!"

Bonds runs off, up near the CP, towards his hooch. I run behind him to share in his thrill. He's falling down, tripping, crying and can hardly talk. He's bumping his head on the bunker hatchway, grabbing for his gear, tripping over untied boot laces. He doesn't know what to do, pack his gear or say bye to everybody. We begin to hear the blades of the Ch-46 re-supply choppers slapping the sky in the distance. Now he's crying like a baby. "Ooooooh, Oooooh, Oooooh!" My own heart starts beating for Bonds as Johnny Long and I watch this madman, while feeling awkwardly sorry for ourselves, staying behind.

"Damn Bonds, you better be careful before you break yo' damn leg." Long says. The same chopper that's taking Bonds out is bringing in a pallet of c-rations and mail and when Bonds gets on, he's still crying with both arms full of gear that he just gathered up and ran with. He gets on and sits down like a little kid with an arm full of school books, crying on his first day of school. The tailgate closes, the chopper lifts up and off, and I never see him again.

LZ Cates - Courtesy Lt. Victor Ludlum

I get a letter from home saying that Ronnie is out of jail and free. I write Ronnie and he writes me back telling me that he got out of jail by using some Voodoo powder. Somehow, he got hold of this white powder from somebody in Savannah with the instructions, "Spread it all over your arms and face before you go in front of the Judge and he'll set you free." The authorities had caught up with Willie somewhere in Connecticut, who'd hit the man with the rusty-nailed 2x4 back in Motta's parking lot in Bridgeton. Ronnie had been held since August, 1967. As I finish his letter I'm reminded of a poem we learned back in Mr. Fletcher's English class, in 8th grade.

I remember I remember The cell where I was kept.

The little window where the sun came peeping where I slept.

It never came a wink too soon, nor brought too long a day.

I needed light to dig a hole and make my getaway.

I remember I remember how Lefty, Moe and Dave

would bring the picks and shovels, and quietly we'd slave.

They stole them from the tool room, and we tunneled nenth the floor.

We dug from 1946 to 1954.

I remember I remember how we'd planned that wondrous day

when we'd come up outside the streets and make our getaway.

But through all of those hardships, our spirits were not downed.

But when we hit that water pipe we very near got drowned.

I remember I remember the Warden's anxious call,

to find out why all that water was running down the hall.

He called me to his office and I stood there straight and brave,

and blamed the whole big bungle, on Lefty, Moe and Dave.

We fly in choppers and land in elephant grass which slices our arms and hands and the salty sweat from our bodies burns into our cuts. We cross rivers with our weapons held above our heads. We encounter tigers, wild boars, elephants, poisonous snakes, leeches, gangrene, malaria and rock apes in the jungles. Somebody said that a marine in Alpha company fell asleep in his foxhole and a rock ape sneaked up on him, punched him in the face and ran down the hill. We have to take Malaria pills and salt tablets daily, issued by one of our Navy Corpsmen, who makes his rounds around the perimeter daily, keeping us in good general health.

Doc Heiser, LZ Cates, Nov. 68 getting a Christmas package from home.
Courtesy, Lt. Victor Ludlum

We patrol, dig holes and camp in areas that are saturated with Agent Orange. I carry my M-60 machine gun by its' port bi-pod and my right hand begins to itch between my thumb and fore finger. We sleep in two-man shelters on the sides of hills and can smell the enemy late at night. I feel wild and free here in Vietnam. I do want to go home badly but this adventure is unforgettable and awesome and as raw as can be.

One day I spend 5 hours cooking do-do in a big pot because I'm on shit-burner detail. The lowest job on a fire base is "burning shitters". If you burn shitters often enough you get labeled a "shit bird". I'm burning shitters because Captain Frye, our new company commander, thinks I need to be more disciplined. He thinks I'm a hippy or something. When burning shitters you approach the rear of the outhouse and open the door. You pull out the half barrel that's filled with waste and you drag it to an area that's clear enough to burn. You saturate the waste-filled barrel with diesel fuel and light it. But that's not the end. You have to stand there and watch it. But that's not all. You have to actually stir it occasionally to make sure all the contents are getting burned and not sticking to the barrel and it takes hours. When you burn shitters you wear a jungle-green handkerchief over your nose and mouth for a mask to filter out some of the fumes. Johnny Long and Slim pass me a couple of times during the day and say, "Who is that masked man?" "I dunno, it looks like the Lone Shit Burner to me!" So you're standing there with a long stick, stirring a pot of do do, and the smell of the diesel fuel combined with the smell of the pot is uniquely di-*stinct.* And you're not finished until everything in the pot has burned to ashes. Then you bury the ashes. So on a fire base you have shitters and pissers. The pissers are usually made out of empty 105mm artillery-round tubes that you stick in the ground with about 2 1/2 feet sticking up and the top's covered with a screen wired around it and you piss into that.

One day I take a piece of bamboo about a foot long, and using some C-4 and a rifle-cleaning rod, I burn holes into it at 1-inch intervals and carve out a mouth piece and a vent hole underneath where you place your thumb, and I make a flute. I attach some string to it and wear it around my neck. Captain Frye sees this and says I'm out of uniform and tells me to take it off. That's when he starts looking at me. That's probably why I'm burning shitters.

I stand 200 feet from a CH-53 helicopter that takes a hard landing at LZ Studd and explodes on the landing pad. I feel the heat of the explosion on my face.

We can see rain coming across a valley like a closing curtain.

We regularly burn leeches off our bodies with cigarettes or salt.

One day in the middle of a company patrol, Gunny Greek gets a leech on the head of his dick.

"Mary, Mother of Jesus will you look at dis shit? Here I am in the middle of the jungle on the other side of the fuckin planet pourin' salt on my dick!"

Major "Peterpan" and Gunny Greek, LZ Cates, November, 1968 Courtesy Lt. Vic Ludlum

I see a new insect each day that I'm in the jungle that I'd never seen before. Every single day in the jungle I say, "What the fuck is that ?" The flies in the tropical rain-forest jungle are extra bold and aren't used to humans and if one lands on a piece of canned pound cake it won't move, even if you pick the cake up and take a bite out of it. Once we're so hungry we eat dog food that was left with us when the Dog Handler scout assigned to our platoon got killed in the middle of the day, on a patrol on a finger of land stretching out from Firebase Argonne. His partner was a marine corps German Shepherd, and when they left on patrol his dog eagerly walked ahead of him as trained. 20 minutes into the patrol we hear automatic fire and learn that he was killed by an NVA who had a machine-gun nest in a tree and opened fire on the patrol but killing only the dog handler. They finally bring his body back to the compound, carrying him in a makeshift stretcher of plastic poncho liner attached to a long tree branch. When they return with his body it's about 3pm and the poor dead scout stays with us until about 4pm the next day and when night fell, we could smell his decomposing body already, in a breeze floating around the perimeter.

One Monsoon day we're wet and hungry and are about to cross paths with Delta 1/4, Rob Zurita's company, and I wait hopefully for Rob to come up the hill in the line of men. I finally see his exhausted body emerge from the thorns and banana trees and I greet him and I ask if he has any chow and I cry as he gives me 4 cans of c-rations which I share with Holland and Slim.

Artillery routinely soars over our heads and we blow up acres of trees with explosives to build firebases.

We see the North Vietnamese through binoculars using elephants to carry artillery cannons, and buy reefer in Cam Lo Ville and along the Cua Viet River from 8 year old kids with cigarettes dangling from the corners of their mouths saying, "Hey Soul Brother, Me got number-one marijuana, don't buy from him, him marijuana number ten."

I've been in the Marine Corps 18 months now and have been with 7 different outfits, always leaving friends behind that I never see again. I've seen none of the guys from boot camp since we were separated in the winter of 1968. We all went to different units and some of us didn't come to Vietnam.

My boot camp buddy, Robert Wanke of Echo 2/1 February, 1969

(2nd kid from left smoking)

We spend Thanksgiving, 1968 on LZ Cates, that overlooks the red airstrip runway of Khe Sahn. When you wake up in the morning on Cates you can't see the land below because it's covered with clouds. You're above the clouds. It's like being in a plane. We swim in the South China Sea during Christmas of 1968. I have never been so hot, miserably cold, pushed, scared, drenched, hungry, angry and hurt. Yet there is joy, laughter, celebration, brotherhood and hope.

X
R&R

One hot morning in early March, '69 I'm sitting in the mud on the banks of a stream at the foot of Dong Ha Mountain, on a squad-sized patrol, exhausted, when word comes over the radio that R&R quotas are in. Thirty-six hours later I'm dancing to Stay in my Corner by The Dells with a 17 year old girl in a bar called the Blue Note in Yokohama, Japan. On the flight to Tokyo I'm sitting between two black Marines I don't know, from other units in Vietnam and by the time we land in Tokyo we're friends. When we land it's snowing and freezing and the first thing we have to do is buy overcoats at the P.X. We take a Taxi to Yokohama and meet three girls and stay with them for 8 days in the same hotel. My girl is the youngest and the prettiest. One of the guys has a girl who looks 35. We awake the next morning in a Japanese-style hotel called the Hotel Ka Sen. It's snowing outside, the TV is on, and we're watching The Beverly Hillbillies in Japanese. It's the first time I ever spent the night with a girl. It's the first time I ever slept in bed with a girl. It's the first time I ever fell asleep with a girl. It's the first time I ever stayed in a hotel.

When you enter the lobby of the hotel you have to leave your shoes In little cubby holes and put on slippers. After checking in at the desk and going up to your room, you have to leave the slippers outside in the hall before going in. I'm with a very pretty Japanese girl named Kikuko Mantani and her nickname is Yuka.

One night she gets a phone call and it's 2 AM and she's talking in Japanese and seems upset and starts crying and hangs up the phone, gets dressed, and tries to explain something, crying all the time. She walks down the steps and out the door as I watch her from the hall window, crying and leaving footsteps in the night snow. I go back up to my room, get in bed and fall asleep, and wake up later and she's there next to me sleeping. But I can't tell if it's her because I don't recognize her with her eyes closed. When she finally wakes up I see that it *is* her and I'm glad to see her. By the 8th day I run out of money to afford her and I spend the last two days in Yokohama walking around the city alone, and getting hissed at by passing construction trucks. One night I go by the Officer's Club and peek in the door and Yuka is there, sitting at a table dressed formally, with other girls and Naval officers in their dress uniforms. She catches my eye and somehow leaves the table and comes outside briefly and I hug and kiss her as the city lights glisten in her eyes and her makeup sparkles. But she has to go back in and it's the last time I see her. I spend $1200 in 10 days and leave Japan broke. The clothes I buy get stolen at the airport in Da Nang. I don't regret anything about R&R in Japan. We knew of many who returned from R&R and got killed in combat. It's the closest thing to going home, back to the world.

XI
Back to the bush

I return to Vietnam and roam the streets of Da Nang by myself for 4 days with no weapon, sleeping in the Marine Transient Barracks at night, sneaking meals in the mess hall, and mesmerized by the song Time of The Season by The Zombies. I'm finally questioned by the M.P.s and sent back up north to a write up.

When I get back to Quang Tri I look for the 9th marines, trying to find Mickey, and I'm told he'd been wounded in the head at an ammo-cache explosion, and is aboard the U.S.S. Repose Hospital Ship. Mickey had a "job" done on himself a couple of months earlier. He got drunk one night at LZ Studd and to avoid going out on operations, he paid a Marine to break his wrist with an e-tool once he fell asleep. He'd revealed his plan to me one night as we sat atop a bunker at LZ Studd, eating pound cake, pecan-cake roll and peaches, and smoking opium that he got from Cam Lo Ville. He swore that he was going to do it, but I never thought he'd go through with it.

"Yo - check this out. You ever had any of this shit?" Mickey's unwrapping a small tin-foil package which reveals something that looks like tar. "What is it?" I ask. "It's O.P. - Opium. I got it from this old mutha fucka in Cam Lo. The kids only sell reefer but if you want some of this shit you gotta talk to one of them old mutha fuckas." Mickey rolled the small piece of tar into a ball then put it in a small pipe, lit it and inhaled, blowing the smoke in my face. "Damn. That shit smell like perfume." I took a drag and inhaled. "It taste like perfume too." We smoked the opium but I didn't really feel any different. "Buck - All you gotta do is let somebody break your arm while you drunk man. That shit'll keep you out of the bush for about 6 weeks." "Sheeeit" I told him. "Fuck THAT!"

The next time I saw him he was sitting on top of an empty ammo box at LZ Studd with his wrist in a splint and bandaged, cigarette hanging from his lips, doing "The Horse", to Wes Montgomery's The Joker. Mickey's buddies in 1/9 have nicknamed him Bogey, because he looks like a black version of Humphrey Bogart and talks in the same tone that Bogart does, with his cigarette jumping between his lips.

There were Marines who'd injured themselves to avoid combat. One recommendation was to rub insect repellent on your testicles. Johnny Long took his K-Bar knife and slowly scraped away the skin on his wrist until raw flesh appeared and he let it get exposed to the tropical elements resulting in jungle rot. I think about Mickey's "job", and I can't imagine paying someone to break my wrist with the sharp edge of a shovel while I'm in a drunk sleep. I think it might give me a heart attack or cause permanent trauma. Now he's on the hospital ship in the South China Sea, probably on his way home.

Shortly after I resume operations with Bravo 1/4 our Battalion Commander, Col. George T. Sargent, who commanded our battalion back in boot camp and inspected my M-14 before graduation, is killed by a mortar attack on LZ Argonne. He had personally led a team in a heroic advance the day before, to secure the firebase. He's the commander of our battalion, a Full-Bird Colonel, a career marine, an officer and a gentleman, known by thousands in the Corps, an educated, middle-class, white American. And look at him now, dead, and I'm still here, me, an 18 year old private-first class from a cellar in Brooklyn, high school dropout who made a baby at 15, left home for the Marine Corps at 17, and slept in a bed with a girl overnight, for the first time in my life, a few weeks ago in Yokohama. I looked up to, admired and liked Colonel Sargent.

LtCol. G. T. Sargent
Battalion Commander

Colonel George T. Sargent, Commander 1st Bn., 4th Marines KIA Vietnam
March, 1969

PFC Edwin S. German on Dong Ha Mountain, March 1969

Finally after 42 days in the jungle we're lifted by chopper back to L.Z. Studd. As we walk from the LZ to the Bravo transient area we're haggard and covered with dry mud. Men have beards and our clothes are mere rags. We'd bathed in streams and rivers, using the same source for cooking and drinking and swimming. We all checked In as usual and by nightfall we're well fed and cleaned up. Holland, Slim, Darnell, Murphy and I stand around in a circle, smoking and talking. Johnny Long sits on the side on the ground drinking a beer and catching glimpses of the conversation, cutting in here and there. We were tired from the long stay in the bush and we're beginning to unwind.

"Hey G-Man, y'all gon sing tonight?" Long asks.

"Yeah man, you know we gon hit some harmony."

There's a couple of new brothers in the company. Anton Bush from Brooklyn, Larry Burch from South Carolina, and another brother from the Bronx who's showing us the latest dance in New York, and we all stand around laughing and learning to do The Funky Four Corners. Murphy learns it right away, and he's making all the dance faces.

"Hey G-man, when y'all gon sing man?" Johnny Longs asks again, looking from one face to the other for an answer.

"What? Oh yeah Long, we gon sing in a couple of minutes."

The Native Americans and the Chicanos are also nearby and a marine nicknamed Chief, because most native Americans here in the war are always called "Chief" and another tall Navajo named Teeth and their boys are laughing, reading letters and guzzling beer. Teeth doesn't laugh out loud, he only smiles broadly. He's big with big hands and big feet and walks almost like he's marching. This entire area, occupied by over a hundred of us, is active in the cool, night air and Right Guard deodorant is being sprayed to further disguise the reefer smell coming from the peppermint joints. Reefer, cigarettes, beer and laughter command the scene.

"Damn G-Man, I thought y'all was gon sing man. Damn. What the FUCK is wrong witchall man?"

"We ARE gonna sing man, in a couple of minutes, shit!"

"BUT I WANTCHALL TO SING NOW! I WANTCHALL TO SING NOW!" Johnny Longs starts breaking down and crying. "I WANTCHALL TO SING NOW, G-MAN, NOW! SING NOW!"

Slim and I take Long by the arms and lift him off the ground and talk him through his crying and finally calm him down. He can't even explain why he's so upset and what he's so upset about. He has no words, just wants us to sing. He feels so far away from home and there's been so much pain and hunger and thirst and sweat for the past 42 days. The group comes together and we open up with Since I Lost my Baby by the Temptations.

Johnny Long and Jose Santos, Camp Pendleton, Calif. 1968

Photo Courtesy Jose Santos

We sing for over 3 hours, through our whole repertoire and by 1 AM we're drunk and tired. Johnny Long applauds after each song and sits impatiently awaiting the next number. He needed to hear us sing bad. He's been affected by some pressure and doesn't seem himself. We had a big audience tonight and the Navajo, Chief and his boys enjoyed the impromptu concert as well. I'm talking to Holland who's sitting at the edge of the tent when I hear a high-pitched, unfamiliar voice from behind me. "Hey G-Man".

I turn around and it's Teeth. I'm hearing him speak for the first time but from his size I expected to hear a deep voice. He sits on the ground and leans against an ammo box.

"G-Man, I just wanted you to know that I really love when you guys get together and sing. It's so beautiful when you and Holland and Slim and Spivey sing just like The Temptations. And sometimes you sound like The Miracles. I just love it man, I could listen forever."

"Hey well, thanks man. I really appreciate that Teeth. We love to sing." When I finally crash on my cot I crash hard but I'm shaken awake by Johnny Long, talking urgently and rapidly.

"G-Man, G-Man. C'mere. Hurry up. Quick man. Check this shit out. C'mon!"

"What, man, what is it?"

"It's Teeth. Look!"

Teeth is sitting on the ground before a crowd of marines, including the Skipper, Captain Frye, who's shining a red-glow flashlight on Teeth's face. As I get closer and can see through the crowd to Teeth I recoil from the picture before me. An American Indian sitting cross-legged with an M-16 rifle pointed under his chin, his thumb on the trigger. All is quiet except for the Captain's voice and sniffling coming from Teeth, who is crying quietly. The Skipper makes certain that we all keep a safe, respectable distance.

"Teeth, listen to me. Tomorrow we're going to Cua Viet for some in-country R&R. You'll feel different then. I want you to take the rifle from under your chin, come into my hooch and talk. There's something I want to tell you."

We're gathered here the way spectators do at parades, trying to see past those in the front. Teeth's head is tilted back and he looks up at the Skipper, the tears rolling down his wide cheeks. His eyes seem to look through the crowd towards Chief, who looks helpless and stands right next to the Captain who's searching for words and means.

"Teeth, it's going to be OK. What you need to do is talk to someone, get some rest..... talk to me.....or whomever you want. Will you do it?" Teeth seems to consider. He looks up at the Skipper and says "Sir?"

I'm not looking at Teeth's thumb, positioned on the trigger of his rifle. My focus is on his desperate, fearful face and his shaking cheeks. We hit the ground at the blast of the rifle as its muzzle explodes under his chin knocking him backwards into a somersault, from the bullet that grotesquely tore his head open. Marines scream and cry and panic. Corpsmen immediately run to Teeth then instantly abandon their efforts seeing that he's dead. I run off, getting as far away as possible, breathing hard with the taste of iron in my mouth and I throw up hard. The shot rings in my ears, as well as the sight of his body falling backwards. Men are hollering OH SHIT! OH SHIT ! FUCK! FUCK! Teeth's friends cry out loud and order is a long time being restored as his body is eventually removed. He lay there bent in half with his head in a big, red puddle, oblivious to the pandemonium he created, unable to comfort anyone, bleeding on our rest area, waiting for us to move him, unaware of the churning in our hearts and stomachs, as if not caring, like an abandoned car waiting for a tow. He finally spoke to me, surprising me with his high-pitched voice. He'd smiled and mused momentarily over our singing in a drunken state as I listened.

Did Teeth, in his drunken desire for attention find himself on stage with an M-16 under his chin and a waiting audience that he'd called to theatre, now unable to disappoint them? Did he find himself in the final seconds unable to decide, then losing hold of reality and rationale until death finally sent its impulse to his thumb? Did it all start as a joke that got out of control? Did he know something about the other side? Did a spirit call him? Did he come here to die? Had he thought about this before tonight? Did he know he was leaving everything he knew? Did he think he might live? Wasn't he afraid of hell?

Holland, Slim, Murphy, Darnell and I lay 5 across with our "rubber lady" air mattresses positioned on the ocean. A good wave threatens about 150 yards behind us, as we curl our feet around the ends of our individual rafts, forming a surface for the coming wave to smack against, propelling us to shore about 15 miles per hour. The sun is hot and the cool, salt water foams on our skin and in our hair. The sky is 100% blue and after our drunken, tragic night at LZ Studd, we're now back at Cua Viet where the sunshine and salt air is medicine for my tense muscles as I cover myself within the cool, bubbling water and dig my toes into the fine, white sand. As the waves hit our mattresses we holler like cowboys, free from our gruesome weapons and heavy burdens. Temporarily free from hunger and thirst and grief. Some men just lay on cots under the rolled up tents with the comforting breeze of the giant gulf whipping therapeutically across their sleeping faces. Marines play naked in the South China Sea while bar-b-cue grills sizzle hundreds of steaks, and beer is everywhere. Johnny Long lingers on the shore with his boots still on and his trousers rolled up just under his knees, like a mother watching her children play on the beach. When we go back to the jungle, Long won't go with us.

Night has fallen and we listen to the radio, AFVN - Armed Forces Vietnam Network where they broadcast The Johnny Carson Show live, and later to the far away, static voice of Hanoi Hannah, who broadcasts propaganda radio from Hanoi and between her messages plays the latest soul, Latin and rock n' roll hits that we can't hear anywhere else. It's her way to get us to listen and hear her message:

"Hey black G.I. Hey Soul brudda. Why you over here? This is not your war! What you gonna do - you from Mississippi and Alabama - who can't go home and sit in a white restaurant for a hamburger while the U.S. Government kills people of color, the same as you? Don't be fooled about this. The big companies of the U.S. are profiting from your unnecessary death over here. Your war is back home, helping people struggling in discrimination and poverty. Turn away! Don't let your country kill you. Listen to the music."

The following morning as we get ready to hit the ocean with our rubber ladies Lieutenant Ludlum calls.

"G-Man, Holland, c'mon back. Second platoon saddle up, we're movin out."

"What? Damn. We just got here sir!"

"I know. I just got here too. Saddle up. We're movin out." He says with a smile and walks away. "Well what the hell is he grinnin about? Where we goin sir?" Slim asks.

"We're goin on patrol."

"Damn. We never git no damn rest. Man, Um sick of this shit. Um tired of these lifers. They just always gotta be doin somethin'. Can't leave nobody alone." Holland complains as we walk from the beach back to our tent and our gear. Harper, who has now made corporal, hears the word "Lifer" and starts singing his lifer song.

This train don't carry no lifers, this train.

This train don't carry no lifers, this train.

This train don't carry no lifers, no staff Sgts,. no six stripers.

This train don't carry no lifers, this train.

This train don't carry no Gunnys this train.

This train don't carry no Gunnys this train.

This train don't carry no Gunnys, cracks them jokes and thinks he's funny,

This train don't carry no Gunnys this train.

This train don't carry no mortars this train.

This train don't carry no mortars this train.

This train don't carry no mortars just sluts, prostitutes, and a few whores

but this train don't carry no mortars, this train.

"Aw shut up Harper, you a damn lifer too." Holland tells him.

Cpl. Harper, Lt. Ludlum, L/Cpl. Boyd - L.Z. Studd, Vietnam, April 1969

Courtesy Lt. Victor Ludlum

No trucks or choppers or amtracs carry us out of CuaViet. We came here by amphibious tractors but now we simply load our gear and walk off. We walk along the tree line, along the Cua Viet River Estuary until about 3pm, and on the way kids come from a little nearby village and stroll beside us asking for candy, gum, food and cigarettes or toilet paper, or sugar or instant coffee or cocoa, things that come in C-ration meals. We re-enter the open beach area along the South China Sea. It's a sunny, breezy area like a tiny gulf, and to our amazement there are fortified bunkers and foxholes in place.

"Alright 2nd platoon, settle in, this is it." Ludlum smiled.

"What? You mean we gon stay here?"

"As long as we can." Ludlum says.

"ALRIGHT!" We shout.

It's appropriately called Oceanview. It's like a private beach and there is really no threat of enemy here. Charles is not coming out of the ocean and we certainly didn't leave him behind us. It's beautiful. The water in this cove-like area is placid but the breeze is pure and comforting. The sand is so fine and white that is hurts my eyes in the bright sun. Security here will be like a vacation, an extension of Cua Viet, but more intimate. We drop our gear and shed our clothing, grab our rubber ladies and float on the still sea water, establish our positions and gladly settle in to this "good duty". By the 2nd day we're so relaxed we begin shaving and trimming each other's afros.

"Yo G-Man. I wantchoo to gimme a shape up." Slim says.

"Me too G-Man." Holland says.

"Oh yeah? And who's gonna shape up mine?" I ask. Slim says,

"Holland'll do it.......wid his razor-blade elbows."

Our squad corpsman is Doc Chang, who is a real curiosity whenever we're among the Vietnamese because he's Chinese, born and raised in New York and talks with a New York accent, and he's wearing his mustache and goatee Fu Manchu style. Now he's walking around here at Oceanview, completely naked.

Black Murphy from Alabama (because there's also White Murphy-both machine gunners like me) is kind of different. He's part of my machine-gun team but has a way of showing his affection for his fellow marines by winking and throwing kisses at us. He's effeminate and speaks kind of girlish in his deep, southern voice and calls me G-Man Baby and calls Holland Mo' Betta Baby, and he stutters a little. But he's part of the crew and we all just laugh this off. When he sees Doc Chang naked he says, "Uuuuuuum -Um! Ooooooo? Will you L L Look at dat man? Whas' wrong wid him G G-Man? He ain't even sh sh shame o' his tiny little wee wee. Oooooo? Embarassinnnnnn'?"

There are no patrols here at Oceanview and night watch is minimal. We have plenty of food and water and plenty of time to lounge and talk. "Sheeeit! Now this is what I call a good war." Says Harper.

XI
Mother's Day

Letters from Yolanda have become less sweet and more political and critical, as she joins in the popular anti-war movement, and she finally writes, "What are you *doing* there"?

The wonderful security we pulled at Oceanview is snatched from under us. On May 6th we're transported by amphibious tractors and trucks to LZ Studd, our forward staging area to begin an operation called Herkimer Mountain, in the northwest sector of the DMZ. At Studd we draw ammo and food then march to the LZ to be lifted to the remote Hill 304. But the weather socks us in and we don't get out until the next day because of the low, thick clouds. Johnny Long has gone to Quang Tri for medical observation. We have new guys with us now who just got in country two days ago and they're on their first operation. One is assigned to our squad. By now, Delta company is at Cua Viet and I bet Zurita and Saldana are having a good time, like we did.

The view of the jungle from above in a CH-46 Sea Knight chopper is still, green, non-threatening and smooth looking. But once we descend we're immediately overcome by the

treacherous density of the rain-forest jungle. The door
gunners on these birds are throwing bursts of .50 cal.
machine-gun fire as the pilots negotiate their approach to the
zone, and as they drop us off, our chopper never touches the
ground. Instead, it dips in the zone and opens the tailgate
while hovering about 8 feet above the ground, tilts backwards
and spills us out into the elephant grass. We tumble over our
gear and weapons as the big bird covers us with its fierce
wind, its blades slamming the air as it strains to haul ass out
of this notoriously hot area. As far as the chopper crew is
concerned, it's only a matter of seconds before they'd be shot
down.

"Damn. What the hell is wrong wid them? They didn't even
land, G-Man, shit. I coulda bust my ass comin outta there like
dat." Holland says. Helmets had flipped off and marines were
toppled on one another. We were literally emptied out of the
chopper like Cheerios from a cereal box or Good N' Plenty out
of a box into a hand. As the rest of the company lands we set
up perimeter and immediately begin patrolling the
surrounding area. Hill 304 is a relatively old outpost and had
been previously occupied by marines. Remnants of weather-
beaten c-ration cartons and burned out trash pits show that
some company had been here about a month ago. It's like
moving into and old, littered house.

Hill 304 May 9th, 1969. Me center. Cpl. Boyd from Brooklyn right of me.

Courtesy Lt. Victor Ludlum

We begin pulling platoon-sized patrols in the valleys below and the new guy assigned to our squad starts catching hell. This is his first patrol and he struggles with his heavy gear and the elements. His skin is pale with red blotches showing on his face and arms. He breathes hard and pants and struggles to keep up the pace, climbing the steep hills and losing footage several times on the oily, red clay of the jungle. He keeps dropping his rifle and then begins bruising his legs badly, falling down and cutting himself on sharp rocks and thick tree limbs. By the 2nd day of patrol he 's suffering from diarrhea.

We assist in every way we can, pulling him along and sharing his heavy gear, but it seems that he isn't willing to conform, and that he has hopes of getting out of the bush because he simply "can't hack it". He is also a burden to us.

The CP on Hill 304. Lt. Converse sitting left center, Captain Frye bottom right
May 9, 1969. Courtesy Lt. Victor Ludlum

"What the hell is wrong wid this fat boot man? He fuckin us up!" Slim says. It's true that his inability to keep up is delaying the patrol but we're not really driving at a fast pace, it's just that he's extraordinarily clumsy. Later on after we'd dug into the old positions at 304, Slim, Darnell, Murphy, Hallett and

Holland and I share adjacent foxholes. At about 2300 hours, the breeze brings the unmistakable, burnt smell of the enemy to our nostrils. "Aw shit. You smell that?" Holland whispers. "I sure do. Charles is passing by." When the enemy is nearby in this thick wilderness he smells like smoke because his clothes are saturated with it from living in the notorious underground bunkers where they also cook, and smoke also comes out when they ventilate the bunkers.

Sunday, May 10, 1969. Mother's Day. I think about Ma as I saddle up my gear for an all-day patrol. Family back home will be having a real good dinner. Ma will probably make a leg of lamb, potato salad, rice and gravy, collard greens and cornbread or biscuits, and candied yams too. Today is also a big day for me because I've finally hit the two-digit numbers. Today I have 99 days left in country and can officially call myself a Short Timer.

"Hey y'all ! It's 99 baby! Y'all know what that means? It means the G-Man is gettin short !! Look out New York, Um gettin ready to come in!"

"G-Man, you got your gun team ready?"

"Yes sir......Happy Mother's Day, sir." Lt. Ludlum looks at me puzzled. "Is is Mother's Day?" "It is." I say.

"Well Happy Mother's Day to you too G-Man." He grinned. "Now remember if we need the gun team the word is gonna be Buddy Up."

"I got it sir."

After a breakfast of cocoa and crackers with peanut butter and jelly I saddle up with ammo and water. Black Murphy will carry the M-60 and the new guy will be coming with us too. This will be a squad-sized patrol plus Lt. Ludlum and his radio man.

At 0800 hours we stand stretched out, on our steep descent into the valley, and as we pause momentarily I glance back at Murphy, my A-gunner, who winks, throws a kiss and says "Happy Mother's Day G-Man, baby", with a contrived, shy smile on his face. I tell him, "No, No! Happy Mother's Day to YO ass Murphy!" He laughs. Murphy doesn't mind being teased.

By 0830 we're patrolling the area of our first checkpoint and we find two .50 cal machine-gun positions with bunkers, empty ammo cans and some benches and tables. This stuff looks to be about two months old. The challenge of patrolling the highlands is that it takes 1/2 day just to travel 1,000 meters because of the hilly terrain. There's no way of getting around the hills, which are taking their toll on the new guy and he's again halting our progress. By 1500 hours the decision is being made about getting him out, because by now his legs are incapable of carrying him. They're beat up pretty bad and the jungle rot will require immediate medical attention. He's been shitting his pants for two days now and his loose bowels have given him a putrid smell and the edges of the sores on his legs are turning green. Whether he can walk or not is a question. When a man makes up his mind he can't walk anymore only he knows for sure. But we're in no position to carry him.

"Bravo, Bravo, this is Bravo 2 Papa, over".........

"Roger 2 this is Bravo, go"......

"Be advised we're gonna need a Michael Victor, over."

"Roger 2 lemmy raise Grasshopper, over"....

The 46 Sea Knight skillfully lowers into the small landing zone we've cleared, lets down a vertical stretcher, receives the ailing, new marine and is gone. It created much noise and wind and probably attracted attention to our position.

"Well if Charles didn't know where we are he sure does now." Lt. Ludlum says.

We lost time getting the new guy out and now we resume patrol with a specific determination to cover our remaining checkpoints and get back to 304 before nightfall. By 1630 hours we're traveling north through a draw, actually walking in the fresh-flowing water, over the slimy, moss-covered rocks that had tripped the new guy, causing him to drop his rifle in the water. We're spread out 10 meters apart from each other. The point man is Hallett from Pittsburgh. If you saw him out of uniform you wouldn't take him for a marine because he looks frail, wears thick eyeglasses, has red acne and his nose is always running. But he's a true grunt and walks point often and doesn't seem to mind it.

AUTOMATIC GUNFIRE RATTLES UP AHEAD AND I FALL TO THE GROUND HITTING THE WATER. MY HEAD QUICKLY TURNS BACK AND FORTH AND AROUND, LOOKING FOR SIGNS OF

AMBUSH. SCREAMS OF PAIN COME FROM THE FRONT OF THE
SQUAD AS LT. LUDLUM INSTANTLY CALLS FOR ME AND MY
GUN TEAM. "ALRIGHT LET'S GET THAT BUDDY UP HERE. LET'S
GO...BUDDY UP!"

"Murphy, Darnell, let's go!" I order. "This is it!"

We take up positions on the west side of the draw and I direct
machine-gun fire. "Murphy, hit that rock and let the fire
ricochet to the right." The stream curves sharply to the east
and Hallett and the 2nd man from point had been fired upon
with a burst of automatic weapon fire. They've both been hit
in the legs but manage to still walk. BAM ! BOOM. Grenades
are being tossed at us from the west, up the hill. We can see
no one. Our men are scrambling in the stream and on the
banks.

"LET'S TAKE TO HIGH GROUND" Ludlum orders. "SPREAD IT
OUT - LET'S GET ON LINE."

We begin an on-line assault moving west, up the hill, in the
direction the grenades are coming from. Then AK-47 rounds
come zipping past my head like tiny rockets. The unmistakable
Kak-Kak sound of the AK calls our attention further up the hill.
As I look to my right at Darnell, who lags about 5 meters
behind I see the sniper bullet rip away flesh from above his
right eye and he goes down.

"DARNELL!" I scream. "DAMMIT THEY GOT DARNELL,
DAMMIT." "WHERE?" Doc Chang calls. "Over there" I point.
But when I look to where Darnell had fallen he suddenly gets
up, standing straight up, staggering in a daze. "GET DOWN

MAN!" I scream at him. Thank God he's only been grazed by the bullet. "GRENADE!" I yell. The elusive NVA are raining Chicom grenades at us and even though we can't see them they're close by. They're so close that we can hear the spoons flying off the grenades as they are let go. "GRENADE!" I call out again. Then I hear something like a firecracker explode next to my thigh. It was a defective grenade that didn't completely explode. Only the blasting cap. We creep our way up the hill, taking ground a few feet at a time. Grenades and snipers are trying to pin us down and are frustrating our efforts to take the hill to safer, higher ground. Slim gets mad when his M-16 jams and he grabs Darnell's weapon. He forgets his cover and stands, doing what we call a John Wayne, firing into the thick bush. "YOU FUCKIN SON OF A BITCHES!" He screams while blasting his rifle. "GIT DOWN SLIM - GITCHO ASS DOWN, MAN!" I scream.

We keep our weapons on semi-automatic to conserve ammo and nobody panics. As soon as we got that first blast of automatic fire down in the draw we began working to repel the enemy, and Charles is keeping us too busy to hesitate or be afraid. We're working our way out of a U-shaped ambush. I lay on the ground looking all around and ahead of me. Up the hill about 11 o'clock I see a hand come out of a bush and toss something. "GRENADE"! We cover ourselves while it explodes and it sends shrapnel flying into Holland's shoulder. I immediately return fire into the bush where I saw the hand come out of, firing about ten rounds into it. We move up and when we pass the area where I'd seen the hand, there's nothing. They're working out of tunnels and underground bunkers and they're moving around right under our feet. We were ambushed about 5pm and it's now 5:45.

"GRENADE! GRENADE!" The flinging sound of the metal spoons from the grenades can still be heard and we're blindly returning fire in suspected directions. The chicom grenade explodes near me and a miniscule fragment of shrapnel the size of a needle rips into my left knee. Holland's wound stops him long enough for Doc Chang to bandage him but he's now wincing in pain and his movement is hampered. We keep taking higher ground for the next thirty minutes, moving a few feet at a time while artillery and air support are called in from LZ Stud and nearby firebases, along with Huey Gunships and F-4 Phantom jets are arriving over our heads, working in the draw where the ambush began. We come across a huge, fallen tree and have to step on top of it in order to climb over it. There's no other way to get around it and as I negotiate my footing to climb over the huge, ancient carcass I feel that something is about to happen but I can't stop it. I know it's coming but it's too late. As soon as I step on the log and am about to jump over it the AK-47 bullet smashes into the upper part of my flak jacket, hitting me in the back and entering a half inch to the left of my spine. The impact knocks my face down in the dirt. The bullet has gone straight through me and causes me to see blackness briefly and I let out a loud cry when hit and knocked down. The blood pours down my chest from my upper-left shoulder where it exited and I can smell my own flesh, hot and raw. I'm crying from the pain. But I know I'm not going to die, because it hurts too much.

"Who's hit. Who's hit?" Ludlum calls. "It's G-man!" Yells Doc Chang. "They got me pinned down G-Man, can you make it over here?" Snipers are firing at Doc and men are returning fire in the directions of the shots. I crawl over to Doc Chang who tends my wound as we find cover in the thick brush. "Damn G, they gotchoo pretty bad but I think you're gonna be OK. Um gonna fix you up with battle dressings and make a sling for you." I can't lower my left arm because the muscle in my shoulder has been torn apart. "Is he gonna be alright? Can he walk?" Ludlum asks. "Do you think you can walk G-Man?"

"Yeah, I can walk. We gotta get the fuck outta here man!" "That's the spirit". Says Doc. "Yeah he can walk".

As soon as the Doc finishes with me we climb another 45 minutes to a clearing near the top of the hill so we can clear an LZ and get the wounded out. My adrenaline flows and though I'm weakened I'm strengthened by our determination to get out of this place. We pause and I lean against a tree. "We're almost there G-man". Ludlum says quietly. He looks like he's sitting a little exposed and I tell the Lieutenant to move a little more into the bush and he takes my advice and moves to where he's covered better. "Thanks G-Man".

It 's taken 90 minutes from the time I was hit until we reach the top of this steep, endless hill. The valley below is vibrating with activity from artillery and bombs exploding from F-4s and rockets from Huey Gunships. Evening is descending and the sun is beginning to set. We've reached the top and men are busy chopping down brush. The radioman is talking with approaching aircraft and coordinating our position on the map. Soon we can hear the sound of 46s approaching.

"HERE THEY COME, LET'S GET THAT YELLOW SMOKE READY!"

A yellow smoke grenade is popped so the pilots can see us. The medevac chopper hovers bravely over us, a hundred feet in the air and lets down a metal cable with a vertical stretcher attached to it. The gunners are pumping .50 cal. rounds into the surrounding brush as the bird hangs perilously in the air, a perfect target for snipers. The cable descends and the stretcher is on hand for the most badly wounded first and that's me. My helmet and rifle are taken away along with my cartridge belt and my men strap me into the stretcher and hoist me into a standing position. They signal for the lift and I bid farewell from this remote, battered hill far up in the highlands. As I'm pulled into the sky, up into the waiting chopper a hundred feet above, I get a real view of the F-4s dropping bombs in the ravine. Then a final horror comes into my mind. "What if they shoot me now, on my way up?" I start praying. "Oh God, please don't let 'em shoot me now." I close my eyes and grit my teeth. "Please don't let 'em shoot me now." As I get higher into the air the stretcher starts spinning like a yo yo when it's just dangling on the end of the string. I try to see my friends below but they've disappeared in their camouflage, amongst the green vegetation. "Please don't let 'em shoot me now".

The growling propellers of the huge craft get closer and I look above me, into the giant belly of the 46 from its bottom, through a hole in its floor. The crew members receive me and the stretcher, pull me aboard then attach another one to the cable and send it down for the next wounded man. The door gunner, seeing the pain and shock on my face, gestures to me with two fingers on his lips, asking me if I want a cigarette. I do. He takes out a Benson & Hedges 100, lights it and hands it to me, then resumes firing into the valley below. He's clean and crisp with his neat haircut, clean shave, brown, spit-shined jump boots and starched uniform, a contrast to my mud-faded, bloody and ragged appearance.

The sling is let down 3 more times while the chopper hovers a harrowing 30 minutes. Finally, with Holland being the last to be pulled up, the deck hatch is secured and the big bird angles out of the battle zone. By now our men on the ground are in the pitch black of the jungle night waiting for reinforcements. They'd done their jobs well. We all did well today. The 14 of us fought for almost 2 hours and none of us got killed. My last visual image of the jungle and my men is when their poor, dirty faces and their camouflage uniforms dissolve into one. The Sea Knight finds its flight path and I catch a glimpse of the hot-orange sun slipping away slowly, over the mountains of Laos. I'm covered with blood, sweat and tears and I hope I can make it to Brooklyn.

XII
Repose

They take us off the chopper at Charlie Med on LZ Studd in the dark night and bring me into a dim medical bunker where I'm received by a corpsman and transferred to a cot.

"Doc, can you do me a favor?"

"Sure what is it?"

I reach into my right trouser pocket and pull out a plastic bag that has 4 joints in it. "Can you get rid of this for me?"

"Sure."

He sedates me and when I awake the next morning I'm at 3rd Med. Bn. in Quang Tri. and Johnny Long, Fee and Elwardo Roach are standing around my rack. They're smiling.

"How you doin brother G-Man?" Says Fee.

"Hey Fee.......Um in Quang Tri ?"

"Yeah brother, you goin back to the world". Johnny Long says.

"Hey Long, how you doin?" "Um doin OK G, but Um glad to see YOU doin alright. Damn. They tried to blow yo head off, G!"

"I know."

"I mean damn. Um tryin to get back to the world too but I don't wanna git shot doin it, you dig?"

"Yeah, I know". I say, feeling the soreness of the hole through my back and the dryness of my throat.

"Yeah well, the brothers in the rear said you ain't even had no business being out there. "

"YEAH I KNOW!" I say impatiently, not wanting to talk politics now. "It's over with".

My last days in country are spent in the South China Sea aboard the USS Repose hospital ship where General William Westmoreland awards me the Purple Heart on May 13.

My wounds are closed at the U.S. Naval Hospital on the island of Guam. When I arrive at Guam I'm wearing a full afro, because of being on operations in the jungle and not having access to the base barber. But being in the bush is also a handy excuse to wear an afro.

One day about a week after my surgery I'm walking outside on the base and a naval Captain stops me. "Marine?" He says. "Yes sir." I respond. "Aren't you out of uniform with your hair that long ? I want you to go over to the base barber and get a regulation haircut is that clear?" "Aye-Aye Sir". I say and salute the officer and he walks away. I say to myself, "Sheeeit! I ain't gettin no haircut. When I fall back in the world I'm gon be wearin an afro"! Two days later I run into the same officer.

"Marine? I thought I told you to get a regulation haircut."! I stumble for an answer and he says "Alright follow me"! He walks me into the barber shop and tells the barber, "Give this marine a boot- camp special." Then he looks at me and says "You had a chance to get a regulation haircut didn't you?" When I get in the chair the barber shaves my head completely bald. Not goin' home in an afro.

A week later I finally receive military orders with the destination New York. I left Vietnam barefoot, empty-handed and wounded on May 11th, and I'm getting ready to finally leave this dead-end Island of Guam and go back to the world and everything I love. After making stops in Tokyo, Anchorage, Alaska and Andrews Air Force Base I land in Brooklyn on June 1st, 1969 2:30 pm, at Floyd Bennett Field in Flatbush.

XIII
Back In The World

Hugh Masekela is playing Grazin in the Grass, Edwin Starr is singing 25 Miles From Home, Smokey Robinson with Baby Baby Don't Cry, Stevie Wonder's My Cherie Amor, Horace Silver and Psychedelic Sally, and Quincy Jones is Walking in Space. The Astronauts are heading for the moon, it's the Summer of '69, they're getting for Woodstock, and I'm home, happy, 19 and alive.

I catch up with Mickey at St. Albans Naval Hospital in Queens and we examine each other's wounds. There is a 1" indentation on the left side of his head where a fragment of skull is missing and the skin covering it is pulsating. He says they're going to put a metal plate there, later. We become temporarily stationed at St. Albans, where we pull guard duty at the Naval Hospital's main gate. The hospital is bustling with marine corps and naval personnel, young, wounded men just home from Vietnam, all from the New York area.

St. Albans Naval Hospital, Linden Blvd. Queens

When it's time to finally go home I have to literally "beg" Mickey to put on his uniform, so that we can walk down my block together, something I fantasized about so many times back in the jungle. We get off the JJ train at the Halsey Street Station, walk down to Putnam Avenue, turn right and walk up the block. It's a moment I dreamed of for a long time, on the other side of the world. It's Sunday afternoon, Ma's in the kitchen cooking dinner and Dad's laying on the couch with the TV on. When we walk in, the whole house cries, and Dad's hair is visibly greyer. I am immediately shocked because both my younger sisters are pregnant.

No one is interested in uniforms and medals except for the older people. Hurry up and grow your hair long so you can blend in. Do what everybody else is doing so you can fit in.

Home is a new world now for me. Hot summer, streets crowded, disoriented, disillusioned and disappointed. Sunshine and music everywhere. Girls galore. My sister Cathy has a crew of girls she hangs out with across the street at 1125 named Lucinda, Joyce, Karen and Ruth, and they all have afros with blond streaks dyed in their hair. Ma says they look like a bunch of welfare tigers. It's hot, almost summer, 1969 and as the 5 girls sit on the stoop in the late-afternoon sun, Ruth calls me over and says with her beer-wet lips, "C'mere, I wanna bend yo' johnson!"

Yolanda is about to graduate high school and says, "Eddie, if you *do* come to the graduation, *PLEASE* don't wear your uniform. " Our relationship since we'd met in High School had been limited to visiting at her house and making out in the living room, and we'd never gone "all the way" sexually. When I left Vietnam I left empty-handed. My photo album was left on Hill 304 near the DMZ, when I was extracted from the jungle on the medevac chopper. All the photos of the men I served with and the girls I met in Japan on R&R, all left behind. I'd sent some photos to Yolanda but she won't let me have them, only look at them when I come over. Back in the jungle I'd day dreamed and looked forward to passionately embracing and kissing her when I arrived home but when she came to see me at the Naval Hospital she showed up with her Mom. I naively offered to show her where I got shot but she immediately turned her head away and said "No, I don't want to see it". She'd been dating a guy named Joe while I was gone, and the war killed our relationship. I think about the song we sang back in boot camp, while running double time.

Ain't no need in looking down,

ain't no discharge on the ground.

Ain't no need in looking back,

Jodee's got your Cadillac.

Ain't no need in goin' home,

Jodee's got your girl and gone.

On the evening of my second day home Ronnie, me and Mickey, my sisters and a group of friends from across the street are heading down Broadway to the Chinese restaurant and as we approach Madison Street an unmarked police car speeds around the corner so close to us that we have to jump back to avoid being hit and the entire crowd of us lets out a yell and the cops back up, get out of their cars, and a black detective slaps Mickey on the side of his head with his pistol, firing the gun in the air simultaneously. The girls scream and Ronnie protests and yells back, "Hey man, he just got home from Vietnam!" The detective says, "I don't give a shit where he came from! You want some of this?" They jump back in their cars and speed down Madison Street towards Bushwick Ave. Mickey and I are in civilian clothes. Had we been in uniform the police definitely wouldn't have hit Mickey.

It's hard to be good Marines in 1969 because of everything that's going on. Back in Vietnam, the Black Power and Anti-War movements are simmering. The military culture is shattered because we're serving alongside Marines who'd been drafted, and also with those who'd been offered a choice of military service or a jail sentence. Our military service seems nothing to be proud of. Mickey doesn't want to talk about Vietnam, and begins drinking heavily.

Heroin is on the streets and stick-ups, burglaries, purse snatchings and muggings are keeping dealers, pawn brokers and fences busy day and night. There's a Puerto Rican fence on Cornelia Street named Darrio who will buy anything of value. Dope is carried around by street dealers in "bundles", bound by rubber bands, and using dope or cocaine is called "fucking around".......... "You fuck around?" You hear street dealers saying, "I got Dutch Schultz", and "I got Beverly Schneider". Addicts are stealing bottles of nose drops and baby pacifiers and rubber bands to make homemade hypodermic needles which they call "works" or "Gimmicks" or "Guns". Pretty young women are becoming junkies, selling their bodies and losing their teeth, their hands are swelling up like boxing gloves, and they're nodding on the subways with fish mouths. Marvin Gaye comes out with the album What's Goin' On? Mickey and I love the song What's Happening Brother and we bring Vietnam slang home and it spreads through Brooklyn. "It don't *mean* nothin" is Mickey's mantra, and Ronnie can't stand it and keeps hollering back, "It *DO* mean something!" A lot of something is "Boo-Coo", and girls are called "Hammers". Instead of saying "be cool" I bring home "be chilly", which was invented by Spivey from Houston back on Dong Ha Mountain. Back home from Vietnam is "Back in The World", and is confirmed by Curtis Mayfield, making it the title of his song for Vietnam Veterans. Boo-ga-Loo Jazz has entered the genre and Eddie Harris' Listen Here, Les McCann's Compared to What, and Charles Earland's More today than Yesterday are on the charts and in the jukeboxes. Quincy Jones has a big hit with the song Killer Joe.

Mickey and I are stationed at Marine Barracks at the Brooklyn Navy Yard and stand guard over the Admiral's yachts, and also guard at the main-gate checkpoint. The Marine Barracks are on the 4th floor on Flushing Avenue and Vanderbilt, and there's a naval brig (jail) on the 5th floor. All marines stationed there have been to Vietnam and are all from the New York area. Young marines are starting to use heroin, first sniffing, then skin popping, then mainlining.

There's a marine named Reiss from Bay Ridge who's a loan shark and who also sells LSD.

"I got acid - $5 a tab. Sunshine."

"What's acid?" I ask.

"LSD - You mean you never took a trip?"

"Nah". I say. He shows me a piece of paper with an orange spot on it.

"Just let it melt in your mouth, that's all". He says, as I hand him the $5.

It's Friday afternoon about 3:30 and as soon as I put the blotted paper in my mouth and it melts, the Gunnery Sgt., Sgt. Baldwin announces an inspection before liberty call. We're just about to go home for the weekend and now this damn inspection. We tighten up our areas, put on our uniforms. "This acid ain't shit. I don't feel nothin." About 30 minutes after the inspection announcement we're standing at attention in front of our racks and the Officer of the Day and the NCO in charge begin the inspection. The acid kicks in. I'm standing at attention. The black and white tiles on the deck begin shifting and waving and making noise. My palms are sweating. The lieutenant and the gunny are going down the line and when they stand before me their faces are melting in front of me and the veins in their foreheads are crawling like worms. I survive the inspection, change into civilian clothes and go downstairs to wait for the Flushing Ave. bus to take me to Broadway where I'll go upstairs and take the "J" train. When the bus stops in front of me it hisses like a giant snake and when I get on, it's rush hour and standing room only, and I'm standing in front of some elderly women and their faces and noses are melting and their veins are crawling and they look like witches and they're talking like kittens. I feel like I'm going to faint. When I finally get off and go upstairs for the "J" train the train pulls in to the station roaring like a monster and it stops and lets out a huge, loud breath and when I walk in the doors I feel like I'm being swallowed. When I finally get off at Halsey Street and walk back to Putnam everything is very loud and colorful and I can't taste or smell anything except that I feel like I have a mouth full of chestnuts. When I wave my hand before me I see five hands going across, like a film. All noise is amplified and it sounds like there are toilets flushing everywhere. When I get to the house Ronnie asks me what's the matter and I tell him that I just took LSD and he laughs and asks what does it feel like and I tell him that everything's melting into chestnuts and toilets, and he laughs real hard. After about 7 hours of this I get frightened and feel like I'm never going to come back and I tell Ronnie that I'm scared and we're down in the basement and the black and white tiles on the floor are still waving like the ocean and my mouth still tastes like chestnuts and there are toilets that have been flushing in my head for hours now. So Ronnie says, "let's get you something to eat." So we go down to this luncheonette on Broadway and order meatloaf and mashed potatoes but I can't taste anything and it feels like I'm putting the fork into someone else's mouth. I really start to get worried and Ronnie walks me back to the house. After surviving Vietnam, here I am, stuck on an LSD trip for life. Oh God. Please, no. Please. I finally fall asleep about 3Am and when I wake up the next day I'm glad to be back, sober and free and home from the war.

Mickey and I receive good news that we're getting discharged from the military 9 months early. I sign my discharge papers on February 17, 1970, and the next week at an employment agency, the Placement Counselor, a blond-haired woman about 30 looking through her Roll O' Dex keeps glancing at me from her desk and saying "Oh, you're just a baby"!

Hey baby, whatchoo know good ?

I'm just gettin back like you knew I would.

War is hell, when will it end?

When will people start gettin together again?

Are things gettin better like the newspaper said?

What else is new my friend, besides what I read?

Can't find no work, can't find no job, my friend

money is tighter than it's ever been.

Say man I just don't understand what's goin on across this land,

Hey....What's Happening Brother? - Marvin Gaye

The 3 biggest lessons learned from Vietnam were to never take simple things for granted, to never fight over petty issues, and that "If I can make it out of here alive, I can do anything." There'd be no more blood and death and nothing to argue about.

But Ronnie is shooting dope and arguing passionately about religion with Ma and tells her she's going to hell. Ronnie actually shoots dope while reading the Bible, trying to find Salvation but being daily harassed by The Devil who is trying to kill him. The dope makes him like Dr. Jekyll and Mr. Hyde. When he heads into the basement to get off, he's as nice as can be, actually friendly and good natured, even smiling although he's sick from his Jones. As soon as he finishes getting off he starts scratching and arguing with a fish mouth, with anyone nearby. Me, Don, Ma, Mickey, anyone he can find to confront. But not Dad, nobody argues with Dad except Ma.

Heroin makes us steal from our parents and puts guns in our hands and makes us sick and helpless and desperate and unable to function without it. Can't even eat or work. I can't believe that after all I went through I have a stupid, dope habit. I feel, for the first time in my life, that I'm a slave and I don't know how to get free. The daily need to satisfy this habit has trapped me, and I'm annoyed by it constantly.

A Puerto Rican boy from Woodbine Street shoots and kills a boy named Victor over a girl. Victor's cousin Danny, who lives across the street from us, retaliates and shoots the Puerto Rican boy dead and goes to jail.

Robby, Danny's younger brother, chases a boy named Lenny down towards Broadway and stabs him to death in front of J. Michaels furniture store while playing Ring O' Livio, and follows Danny to jail.

Danny's cousin Sidney is involved in a bank robbery and his picture is all over the subways.

One of our neighbors three houses down, a 15 year old boy named Jason, strangles his 13 year old sister Rachael to death with the telephone cord during an argument, and sits on the stoop of his house, waiting for the police to arrive.

The house where he killed his sister and waited for the cops on the stoop.

There's a fat woman across the street named Earline who's the fattest woman I've ever seen, and her upper arms are the size of my thighs, and she's always in the window looking up and down the street. On these hot summer days, Earline is a fixture on the block's landscape, her head, arms and shoulders filling up the entire wide-open window. One day she was hanging out the window and gesturing and talking to someone downstairs and got stuck. Her big body became wedged in the window frame and she couldn't pull herself back in the house. The fire department was called and they were only able to free her by removing the molding around the window. The entire block gathered to behold this bizarre spectacle, and kids pointed fingers and laughed openly, as six firemen wrestled with this huge, sweat-drenched woman, finally setting her free.

Earline's 2nd floor middle window on Putnam Avenue

XIV
The Hustle

Business at the Hotel is regular and paying well, but the record-keeping system is primitive and part-time workers are stealing money from Ma and Dad. Ronnie and I also work there occasionally, manning the desk overnight, changing sheets and sweeping up spent condoms in the rooms, and getting to know the local prostitutes, watching all the traffic and street activity below, the Italian men playing Bocci ball on 1st and 1st, limousines double parking in front of Russ & Daughters to buy delicacies, and double parked in front of Katz's buying takeout, and the "Junkie Policeman", an NYPD patrolman and a known heroin addict. He'd be seen going in an apartment on Orchard Street, then coming out later to resume his foot patrol with a fish-mouth, walking towards Delancey, rubbing his nose and scratching in uniform.

Russ and Daughters on East Houston Street

A local Puerto Rican man named Carmello from Eldridge Street starts working at the Hotel and keeps the hallways and rooms clean and prepares the laundry for pickup, shoots dope and calls me "Eddie Boy", and always says, "My name is Carmello Bonilla Cocholla and I'm a Five-Town Man." After months of saying this, he finally says one day, "You know what is a Five-Town Man, Eddie Boy?" My first answer to this question is a five-town man is from the five boroughs of New York but he reveals to me, "I'm a Five-Town man. I'm from Uptown, Downtown, Midtown, Crosstown..........and *Chinatown*, baby!"

Ronnie has a dope connection in Chinatown, and we walk over there one day and cop from a tall, buck-tooth, skinny Chinese guy who hangs around Chatham Square.

Carmello Bonilla Cochola, The Five-Town Man, at Clinton Correctional Facility, 1975.

Reverse of Photo from Clinton Corr. Fac., 1975

"The Sex Street Tail Market"

One of the regular prostitutes, a heavy-set white girl named
Carmen whose tricks are exclusively Chinese, begins to like me
and starts giving me money, and uses the Hotel to rest after
long, cold nights on the streets. She invites me into her room,
calls me Daddy, and says she needs for me to love her, and

we cuddle up on the bed but I don't have sex with her but she at least wants me to kiss her, so I barely do and she says, "Is that all?" , as she reached up to me from the bed. The poor, fat girl. She hands me $40.00 and I leave and head uptown to Harlem to get high with my cousin Count, who lives on 126th Street and Old Broadway. When I get off the train at 125th Street comedian Pigmeat Markham is standing in the middle of the block on St. Nicholas Avenue among a bunch of locals, playing single action and waiting for the numbers to come out.

"Hey Count, guess who I just saw? - Pigmeat Markham!"

"Shiiiit. Pigmeat always out there - every day. He just a nigga from roun' here, man. You know how I can tell I got some good dope? Cause when I git a hit it go straight to the bottom and make my asshole burn."

"Listen Bucky", says Count, a long-time hustler, pimp and dealer from uptown, as he cleans his "works" and squirts blood and water into a glass through the home-made syringe, nodding and talking with a fish mouth, about the girl who gave me the $40.

"When you git back downtown yunderstand, you got to pull up on her wid the soft mack you dig, she gon' be the base of yo stable, I mean, you can't cop no swag with *one* sway-back nag, yunderstand, it's time to git wid the long-shoe game you dig, be sweet and hard wid her yunderstand, git the swag, start off wid the easy muscle and stroke the thoroughbred yunderstand, let the sweet beat up on the sour you dig, she got to build up a bail pot first you dig, give her the hotel phone

number yunderstand, so you can fall in when she git popped
you dig, then she start to pull and draw, yunderstand, once
she start to pull and draw you cop the ride - I'd start off wid a
nice, black, 98 Olds you dig, when the knot git fat you slide up
to Leighton's and Phil Kronfeld's for the vines yunderstand,
then you can go wid the hog, you dig? I like a Fleetwood. All
the while, you take yo time, TCB, and lay on deep simmer,
yunderstand?" Butchoo need to knuckle down on this Phillie
right now Jiiiimmm, and she'll pull you a full stable of
thoroughbreds. Now gitcho ass back downtown."

Everybody uptown knows Count, who was born in Harlem in
1933. He always keeps his hallway door half open for cross
ventilation and to holler at the neighbors. Years later Count is
found dead by one of his neighbors, sitting in front of his
television in his armchair. Sort of the way Charlie Parker died.

It's 1971 and my cousins Larry and Cedric are deep into the
street hustle and have girls and product in Jamaica and
Brooklyn, and driving big cars. Cedric has a white, 1971 Coupe
De Ville and Larry has a 1971 aqua-blue, convertible Eldorado
with a "no smoking" sign on his dashboard, dressing in clothes
from Leighton's, listening to Bob Dylan and taking his whores
to lunch in the Russian Tea Room. Larry is 22 and Cedric is 23.

One day I'm standing at the bus stop waiting for the B44
Nostrand, on my way to see a girl named Jane who lives in
Sheepshead Bay, and a man pulls up in a 1971 Buick Electra
225 and the windows are down and there's jazz on the radio
and he asks me if I need a ride. I get in the car and Red
Garland is playing You Better Go Now. He drives me all the

way to Sheepshead Bay and says his name is Buster and asks if I'd be interested in a job at a men's clothing store uptown in Harlem. I begin working at Reid's Boss Vines, right next door to the Apollo, and every day after work I pass a man on 125th Street who's standing in the shadows hawking, and he says, "French Ticklers.....................Spanish Fly." Pimping, prostituting and selling drugs is big, and pimp's cars are conspicuous, with their white-wall tires, spoke rims, and license plates from Tennessee. It seems that most of the real pimping and hustling is headed by guys from the south. One such group sets up shop on the corner of Putnam and Broadway and they run their hotel just like Ma and Dad run theirs, but they also sell dope and run the bar on the ground floor, and they have a fleet of hopped up race cars. The head man of this hustling crew is named "Bubba Mack".

What used to be Bubba Mack's hotel, Putnam Ave. and Broadway

Mickey begins to be paranoid and thinks that everybody thinks he's crazy, especially because of the heavy combat and being wounded in the head. He goes over to Paragon Sporting Goods on 17th and Broadway in the City, purchases a crossbow, and begins shooting stray cats in the backyards of St. John's Place, from his apartment window. He comes over our house one Friday night and drinks until he pisses his pants. He loves when he and I sing together,

Permit me to introduce myself,

the name is Mr. Kicks,

and I dwell in a dark dominion,

way down by the river sticks.

The Devil has sent me here because I'm full of wicked tricks,

and I'm such a popular fellow, among all you lunatics.

Now I teach a course in ruination from the Devil's text,

To fools who can't withstand temptation,

Step right up you're next.

Now I hail from a hot old hell on down along the river sticks,

Allow me to introduce myself,

the name is Mr. Kicks. - Oscar Brown, Jr.

I meet a girl named Kathy from Queensbridge Projects who cutely and discreetly sniffs dope, and begin a relationship, then she allows her sister Brenda, who calls me "Daddy", to seduce me into a 3 month affair with her, then Kathy and I resume our relationship like nothing ever happened. I am immersed into the Age of Aquarius. Kathy is adorable, 18, a pure Redbone with a big, brown, soft afro and looks like Nikki Giovanni, and my mother likes her because whenever she comes over, if there are dishes in the sink, she automatically begins washing them and always has a pleasantness about her. When I visit her house she instantly offers me coffee, as soon as I walk in the door. But she can't be true to me and tells me she can't be what I want because of her "free nature". She gives me a tag name, "Equality 550", but never explains it to me. Kathy is a genuine Hippy, mysterious, and she writes on the wall of our psychedelically decorated basement,

"Eddie was clever,

and someone loved him forever."

Dope is getting the best of me and I don't know what to do. There's a drug program called the Rockefeller Program so I sign up for it but when it's time to report I never show up. Three weeks later I'm in the basement and I hear the door bell ring. Before I reach upstairs to answer the door Don is already telling someone that I'm not home so I yell at him. "How you know I'm not home, did you check? Move out the way"!

When I move him aside I see two detectives darkening the doorway, looking for me. They'd come to take me away, to keep my commitment to the Rockefeller Program and get off dope.

"Okay, can you just give me a couple of minutes? I just have to get something from upstairs."

My plan was to go up to the attic, exit through the roof door, go down the block by crossing over roofs, climb down a fire escape and make my way over to Broadway or some backyard and be gone. But Dad saved my life that day. He caught me on my way upstairs and said calmly, "Listen son, you do like I say and go with these people. They tryin to help you." I listened to my father and he saved my life. I was finally home from Vietnam. Six months later I was free of heroin.

My first cousin Tony from Bridgeton starts coming up to Brooklyn with his brother Michael and turns us on to Rudy Ray Moore and we smoke reefer and drink "Fightin Cock" and listen to and memorize epic stories about Dolomite, Pimping Sam, Shine and The Titanic, Hurricane Annie, San Antonio Rose, The Pool Shootin Monkey, and Petey Wheat Straw, The Devil's Son-In-law. We buy reefer from Liz and John on Hancock Street, and every time we go to Liz's house to get a nickel bag they're drinking beer, smoking reefer and cooking greens and neck bones. Tony is my closest cousin on my Mother's side and Tony and Michael come to New York every two weeks sometimes. They take the bus from Bridgeton to Port Authority, and spend a couple of hours in the peep shows on 42nd street before taking the subway to our house in

Brooklyn. When they head home they take the subway from Brooklyn to Port Authority and go back to the peep shows before getting back on the bus for Bridgeton. Tony digs jazz and is knowledgeable about music and knows how to harmonize, plus he's a rustic country man who knows all about the local wilderness in the pine barrens and he knows how to go in the woods and gather herbs for medicinal uses and how to recognize plants and trees and he knows how to hunt and fish and prepare wild game. He knows how to make wine and when to plant and harvest and he works in the land and is extremely observant and cautious. His Mother, my Aunt Evelyn, is my favorite Aunt. Aunt Evelyn says the funniest things about people. When Uncle Pete gets drunk and starts laughing she says he looks like "A mule eatin yellow jackets". While growing up in Bridgeton, Tony gathered lots of information and gossip from listening to grown folks talk, and said he listened to my aunts laughing about some man who likes to "hide his face in the bushes".

Way deep in the jungle far off in the sticks,

the Baboon runs a pool hall with all the slicks.

The Baboon is fast and very cool,

Why, he's so goddamn good he can't find anybody who can shoot him a game of pool.

But up drove the monkey from the coconut grove,

and you could tell he was a hustler from the cut of his clothes.

He wore some alligator shoes and some double-knit slacks,

a continental coat with a belt in the back.

He had a white-on-white tie and matching vest, a diamond stickpin in his mutha-fuckin chest.

He didn't have as much hair as you got on your ass,

but what little hair he did have, he had that gassed.

He drove up in a long Cadillac with gold handles on the doors,

In the back seat he had four, good -cock monkey whores.

He stepped out the car and said girls be cool,

while I go in here and shoot this ugly Baboon a game of pool. -

Rudy Ray Moore

"Dhot is an abomination, ya know,........... me and me wife walkin' down de street just now and a cat come rainin down from de roof! Dem shtupid boys just trow a cat from de roof 'mon, and it fall right in front of we and run down Broadway! Me wife so frighten and she pregnant ya know."

A man from Trinidad and his wife come running around the corner on Bushwick Avenue, sliding as they go, holding hands and gasping for breath as he explains that some boys threw a cat from the roof and it almost landed on them. "Well you gon' laugh now, T'aint funny! Me gwan fetch de police just now. Me know dem was aimin' for we. "Dhot is an abomination ya know." He takes his wife by the hand and continues down the street towards Madison. "Me woman so frighten - de baby mighten be born to look like cat!"

We're standing on the corner of Bushwick and Putnam, me and my friend "Dice", my bike-riding buddy, leaning on our bicycles and drinking a cold beer, after riding home across the Williamsburgh Bridge from Manhattan.

All we can do is grin to hide our laughter. The West Indian couple cross Madison towards Woodbine. My brother Don and his friends Harold, Reggie and Chucky appear from around the corner talking about, "What happened?" A taxi pulls over to the curb with Mickey inside. He pays the driver, hops out, lights a joint and passes it around, then reaches inside his jacket and pulls out a pint of Wild Irish Rose, takes a guzzle and says, "It's nice to be nice - Buck - my niggah - you my nigga if you don't git no bigger - and if you git any bigger you'll be my bigger niggah." He says to Don, "Whatchoo lookin at niggah?" He goes after Don and starts beating him up. I look over to Chucky who's peeping at me and preparing to defend himself. "Yo punk, you want some? C'mere." So Mickey and I are routinely beating up Don and Chucky. Harold, Reggie and Dice stand by laughing, Dice with his hand covering his mouth because he has no teeth left. Whenever we see Don and Chucky we beat them up. Mickey beats up Don and I beat up Chucky because Don and Chucky want to be like me and Mickey and if they're ever gonna try, we have to make sure they're tough enough to face this hard world with all these dumb motha fuckas walkin around out here. Harold lives across the street from us at 1125 Putnam and has the keys to the roof door so we know that they threw a cat off the four-story roof to see if it would just land on its' feet like folks say, and had been wanting to try it for a long time. But that wasn't good enough, because once they got on the roof with the cat they took it to the next level and said, "Let's wait till somebody walks by and aim it at 'em." The cat landed on its' feet, scared the shit out of those West Indians and ran down towards Broadway.

1125 Putnam Ave., where they threw the cat off the roof

Just throwing the cat off the roof wasn't good enough, like just throwing water balloons off the roof wasn't good enough when one Easter Sunday morning, Mrs. Murph's kids were all dressed up in their brand-new Easter clothing, tightly gathered on their small stoop waiting for their Mom to come downstairs and go to church. All the houses' roofs are connected so Don and Chucky go in the house and they get a large, plastic garbage bag and fill it up with water using the garden hose. They carry the garbage bag up two flights of stairs, then up the winding little stairwell into the attic, open the hatch to the roof then Chucky hops through the hatch onto the roof while Don struggles to pass the huge, cumbersome bag filled with water up to him. Once Don gets on the roof they both carry the bag down three houses, perilously lean over the edge, aim and drop the bag right into the middle of the Easter kids, and it splats onto the concrete steps, drenching them all. Ma whips Don with a belt, up and down the stairs.

Reggie, who lives down the block on our side of the street is light skinned, good looking with green eyes and freckles and gets all the Puerto Rican girls and wears long-hair beaver hats and Playboys. Guys from uptown say, "Every time we go down to 42nd Street you can tell them niggas from Brooklyn cause they got on them Beavers and Playboys." Reggie wears lizard shoes and Blye knits and is the first person we hear say "24/7". Don and Reggie and Chucky and Harold and Eric and Keith are always shooting C-Lo in the gutters, rolling the dice, gambling, playing hooky, smoking reefer and drinking wine, riding bikes and going to 42nd Street, and Don and his girlfriend Cindy are doing the hustle on the sidewalk while the Spinners are singing It's a Shame. They're drinking wine and calling at the girls. The war is 3 years behind us, and it's the summer of 1972. WAR is singing Slippin into Darkness, Al Green is on fire, and Ma smiles and says to me at the Hotel one day while A Horse with No Name is playing on the radio, "I like that song......The Horse with No Name."

I went through the desert on a horse with no name,

it felt good to be out of the rain".

In the desert, you can't remember your name,

for there ain't no one there to give you no pain."

I think about the days back in Nam when we spent Christmas at Cua Viet and floated and surfed on air mattresses in the South China Sea, and stood pleasant duty at the beach compound called C-2-Oceanview, where Doc Chang walked around naked and we gave each other haircuts. I remember how Doc Chang was pinned down and couldn't get over to me when I got shot. I think about Yuka back in Yokohama, and the other two Marines and Japanese girls who made up our group. I think about my pictures that were left on Hill 304. I wonder about the 16 year old girl I knew in Cam Lo Ville named Lana.

I keep running into guys who were in the service when I was, and they fake about having gone to Vietnam, like Paul who lives across the street and shoots dope and all he can say is that he was in Cu Chi, but can never talk about any details, and even Artis, who insists that he "went to Nam" when he was in the Army, but was in Germany most of his time overseas. I meet former marines who said they were in Vietnam but when I ask what unit they were with they say they can't talk about it. My friends from high school who didn't go in the military don't know what to say to us about the war. It's like a joke, like it didn't happen, and they want to put it in the background. I feel bad about Mickey, with a hole in his head and piss all over his pants because it was my idea to go in the Marines, and he's not even a U.S. citizen.

I think back to Halsey Street and Johnny next door, sleeping, smoking and scratching on the stoop and now I understand that Johnny wasn't really sleepy at all, but was actually nodding off of dope.

Then I'm reminded of Mr. Sherman, our math teacher back in JHS 35 who used to go out in the hall and secretly laugh after lunch, and I now suspect that he might have been smoking reefer on his lunch hour. No wonder his eyes were always red and he'd step out in the hall and return with them watery while suppressing a laugh.

I'm disappointed because Yolanda won't let me have the two pictures I mailed her from Vietnam, especially the one on the USS Repose hospital ship after I got shot, pictures that are precious to me and help to validate my experience, the few memories I have of the odyssey I took with my poor best friend Mickey. She wasn't my girlfriend anymore and was ashamed of my uniform and when I came home from the war empty handed, she wouldn't give me my pictures. I remember Wes Montgomery's "How Insensitive" before going to Vietnam, back on the beach in Oceanside, facing the Pacific ocean with no one to talk to.

I've known Dice, whose real name is Milton, since I was 14, from Ralph Avenue. We go everywhere together on our bicycles, all up in Manhattan, Central Park and Harlem, and always make our traditional stops. We ride across the Brooklyn Bridge into Manhattan, then make our way over to the Lower East Side and stop at Yonah Shimmel's Knishery on Houston Street and get blueberry knishes and Yoo Hoos for breakfast before heading uptown. Yonah Shimmel has a working, hand operated dumbwaiter they use for bringing orders up and down from the cellar, and Dice always takes a look through its door when we go there, because he has a fascination with old devices and architecture. On the way home we stop in Washington Square Park and smoke a joint in a place we named the corral, then we ride east to Katz's Deli, get two beers and four hot dogs, stuff them in the backs of our Jerseys, ride to the crest of the Williamsburg Bridge and stop and eat our franks and drink our beers, as the Schaeffer Beer brewery is pouring excess beer into the east river, then we continue to Brooklyn.

Yonah Shimmel on East Houston Street

Dice is a printer and works a multilith press. He went to The
Manhattan School of Printing and works for a company in
midtown, in the Theatre District. His hands are always black
with printing ink, and he says "I gotta wash my hands before
AND after I take a piss - I can't touch my dick with all that ink
on my hands!" We laugh about the same things, ride bikes,
listen to jazz and know each other's families. He's like a
brother, just like Mickey. Dice has no teeth because drugs
have abused him. He does have a set of dentures in his house,
but he won't wear them. He lives on St. Marks Place in Ocean
Hill, our old neighborhood on Ralph Avenue, and he still lives
with his mother. He knows all about raising pigeons and can
name the different birds when he sees a flock. We ride
expensive racing bicycles with all the professional gear that
goes with them, and we know that the best bicycles are

Italian, and we're familiar with names like Legnano, Atala, Campagnolo, Cinelli, Fiorelli, and the handle bars on our track bikes are Pista. Sometimes we say to each other "Officine Mecaniche-Marca Depositata, Brev Milan", as an inside joke because no one knows what we're talking about, and it's simply what the trademark says on our Italian-Made Bicycles. We have our own group of neighborhood cycling friends and we ride all over the city and go where the New York Cyclists go.

Cycling New York, 1976

We laugh and laugh about an old wino on St. Marks who saw us on our bicycles dressed in our racing gear and he said,

"Yeah.......... that's good, that's good.........keep ridin' them bicycles and stay outta trouble and stay away from dope, stay away from them grugs and stay away from niggas who be *dealin* them...........them............them *cosmetics*."

Dice likes King Pleasure and Count Basie and laughs and laughs at the lyric in Joe Williams' Going to Chicago Blues.

Going to Chicago,

sorry I can't take you,

cause' there's nothing in Chicago,

a monkey woman can do.

Dice and me, corner of Ludlow and Delancey Street, 1975

Me and Dice on the Brooklyn Bridge

Me and Dice, Tompkins Sq. Park, 1974

It's the fall of 1972 and I start working at Vocational Foundation Inc. on Park Avenue South as a Job Developer, soliciting employment and training opportunities for inner-city youth on the phone, and I begin to learn about the world of business. I'm trying to find jobs for young adults and one day on my home from work I get off the "J" train at Gates Avenue and stop by Al's factory on Monroe Street and ring the bell. Al soon comes downstairs on the service elevator and slides open the elevator gate with a big smile. He's got his doo-rag over his process and he needs a shave. I tell him I have a job soliciting employment opportunities for young adults and was wondering if he had any openings. He says, "Yeah I think so, send me a couple of nice, young girls. I need some secretaries, you knnowwww?"

I start going with my co-worker Vickie from the Bronx , and the first time we kiss is at a Friday-night dance at Hunter College on 23rd Street, where she attends part-time. Eddie Kendricks has a hit, Girl You Need a Change of Mind. Vickie comes and spends the night on Putnam and one morning Dad sees us leaving for work because we work in the same office, and pulls me to the side and says, "Listen, if that's whatchall gon' be doin, you gon' have to find your own place to do it in, you hear?"

I hear him clearly and now we have an apartment in Jersey City, on Pavonia Avenue, one stop from Manhattan on the PATH, and the PATH just a five-minute walk from our place, a four-room, three-flight walk-up cold-water flat for $100 a month. We take the PATH from Pavonia and get off at the 23rd St. 6th Avenue station and walk over to Park Avenue South and 27th Street where we work, just down the street from Tin Pan Alley, where the Irving Berlin Publishing Company is. The ride on the PATH from Jersey City to Midtown is 30 cents.

A young, white couple with a tiny, toddler daughter roaming around in a walker with drool on her mouth live on the ground floor where we live, and on a hot, 1973 August evening we share a joint in front of their place, and from their record player inside I hear a piano playing block-chord blues for measures and measures, then, unexpectedly, John Coltrane's horn enters the scene, capturing my attention nicely. "What's

the name of that?" "By The Numbers" the girl says, and I
think, "By the Numbers"....... then I remember, that's how I
used to make oil paintings, way back down in the cellar on
Willoughby, by the numbers.

We live in our first apartment in Jersey City for a year, then we
find an apartment on East 10th Street between Avenue B & C,
a one bedroom for $125 a month. We become friends with
our neighbors from Trinidad, Haydn and his wife Christine and
Gerry and his wife Charmaine. Haydn and Gerry are brothers
and Christine and Charmaine are sisters. We start having lots
of house parties and we go out to the clubs in Manhattan and
I teach Vicky to do the Brooklyn Hustle, because she's from
the Bronx, and we learned to do the hustle in 1964 on Park
Place, and it was called the Hustle back then too. Now the
Puerto Ricans are getting hold of it and calling it the Spanish
Hustle and Van McCoy makes a silly disco song called The
Hustle and it becomes commercialized and now it looks like
anything BUT The Brooklyn Hustle. It used to look very local
but now it's starting to look like International Ballroom. One
day some of Gerry's radical friends from the Bronx come over
our house with a couple who have a 4 year-old daughter, who
rolls and smokes reefer.

In front of 382 East 10th Street, 1974 Photo-Tori Geter

I ride my bike to work from here, taking it on the elevator at 353 Park Avenue South and parking it in the hall outside our office. We sometimes eat lunch at the Bellmore Cafeteria on Park Ave. South or at the Butcher Block on Madison & 28th. Madison Square Park is filled with people openly smoking reefer every day during lunch hours and after work at 5pm. You regularly smell reefer drifting down the busy sidewalks of the City, in the movie theatres, in and on the subways. There's a hippie couple who always dress in tie-dyed purple clothing and ride purple bicycles, and you see them all over the city scooping up horse manure and depositing it in purple, plastic-lined boxes attached to their bikes. People are drinking beer and eating chic peas at the bar in Max's Kansas City on Park Avenue South & 19th, and Stevie Wonder is on the jukebox singing Superstition.

I'm having fun living and working in vibrant Manhattan, and whenever funds run low, I go by the Hotel and pick up 10, 15 or $20, sign a slip and whoever's working puts the slip in the drawer along with the cash. We all use the hotel like a cash machine but Ma and Dad don't complain. I go there about every ten days. Linda goes there, Cathy and Sissy and Ronnie and Don. But they probably see me more, since I live on the Lower East Side.

It's a warm, sunny morning in July, 1974 and I'm riding my bicycle down 2nd Avenue crying, wearing a suit and tie and approaching 14th street, sobbing and heading home. I had to leave work because when the phone rang at my desk it was Mickey's brother Berto, telling me that Mickey was found dead in the 16 feet at Betsy Head Pool in Brownsville and I lost it there on the spot and my supervisor told me to go home. There's a crowd that hangs out around Betsy Head pool at night when it's closed, and they play radios and drink and shoot C-Lo and Mickey was drunk and had plenty of money and was gambling and somebody knocked him in the head, into the 16 feet.   Mickey was a good swimmer. He grew up swimming in Panama. He wouldn't have drowned in Betsy

Head. Someone took advantage of him and everybody abandoned him in the water and left through the hole in the wire fence and went their ways. No. I wasn't there, and never saw Mickey swim until we were in Vietnam, and it was at the swimming hole above LZ Studd, at a place called Ca Lu, and there, in a hidden gulley where a waterfall cascaded into a small basin, Mickey was diving off the cliffs into the water, disappearing for like 30 seconds and he'd surface, climb up the rocks and dive down again. He did this as I stood by in full jungle utilities watching, because I wasn't confident enough to swim there, and he'd holler "C'Mon Buck, git in. This shit is nice man!" I never imagined that we'd survive the combat in the war, both wounded, and after surviving battles in the Ashau Valley and Hamburger Hill and being wounded in the head while surveying enemy ammo, that he'd die in a swimming pool on Hopkinson Avenue.

He'd never had the metal plate put in his head and probably shouldn't have been under water. He didn't even know how to drive a car.

Mickey and Diane Cooper , at the house on Putnam, December, 1970

It's 1975 and Don and Chucky have been friends since 1966 when they were 9, always looking up to me and Mickey, and me and Mickey always roughing them up when we come walking up our block on Putnam. They've been talking about joining the Army because they have the same feeling that we had when we were tired of school. I'm living in my new apartment on Lincoln Place in Crown Heights and the phone rings and it's Sissy and she's furious.

"Buck, did you talk to Don? - Them fuckin' Puerto Ricans from Woodbine shot Chucky to death last night right in front of the house and he died under Daddy's car. Oh God, I never seen nothing like it. I'm so hurt, Buck. Don was upstairs leaning out the window talking to Chucky, and these bastards came from around Bushwick just walkin like they was headin up Broadway and they just shot him dead, and the poor boy tried to duck and crawled under the car and that's where he died. I had to hold Don by his shirt tail to keep him from jumpin' out the window. They shot him over some fuckin' girl. They was leavin' for the Army in a couple of weeks !"

Chucky was always smiling with his big eyes and nappy head, and he didn't even know how to drive a car.

Michele Wilson and Chucky, 1975

Donald H. German, U.S. Army Ranger-Pathfinder

My sister Linda is a jet setter and she and her friends do all the things that most young people wish they could do. They travel out of the country, drive big, brand-new cars, dress in the latest fashion and keep money in their pockets. They go to all the hippest night clubs and discos, and know some of the biggest hustlers and pimps in Brooklyn who drive Rolls

Royces, and Linda and her friends have jobs in banks on Wall Street. Linda's best friend is Sheryl, who soon becomes my girlfriend. One evening we piled into a limousine and went to see the film Apocalypse Now with Linda and her boyfriend Ed and their crowd. I'm the only one in the crowd who was ever in the military and actually went to Vietnam, and after the movie on the way back home to Brooklyn in the limo, no one says anything about the film or the war to me, or even asks me anything about my time there, after being in combat and being wounded. Instead, all the way home to Brooklyn we're listening to a tape of the Marvelettes and everybody in the car is singing along to the song, Destination Anywhere.

They just don't know what to say to me.

Me, Don, Ronnie, Sissy, Cathy and Linda 1975

The party scene is driving Brooklyn, and neighborhood clubs are active. Big parties are being promoted by The Dow Twins, and DJs are becoming famous like Pete D.J. Jones, and Flowers, and young people are going to Town Hill and Club Ecstasy on Eastern Parkway, the Iron Rail on Sterling place and Bedford, the C.O.C.P. on Fulton Street, Satan's Pit in Brownsville, and private after-hours clubs like Brown's Guest House on Waverly, New World, Timbuktu, Maxines and Cadillac Rose on Nostrand Avenue. Hustler's names are in the air like Pete Mooney, The LeGrand family, East-Side Charlie and Gloria Love. I get an idea that I can make money DJing, but not just disco and dance music but as a Jazz DJ, because I have the records and know the music, and I'll appeal to a more mature crowd of people who have money and will appreciate hearing Dakota Staton, Joe Williams, Gloria Lynne, Ray Charles, Jimmy Smith and Charles Earland in the local bars. Ma lends me the money to get some equipment and I go down to Canal Street in the City and get speakers, turntables, equalizer and mixer and have some business cards made up advertising myself as a Jazz DJ, and give them to local bar owners.

Soon I'm playing Wednesday and Saturday nights at a bar called Cuzzins on Rogers Avenue, then I get stolen from there by a woman named Maxine who has a private after-hours club on Nostrand Avenue called Straight No Chaser, that opens at 2am, and one of Maxine's handymen named Jenkins hooks up the wiring for my speakers from the front to the rear of the club. The patrons are drug dealers, gamblers, pimps and prostitutes. People drink Piper Heidsick champagne and smoke reefer and sniff cocaine openly at the bar, where their

coke sits in half-folded dollar bills, and every night around 4am
the prostitutes come in off the streets followed by their
pimps, and the gamblers come from the game house on
Nostrand and Fulton, and I'm spinning jazz and disco from a
little room that has a glass window with a view of people
sitting at the bar. By 12 noon, everybody in the entire club is
fucked up, and women who think they're sophisticated are
talking with frozen mouths and breath that smells like the
garbage truck, gesturing and pointing noses at you filled with
cocaine boogers.

The man who keeps things clean at Maxines and checks
people at the door is in his 50s, short and fat and called
"Flatbush", and he hates hip-hop. He reminds me of the
singer Jimmy Rushing, "Mr. 5 by 5". Kurtis Blow's record The
Breaks is a hit, Luther Vandross is making his debut with a
group called Change, The group Sky is singing Skyzoo, Loleatta
Holloway is singing with The Salsoul Orchestra, and the
Miracles have a record singing, Ain't nobody straight in L.A., it
seems that everybody is gay...........homosexuality is a part of
reality, and Diana Ross has a record called I'm coming out,
both tributes to the coming-out gay community. The pimps
are driving 1978 Cadillac Sevilles and I see them slapping their
whores in the mouth and one Sunday afternoon when the
club is about to close a pimp named Yaku slaps a girl so hard
that her panty hose falls down. The Whispers come out with a
record called Olivia, about a girl who gets turned out by a
pimp, and the lyric goes, *She has a certain quota to fill, he
wants to buy a new Seville.* A short pimp with long, straight

hair and who calls himself Andre Champagne is famous for walking in the door and setting up the bar with Pipers.

I'm mixed up in this night-life circuit and one Sunday morning after spinning music all night I'm driving Ma's car and stop to cop some blow and a Jamaican dealer slides in the car beside me and sticks a 44 magnum in my rib cage demanding all my money. I have $200 in my wallet but $20 in my hand. I offer him the 20 but he says "No Mon, gimme yuh purse from yuh back pocket." He's sitting in the passenger seat beside me and I hesitate, thinking I can open my door and jump out and run, but as soon as my left hand flinches for the door, he takes the gun out of my rib cage, pushes it into my thigh and says "Listen mon, me gwan hurtchoo right no." He takes the gun out of my rib cage because he doesn't want to kill me and when he pushes it into my thigh I know he's going to shoot me. I give him the money and say "Here.......... Now get the fuck out". He says "No Mon, *YOU* get dee fuck oat!", still pointing the gun at me. I get out and he drives Ma's car fast down Park Place towards Utica Avenue. I'm frantically trying to flag down drivers passing in cars because I've just been robbed and car jacked and people are on their way to Church and looking at me like I'm crazy. My mother's car is found three days later and the front seat is filled with blood and a sweat-shirt that I'd left in the car is also soaked with blood. When he had the gun pointed at me it was cocked and I think he accidentally shot himself while getting away, or something.

I'm spinning records one night about 4am at Maxine's and the stick-up men come through. I'm inside the DJ room and I hear banging and mirrors breaking and men shouting, "SHUT UP,

DON'T LOOK AT ME! - EMPTY YOUR POCKETS, TAKE OFF YOUR JEWLERY, PUT EVERYTHING ON THE BAR. DON'T LOOK AT ME." I realize what's happening and quietly lock the door to the room I'm in, take the $80.00 I have and slip it between my albums. If they come in here I'll tell them I haven't been paid yet, which is true. I turn the music down so I can hear better. "TURN THE MUSIC BACK UP"! They demand.

During this time I live in Crown Heights in a three-story Brownstone at 845 Lincoln Place between New York Avenue and Nostrand, on the second floor.

My apartment on Lincoln Place from 1975-1981

One Saturday afternoon I'm at Reiss Beach with my girlfriend Sheryl, and I look across to my right and there's Patty, my old girlfriend Cathy's best friend. I walk over to her blanket and she's surprised and glad to see me. She immediately tells me the bad news that Cathy's dead. She died of an overdose. She was the only girl I couldn't get to be completely mine. I always loved her, with her red-bone complexion and soft, brown afro. She was the sweetest girl I ever knew, and Ma loved her too.

There's a new night club around the corner on Eastern Parkway named Club Ecstasy, and me and my friend Grief from Trinidad whom I met when I lived in Alphabet City on East 10th Street pay our way into the club and we're wearing suits and ties and hats. The club attire is that men have to wear jackets. After they stamp our wrists and we're about to go in they say we have to take off our hats. So we take off our hats and go in and sit at a table and the dance floor is crowded with people doing the "Freak", guys rubbing up against girl's behinds, and people are in the bathrooms sniffing coke and the bar is six deep. So I ask a girl to dance and then another girl, and it starts to get warm so I take my jacket off and drape it on the back of my chair and go back to the dance floor. A guy who works in the club weaves his way through all the dancing people, all the way out to the dance floor to me, and says, "Excuse me Sir, but jackets are part of the dress code here so you have to put back on your jacket." Ecstasy is located underground in a black neighborhood and people are in the bathroom sniffing coke and this West Indian works his way to the middle of the dance floor bothering me about my jacket while I'm dancing with a fine girl, and I'm wearing a white shirt and tie but without the jacket, buying drinks and being decent and I snapped at him and he touched my arm and then I pushed him off me and me and Grief started fighting with the bouncers and got put out.

But I met a girl named Celia there who lived in Harlem and was a student at F.I.T. and got her phone number. She was from Chester, Pa. and lived in a first-floor apartment on 149th Street off Amsterdam where the bathroom was outside of her apartment in the hall, shared by other tenants on the first floor. We started going together and I spent the night at her house in Harlem and got real drunk and in the middle of the night I went out into the hall to use the bathroom and got disoriented afterwards, and the sun awoke me the next morning blazing in my eyes, and I was sitting on the staircase leading upstairs to other apartments, buck naked in the hall. I jumped up, ran into Celia's apartment where she was sound asleep, and got back into bed. I wonder how many people, if any, walked past me on their way up the stairs.

My son Darren is twelve years old and his best friend is Chris Rock. Darren lives at 551 Decatur St. on the next block east of Union Baptist Church where Dad goes. He lives with his Mom and his two sisters and Chris lives on the same block. They're also in the Boy Scouts together, and I drive through and see them sitting on the stoop, playing ball in the street and shooting skelly. Darren is handsome and All American and idealistic and I love him and I love his mother Diane, too. It's just that I'm in a different world now.

On July 1st, 1980, my second son Vaughn is born and he is a joy in my life and an amazing boy, bringing a feeling to me that I never had and never expected.   I instantly love him and I'm closer to him than Darren because when Darren was born I was just a boy and he never lived with me. But now I'm 30 and I'm in the delivery room when Vaughn comes into the world and God bonds us together at this moment.

Sissy and Vaughn on the stoop of 1124 Putnam, 1981

"You know what I always wanted to do?"

It's 3 a.m. and I'm at the Hotel and Ma's sitting at the desk, ready to check out, with about 300 old registration cards in her hand, and we're about to leave and drive to Brooklyn.

"I always wanted to throw these in the East River from the Bridge, and watch 'em float down to the water."

She laughs a little.

"You reckon we might can do that tonight? It's late and there ain't no traffic this time of morning."

She's looking up at me through her glasses with a mischievous, daring grin, holding the stack of 5 x 7 cards with two hands. I say OK and we're in the car and the streets are quiet and I'm driving. We turn the corner by Katz's and go down Ludlow Street and turn left onto Delancey, get on the bridge and take the far right lane to Brooklyn. We approach the crest of the bridge and it's about 3:30am and we pull over and stop, put the hazard lights on and quickly get out, Ma with the thick stack of 5x7 registration cards, and we lean over the edge on the rail and she looks at me and says, "You ready?" She lets go of the cards and they flutter in the wind down into the dark night for about 12 seconds like white birds above the crisp river, disappearing under the bridge, out of sight and she smiles wide like a little girl and I see the night-time Manhattan skyline reflected in her eye glasses and I'm glad that I'm here to do that for her, and share the moment with her, and do something I'd never done before, stopping a car at the top of the Williamsburgh bridge with my mother to toss registration cards that had been filled out by whores who helped us buy our house, into the East River, a rare thing indeed, a cherished moment.

Dad would never do a thing like that. They're different in those respects. Dad is conservative and Ma is more liberal and more flexible. We can play dirty records by Rudy Ray Moore and the profane poetry of Gylan Caine around Ma, but not around Dad. Ma wants to go down to Pier 1 at Riis beach to look at the nude bathers. We can even smoke reefer in the basement if Ma is upstairs, but not Dad. Dad goes to Church every Sunday at Union Baptist and has been going there since 1953 but Ma doesn't like going there and doesn't like Rev. Woods, the Pastor. She jokes about the way Dad pronounces church, and says he calls it "Chuch". When Ma was a little girl in Georgia, standing outside after Church with a crowd of people, she was hit in the shoulder by a bullet from a man who fired a gun into the crowd, and the bullet is still in her shoulder. Ma doesn't want any of us to get married. Whenever she hears someone mention getting married she immediately says *"FOR WHAT ?"* Ma has a daring sense of humor. She took this photo of the kids and suggested the pose.

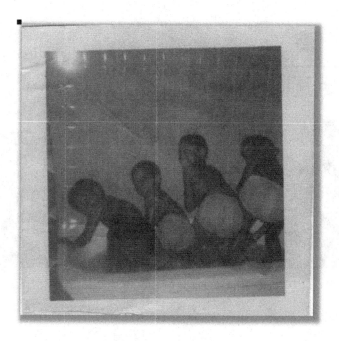

Will, Peter, Tonya and Jeri

Union Baptist Church, Decatur Street Brooklyn

Ma is kind to everyone and feeds people when they're hungry and gives beggars change and picks up Jews and drives them across the bridge and makes enough lunch in the summertime to feed 10 or 12 kids playing outside in front of the house, and goes down to Pitkin Avenue shopping and comes back with T-Shirts, shorts and sneakers and gives them out to the less fortunate kids on the block, and she'll pile a bunch of other people's kids in the car and take them to Coney Island and they all call her Grandma. Ma's worked hard all her life, so hard that her hands always smelled like onions when she'd tie my necktie for me before I learned to myself. She'd work all week at the Hotel, then on the weekends she'll have a bar-b-cue in the backyard and start cooking and cleaning early Saturday morning, then drive and pick up Aunt Toots and Miss

Hipp, bring them back, serve people, feed them, play cards and dance with them and get them drunk, and then have to drive them home late at night. If you say to Ma, "I'm bored", she says, "You mean, you're bo-ring"! She feels sorry for "all the poor Puerto Ricans" and feels sorry for mice when one gets caught in a trap. If I make it to Heaven and Ma's not there it won't be Heaven for me. A big lesson I learned in life is to respect my mother and father. Like my Aunt Lil says, "If you *EVER* disrespect your parents, you'll curse the day and damn the hour".

When Ma dies unexpectedly in the cold winter of February 1982 there is standing room only in Union Baptist. One of her favorite songs was "Release Me" by Esther Phillips. Dad's nickname for Ma was Monk, and one week after she dies on February 10th, Thelonious Monk dies exactly a week later, on February 17th, 1982. Ma had grown up in the south like Dad, doing farm and domestic work, and she never learned to ride a bicycle. I'd wanted to buy her one of those tricycles for grownups but didn't get the chance.

I think an angel helped me when Ma died. On the late evening of February 9th Vicky and I were watching TV in our apartment in the Bronx and Vaughn was in the bedroom asleep. He was 18 months old. The volume on the television was low enough to hear Vaughn in the bedroom. During a pause in the TV program we heard sniffling from the bedroom, quiet crying. When we looked in, Vaughn, a baby, was quietly crying, as if he were crying in private, uncharacteristic for a baby. Vicky and I looked at each other puzzled, comforted him, and later went to bed. The telephone jumped us awake at 3am and I knew something was wrong. It was Linda's voice, crying, saying that Ma was dead. She'd had a bad asthma attack and her heart couldn't take it anymore. I cried and cried the rest of the night and Vicky, Vaughn and I took the subway the next morning to Brooklyn. I cried and cried on the train all the way to the Halsey Street station. The house on Putnam was filled with crying family and friends and funeral services were being prepared.

At the end of the day Dad let me take Ma's car to go back to the Bronx. I'm driving on the Interboro Parkway heading for the Whitestone Bridge, crying on and off. As I'm going up the winding ramp to get on the Van Wyck Expressway I suddenly lose acceleration and hear something dragging under the car. I get to the top of the highway and I pull the car over to the right side and get out to look under the car. The universal joint had come lose and the crankshaft was hanging down on the ground. It's extremely cold and windy, about 18 degrees, and rush hour has begun. This is all I need right now. I'm standing on the busy highway in the cold wind trying to wave anyone down for help. By this time Vaughn is crying inside the car so I grab him up with the blanket around him and I'm standing on the highway with him in my arms, both of us crying and I'm waving for help. No one is stopping and my heart is broken. Finally a yellow Volkswagen pulls over and stops and a young white guy is driving and welcomes us in out of the cold and offers to drive us off the highway to a pay phone. I get in the front seat next to him, holding Vaughn, and I'm so grateful for his kindness. I'm cold, exhausted, my baby son is crying and my Mother is dead. As we head north up the highway I notice stickers and decals on his dashboard, and one of them says something about being in the presence of angels. At that very moment I look at this young man and his eyes meet mine, and he slightly smiles and I feel that I am surely in the presence of an angel, who'd rescued me and my boy from the windy, dangerous and busy highway. He came when I needed help the most.

Ma

"Buck! Mike is laying dead in the street on Howard Avenue!"

It's 1986 and Sissy shouts from the upstairs window on Putnam as I'm about to park my car. It's a sunny winter morning. I head down Putnam, cross Broadway and when I get to Howard Avenue the street is blocked with yellow crime-scene tape and there's a small crowd on the corners of Howard and Monroe Street and Mike, my sister Cathy's boyfriend, is laying face down in the gutter across the street from the RKO Bushwick, just a few steps from his bullet riddled Cadillac, face down with his legs crossed behind him. He and Cathy were sitting in the car talking when the Colombians he owed drug money approached from Broadway and carefully shot through his front windshield with automatic fire, avoiding Cathy. Mike, after being hit, opened his door to get out and run but it was too late. He got about 20 feet from the car and collapsed while trying to run, which is why his legs are crossed behind him. Cathy jumped out of the car and ran south on Howard Avenue. He was a no good, mean and ugly dealer with a nasty disposition, and had crossed many lines and many people.

"Buck, Reggie is in the house dead. He overdosed this morning!"

Terry Simpkins greets me quietly as I'm about to park my car. He lives right across the street from Reggie. It's another sunny, winter morning just two weeks later. I follow Terry into Reggie's house and his mother is in the front room sitting quietly in a chair by the front window. Neither the police nor the coroner have arrived yet. Reggie lies dead in a lower bunk bed in the dark, across the hall from the bathroom where his mother found him.

Mrs. Miller's first-floor apartment on Putnam Ave.

She'd called out to Terry from her front window and he helped carry Reggie from the bathroom to the bunk bed. I take a good, long look at Reggie, run down to the house, go upstairs and wake up Don and call him out in the hall and after I tell him, he stands there under the skylight, gripping the banister and cries helplessly and pitifully. Three weeks ago I'd come around the block with a grey, pin-striped suit I no longer needed, and Reggie saw it and said, "I can fit this Buck, it's just my size man thanks, I need this suit. I really need it".

Good lookin, light skin, long-hair beaver wearin, lizard wearin, checker-board leather wearin, c-lo shootin, shit talkin, money gittin, wine drinkin, can't sing a note, Puerto-Rican girl gittin', Don's Ace Boon Coon, Irish great granddaddy Reggie Miller, laying in his coffin in a grey, pin-striped suit, done did it all.

Don German and Reggie Miller

It's 1987 and I'm driving my new car, on my way to see Dice and show it to him. I run into my son Darren and Chris Rock on Howard Avenue. "Wow Dad, I like your car, when you gonna let me drive it?" I tell him he doesn't know how to drive a stick and he says, "I can drive anything". I ask him where they're going and he says he's going with Chris to "Catch". Chris is doing his stand-up routine at Catch a Rising Star and Rodney Dangerfield's, just breaking into the business. Darren and Chris nickname me "Speed Racer", because I regularly come riding through the block with Dice on our bicycles.

Chris Rock far right with Darren to his right

It's 1987 and there are still gangs around, but the focus isn't on turf for identity purposes only. It's money and drug dealing, gun toting and drive-by shootings. The big gang in Brooklyn is the Tomahawks. Kids are wearing their pants hanging down with their drawers and the cracks of their behinds showing. This comes from jail. It starts on Riker's Island and comes about in the late 1970s. Riker's Island is a detention facility for young men between 16-21, and the first thing that happens upon arrival is they take away your shoestrings and your belt, to reduce suicide risks and minimize potential weapons. So a guy spends a couple of years at Riker's, and he's eating 3 square meals a day and working out in the gym and gaining weight, and on visitation days his people bring him new jeans and sneakers to wear with pants oversized, allowing room for weight gain, and you don't want to wear tight pants in jail anyway. So when you get these new clothes, including nylon and silk drawers, you have no belt and shoestrings, so you walk around the jail in your new sneakers with the tongues hanging out, and your new jeans hanging down below your behind showing off your new silk drawers, and it shows that you have power on the outside. Those who get no visitors get no new clothes and they wear strictly prison garb. After 2-3 years on Riker's you come home to the streets and you're seen by your peers on the block as a hero, a bad dude. You got muscles and tattoos, you did a bid, you made connections, your "pants is hangin' down" and your "sneakers is loose" and you "got that walk".

"Hey Dice - wanna come downstairs and see my new car?" Dice hasn't worked recently because he's been sick and is sitting in a chair across the room from me, at a small table with electric wires hanging from a transformer, the control box for his set of Lionel trains that he's owned for 30 years. He slowly cranks the transformer and the engine lights up and the locomotive pulls the freight cars around the circumference of his mother's living room, up on the 4th floor on Sterling Place. Next to the transformer on the table is a can of 3-in-one oil, some tiny tools and baby diapers used for wiping cloths, and everything is neat and in its place. Dice looks straight past me and shakes his head "no". The train pulls past me and the smoke from the engine trails behind. "Hey Black, don't that smoke smell just like the subway?" Black. Dice calls me Black - that's his nickname for me. His nickname for Don is Draulics. This immaculate Lionel train set is all he has in the world, except for a very nice grey-Fedora hat. He'd parked his Atala bicycle outside a liquor store 6 months ago and it got stolen, and he had to walk home wearing cycling shoes with metal cleats, black tights under black cycling shorts with the crotch completely worn out, just like the teeth from his mouth. Now he's sitting here dying. "What kind of car is it Black?" "It's beautiful. I bought it used. It's a black, 1981 Audi, 5-speed." Dice has no expression, only a blank, soberly hypnotic stare past me. "I'm not goin' outside no more, Black".

I knew Dice since we were 14 and he was the first guy I saw with a professional track bike, and one day when we had my mother's car and were listening to jazz on WRVR, Red Garland was playing the piano and Dice said, "I know that song, that's East of The Sun". I learned from Dice that Miles Davis' middle name was Dewey. Dice wasn't a musician and couldn't hit harmony and never finished high school, and never learned to drive a car.

Dice in his grey Fedora

I tell this story for those who are dead and cannot tell it, for there are so many and I've only mentioned a few. All of my nieces and nephews have one deceased parent and my niece Tonya has lost both her parents. My sister Cathy, who surrounded herself with friends who were down and out and who was famous for making friends with everybody, died in 1998. Cathy eventually became bi-sexual and sometimes I think I had something to do with her doing so, because whenever she'd bring a new friend to the house, she'd introduce me to the girl, and I made sure I got to know her. Cathy once complained, "Every time I bring one of my friends home, Bucky take her right in the basement." Linda's son Peter, has never seen his father Darnell, who died young from drugs abusing him, his family has disappeared and we don't even have a photo of him.

Seventy percent of the people we grew up with are gone. God has pulled me from the grip of death many times, more times than I mention here, and I am grateful for His friendship, salvation, provision and promise. All the gambling and pimping and drug selling and drug using were life styles that trapped people, and their dreams and ideals escaped like helium-filled balloons let go.

One afternoon when Vaughn is five years old we're riding downtown on the D train, and above the clattering noise of the subway tracks he looks up to me and says, "Daddy, isn't it great to be alive?" Yes it is.

Me and Vaughn Cape Cod, 1982   Photo, Tori Geter

Author's Note:

I am an American Negro because of my culture, which is American. I am an American Negro because I am more than African American. There is Native American and European in my ancestry. My great-great grandparents were born in America. Langston Hughes and Fats Waller and Louis Armstrong and Duke Ellington and Count Basie and Mary Lou Williams and Oliver Nelson and Billie Holiday and Dakota Staton and Gloria Lynne and Ray Charles and Billy Eckstine and Joe Williams and Martin Luther King and Oscar Brown, Jr. are just a few of the icons who formed and influenced 20th century American culture, and my perception of being American.

People who live in the large African community around West 116th Street uptown in Harlem who become U.S. citizens are African Americans. I am not the same as them. There is more to me. By the Grace of God, my heritage and lineage have come full circle.

When Yusef Hawkins was killed by those Italian boys in Bensonhurst, Rev. Al Sharpton led a group of protesters in their community, and arrived in Bensonhurst carrying red, black and green flags. When the Italians saw this they went in their houses and retrieved their American flags and waved them in the protesters faces. They didn't come out with the red, white and green flags of Italy, they came out with American flags, as if to say, "Oh - You're African? Well, *WE'RE AMERICAN !* "

Rev. Al Sharpton and the protesters should have been carrying American flags, to say "This is My Country". Do you think you're more American than I am?" What country does the red, black and green flag represent? I'm not a Negro American, but an American Negro. Negro *means* Black. To say you're African American is to say that you're African first. If I'm African American all Americans are African American because science and DNA have shown that all humanity originated in Africa. So if I'm African American the adorable Dolly Parton is also African American. I am what I am. I am American first.

Ronnie is an ordained minister and has given his life to God.

Don is a professional carpenter and an extremely talented comedian.

Out of our 20 aunts and uncles, there is only one left.